D1648249

Digitized Lives

In a remarkably short period of time the Internet and associated digital communication technologies have deeply changed the way millions of people around the globe live their lives. But what is the nature of that impact? In chapters examining a broad range of issues—including sexuality, politics, education, race, gender relations, the environment and social protest movements—*Digitized Lives* seeks answers to these central questions: What is truly new about so-called "new media," and what is just hype? How have our lives been made better or worse by digital communication technologies? In what ways can these devices and practices contribute to a richer cultural landscape and a more sustainable society?

Cutting through the vast—and often contradictory—literature on these topics, Reed avoids both techno-hype and techno-pessimism, offering instead succinct, witty and insightful discussions of how digital communication is impacting our lives and reshaping the major social issues of our era. The book argues that making sense of digitized culture means looking past the glossy surface of techno-gear to ask deeper questions about how we can utilize technology to create a more socially, politically and economically just world.

Companion website available at culturalpolitics.net/digital_cultures

T. V. Reed is Buchanan Distinguished Professor of English and American Studies at Washington State University and Distinguished Visiting Professor at York University, Toronto. He is the author of *The Art of Protest: Culture and Activism from the Civil Rights Movement to the Streets of Seattle*.

Digitized Lives

Culture, Power and Social Change in the Internet Era

T. V. Reed

Routledge
Taylor & Francis Group

NEW YORK AND LONDON

First published 2014
by Routledge
711 Third Avenue, New York, NY 10017

and by Routledge
2 Park Square, Milton Park, Abingdon, Oxon OX14 4RN

*Routledge is an imprint of the Taylor & Francis Group,
an informa business*

© 2014 Thomas Vernon Reed

The right of Thomas Vernon Reed to be identified as author of
this work has been asserted by him in accordance with sections 77
and 78 of the Copyright, Designs and Patents Act 1988.

All rights reserved. No part of this book may be reprinted
or reproduced or utilized in any form or by any electronic,
mechanical, or other means, now known or hereafter invented,
including photocopying and recording, or in any information
storage or retrieval system, without permission in writing from
the publishers.

Trademark notice: Product or corporate names may be trademarks
or registered trademarks, and are used only for identification and
explanation without intent to infringe.

Library of Congress Cataloging-in-Publication Data

Reed, T. V. (Thomas Vernon)
Digitized lives : culture, power and social change in the Internet
  era / T.V. Reed.
    pages cm
  Includes bibliographical references and index.
  1. Internet—Social aspects. 2. Information technology—Social
aspects. 3. Social change. I. Title.
  HM851.R4336 2014
  302.23'1—dc23
  2013042434

ISBN: 978-0-415-81930-5 (hbk)
ISBN: 978-0-415-81931-2 (pbk)
ISBN: 978-0-203-37467-2 (ebk)

Typeset in Stone Serif
by Apex CoVantage, LLC

To Hart
—the best kind of digital native—
with love and appreciation

Contents

Illustrations

⬚ FIGURES

⬚ TABLES

Preface

Why Buy this Book?

Have you been tweeted, blogged, YouTubed, Kindled, interacted, texted, sexted, crowdsourced, wiki-ed, and socially networked to the edge of your sanity? Are you tired of being told that digital technology will solve all the world's problems, or that it is bringing an end to civilization? Do you want to make common sense of all this digital stuff without the hype, the paranoia or the jargon? Then maybe this book is for you.

There are many books that promise to tell all about the Internet and new communication technologies. Most fall into one of three categories. The most common type is the "how to" book that provides step-by-step ways to use the technology. While these tend to go out of date quickly, they can be useful, even when they call their readers "dummies." The second type is written in a form close to a rant by people either so enamored of or so afraid of new technologies that they profoundly exaggerate their positive or negative impact. The third type of book is written by experts who generally tell way more than most of us want to know about a small aspect of these new media technologies in a language that seems to have come from another planet (the planet Geek, to be precise, a planet I love and visit frequently, but do not live on). Only this third category is relevant to my aims in this book. Many of these works by experts are very important, and this book would not exist without them. But they are not for everybody. They are aimed at a fairly exclusive community of scholars and advanced communication students, not the rest of us.

This book is different. What I hope to do is provide a framework for readers to think about questions like: Why use these technologies at all? What are "new media" doing to our brains, to our sex lives, to our parent–child interactions, to our politics, to our education system, to our identities as individuals and as community members? In other words, how do these new technologies fit into the bigger picture of society and culture in the twenty-first century? This book is less interested in programs, apps and devices that come and go in the blip of a computer screen than in asking, in as clear and jargon free a way as I can, some enduring questions about what we can and should make of these technologies, about how we can take control of them rather than have them control us.

We all sense that the Internet and the ever-changing array of new digital hardware and software are changing the world, changing us. But most of us aren't so sure what those changes are, and whether they are for the better or for the worse. Indeed, anyone who tells you they *do* know for sure what those changes mean is probably about as reliable as that e-mail from the stranger who wants you to help him transfer his million dollars into your bank account. From the dawn of the Internet era, there has been a duel between the techno-phobes and the technophiles as represented by the contrast between Neil Postman's relentlessly pessimistic *Technopoly* (1993), and Nicholas Negroponte's equally relentlessly optimistic *Being Digital* (1995). Avoiding these two speculative extremes, this book seeks to examine some of what is actually going on in digitized spaces, noting both the dangers and the pleasures involved.

For many of the more than two billion of us now taking part in the digitized world, asking these questions is like a fish trying to think about water. We take that water for granted. It's just where we live. But just as the quality of water is vital to a fish's health, so too is it vital for us to think about the quality of digital culture, to try to sort out the healthy from the polluted or the toxic waterways, to try to make things a little less murky, a little more transparent.

Reportedly the great modernist writer Gertrude Stein, when asked by her lover on her deathbed the presumably metaphysical question, "Gertrude, what is the answer?" replied, "What is the question?" I'm on Stein's side of this exchange. I think most often good questions are more important than answers. I'd like readers of this book to enter a conversation about how to think more carefully and deeply about these new forces that we have unleashed upon the world. I have tried to identify some key questions to help you come to your own conclusions about how you are going to involve yourself in (or sometimes wisely run away from) what these new digital cultures offer. The great science fiction writer Theodore Sturgeon had a motto that more of us might take to heart: "Ask the next question." What does that mean? Good question. Well, one thing I think it means is always ask the question that leads beyond what you think you already know. That's what I hope my questions will lead you to do—ask the next question neither you nor I have thought of yet.

One question asked often about new communications media is whether or not they are creating a new "generation gap" between adults and youth, between members of the "digital" or "d-generation" and the analog one. If you are a reader under 30, you may well have grown up with digital devices utterly woven into your lives. You are what some call "digital natives," as opposed to "digital immigrants" who come to new media as adults. Not all digital natives are young; aspects of digital culture now go back several decades. And not all digital immigrants are older, since not all youth grow up with digital devices. But generally speaking, the digital native/digital immigrant distinction has an age dimension. More important is the distinction itself. Think of it as analogous to being a native speaker of a language. If you grew up immersed in digital culture and speaking "digitalk" naturally, you have a different experience to that of folks who came to digital culture after having spent a good many years in the pre-Internet age. Many digital immigrants have gotten very good at using new digital media, but just like someone who becomes fluent in a second language, they never have quite the same command as those who speak the language as natives. So those of you under 30 reading this book may understand some things about digital life that your over-30 parents and teachers will never quite get. On the other hand, digital immigrants have some knowledge that digital natives do not, namely knowledge of the olden days BW (Before the Web) that may allow them to see some things about digital culture that are not as apparent to immersed natives. In any event, one hope for this book is that it will spark cross-generational dialogues about the pros and cons of various digitized experiences.

One key question we will return to again and again as we look at various new media and the cultures surrounding them is what is truly new here and what is not? And to understand what is truly new, as opposed to merely newish-looking or newly hyped, you need to know what went before (or at least more about the undigitized world). Hence the value of those who grew up BW. As for those of you (natives or immigrants) who have been assigned to read this book in a class, if you don't like your teacher's questions, or mine, ask your own. This is not a textbook where you are told just the facts, ma'am, or the scholarly Truth. This book is a set of provocations.

◨ OUTLINE OF THE BOOK

Chapter 1 looks at questions of technological determinism, questions about the extent to which technologies develop a life of their own beyond human control. It also introduces some crucial terms useful in thinking about the culture–technology relationship, and describes some of the ways readers might follow digital culture scholars in tracing the social impact of new media. Chapter 2 deals with the often-overlooked forces that make digital culture possible, the production process that creates the devices and the networks that carry digitized cultural materials around the world. It also deals with another largely hidden part of digital culture, the environmental devastation resulting from the production, use and disposal of digital communication devices. Chapter 3 takes up one of the most discussed aspects of digital culture, the impact of that culture on individual and collective identity, including issues of digital cross-dressing (impersonating someone you are not), the loss of privacy in a highly networked surveillance society, and the notion that we may be turning into "posthuman" creatures, into "cyborgs" (part human, part digital machine). Chapter 4 continues the discussion of identity by looking specifically at how questions of gender, ethnicity, and physical dis/ability have been reshaped by digital cultures. Is the digital world creating greater social equality? Chapter 5 takes up the multifaceted question of sexuality as impacted by new media spaces, looking at online sex education, various cybersex practices, issues surrounding online pornography, and the representation of alternative sexualities online. Chapter 6 looks at a variety of ways in which political cultures, from mainstream parties to dissident social movement protesters to revolutionaries to terrorists, have had their actions reshaped by digital technologies. Chapter 7 is devoted to digital games and the various controversies that have surrounded them, from allegations that they promote mindless violence to those who argue that games can be used creatively to solve many of the world's problems. The chapter also looks at the ways that digital gaming has contributed to the phenomenon known as "militainment," the increasing fusion and confusion of militarism and popular culture. Chapter 8 takes up another controversial area where digital technology is having a huge impact, the arena of education, from pre-school through graduate school and out into the wider world of life-long learning. Chapter 9 explores the vital question of who does and does not currently have access to digital cultures, and what the reasons for this might be, including why some people intentionally and thoughtfully opt out of the digital world. Chapter 10 concludes with a brief glimpse of some likely future developments in digital technologies that will offer new possibilities and challenges for bringing greater cultural richness and social justice to the world.

⊟ COMPANION WEBSITE

This book has an accompanying website—culturalpolitics.net/digital_
cultures—that includes a bibliography with books, articles and relevant websites for further exploration of key digital culture issues,
and a timeline on the evolution of digital cultures. The website is a
resource and a reminder that this book can only introduce topics that
deserve much deeper understanding. The website also has a response
section where you can send me comments or questions about the
book or about digital culture issues more broadly. I appreciate getting
feedback (most of the time).

Acknowledgments

This book grew out of many years of teaching courses about digital culture to undergraduate university students at Washington State University (Pullman) and York University (Toronto). Students in those classes contributed significantly to this book, and I thank them for educating me.

I also want to thank several individuals who read the manuscript in total or in part and offered valuable suggestions. In particular, I single out Hart Sturgeon-Reed, to whom this book is dedicated. Over many years and dozens of conversations, and as a very astute reader of the manuscript, he has contributed more to the book than anyone apart from the author (who is, of course, responsible for all the mistakes and dumbnesses within). Noël Sturgeon, Katie King and Jason Farman also offered valuable suggestions at key moments in the writing process. I thank Noël and Hart for far more than editorial assistance. One couldn't design, digitally or otherwise, better partners in life.

Lastly, I want to thank the staff at Routledge, both those whose names I know—Erica Wetter (instigator), Anna Carroll (word wizard), Simon Jacobs (helper in all ways) and Bonita Glanville-Morris (finalizer extraordinaire)—and those behind the scenes whose names I know not but who also contributed to the collective effort that has made the publication of this book possible. Thanks all.

1

How Do We Make Sense of Digitizing Cultures?

Some Ways of Thinking through the Culture–Technology Matrix

Computers are incredibly fast, accurate, and stupid. Human beings are incredibly slow, inaccurate and brilliant. Together they are powerful beyond imagination.

—(Leo Cherne, Discover America conference, Brussels, June 27, 1968)

→ Does Technology Make Us More than We Make Technology? Techno-logical Determinism vs. Technocultural Analysis

→ Components of Digital Culture Analysis

→ Is There a Virtual World/ Real-World Divide?

→ Terminal Confusion?

→ What's in a Name? New Media/Cyber/Digital Culture/Etc. Studies

The Internet includes an unimaginably vast sea of data that is profoundly changing the range and nature of human communication. Not only has it greatly decreased the cost of communication and enabled heretofore-impossible distances to be crossed instan-taneously, but it is also increasingly subsuming all other media into itself. Mail, phoning, film, television, music, photography, radio—all have been translated into digital form and made available in far more accessible ways to the roughly two billion people (now rede-fined as "users") around the world. No book can hope to fathom the immensity of the Net and other "new" information communication technologies (or ICTs, as they are known among professionals). But we can examine some of the key patterns of human social interaction made possible, fostered, or transformed by these "new media." Note that this is the second time I have put "new" in scare quotes. Why? Because one of the recurring questions in the fields upon which this book draws is: What exactly, if anything, is really new, as opposed to seemingly new, about the world of digital media? This book draws deeply from various academic fields that examine the social impacts of information and communication technologies. The chapters that follow draw ideas from anthropology, sociology, communication, rhetoric, ethnic and women's studies, cultural studies and half a dozen other disciplines. The interdisciplinary field that most directly addresses the set of issues raised in this book looks at digital cultures—the *social relationships* that occur through immersion in the realm of the Internet, video games, smartphones and other high-tech platforms and devices. Studies of digital culture ask how communication technologies reflect the wider social world, how they create new cultural relations, and how those new online experiences in turn reshape the offline world.

Culture is one of the most complicated words in the English language, but for our purposes we can simplify it to mean the values, beliefs and behaviors that are typical and defining of a group. In this sense, we are all involved in many cultures. We can think of cultures as like the Russian dolls that have smaller and smaller dolls inside. At the broadest level we can talk about global culture, at the next level national cultures, then perhaps ethnic cultures, and so on down the line to the cultures of small groups (clubs, workplaces, etc.) in which we take part. In terms of digital cultures, we can think in terms of Twitter culture, or Facebook culture, digital classroom cultures, smartphone cultures, digital activist cultures, gamer cultures and so on, each of which could be divided into smaller groups (e.g., Grand Theft Auto 5 players or iPhone user cultures).

The analogy breaks down, however, in that Russian dolls are far more clearly demarcated than are cultures. Cultures are fluid, not neatly bounded entities. Recent anthropology theory argues that "cultures" are always fictions, are always artificial constructions of observers. The question of what typifies or is essential to a given cultural group is always subject to debate within that group. The boundaries or key characteristics of any imagined cultural group are always blurry, and often in process and changing. Cultural meanings are in fact never settled; they are always subject to contestation, both among outside observers and internal participants. This simply means that anything claimed about a given cultural group can be challenged, and that is a good thing. It keeps cultures from becoming static and keeps those who analyze cultures from becoming complacent or arrogantly sure of their interpretations.

At the broadest level, digital communication technologies have played a very significant role in our current international configuration of economics and culture, the period of the last several decades that is generally referred to as neo-liberal or "free market" globalization. Globalization is not a new phenomenon in history. There have been many forms and periods of significant global interaction for hundreds of years. Precisely what is new about our current era is up for debate, but among the new features of this particular phase of globalization is the spread of new digital communication networks. Most scholars agree that our current brand of globalization would be impossible without the rapid movement of money, data, knowledge, and non-material commodities across national borders via the Internet and other digital technologies.

To address some of the human-to-human issues surrounding our digitizing world, we need to get beneath the glossy surface of ever-cooler new tech devices to ask questions about what these devices are doing *to* us, and what we can do *with* them to make our lives and the lives of others better. My aim is to avoid both the pro-tech hype driven by profit-hungry electronics corporations, and the equally dubious tech haters driven more by fear of the new than by clear thinking about some of the downsides of high-tech cultures. Instead this book tries to provide some useful ways to think through the many and varied social impacts of digital cultures, and hopefully provides some tools to help readers play a stronger role in shaping new technologies in ways that improve the world.

Few of the questions this book addresses have simple answers. One reason there are no easy answers about what new technologies are doing to us is that the subject is incredibly vast, and changing at a phenomenal rate. Though no one really knows how to count them with complete accuracy, by the second decade of the twenty-first century there were over 1,750,000,000 (1¾ billion) individual web pages indexed by Google (with several million more unindexed). Moreover, between the time I wrote that sentence and the time you are reading it, several million more were created. If Facebook were a country, it would be the third largest nation in the world. YouTube broadcasts more in a day than all major TV networks have broadcast in their entire history. In the history of the world, counting every language, there have been about a hundred billion printed books; the amount of information contained in that number of volumes is uploaded onto the Web every month. How could anyone claim to know what is going on across all those sites and in all the other arenas that make up digital cultures? Trying to understand digital cultures is a little like trying to interpret the lyrics to a song that adds new verses every day. Sometimes the new verses seem to continue the song's main themes, but at other times the new verses go off in totally unexpected directions because the song has two billion co-authors.

As a result of the rapidly changing nature of new communication networks, the question of what new technologies are doing to us covers a territory that is riddled with contradictory evidence. Are they helping create a more just world, bringing down dictators and opening up societies, or are they giving hate-mongers a new, safely anonymous space to recruit? Are they giving women and ethnic and sexual minorities new platforms to be heard, or offering new space for dominant cultures (and the English language) to overwhelm everyone else? Are we creating a new "(digital) generation gap," or finding new ways for parents and children to communicate across differences and distances? Is the Web truly world-wide in terms of who can use it, or are we creating a world of digital haves and have-nots? Is the Web a space of free and open public discourse, or one controlled by governments and huge corporations? Is the Web creating new transnational, person-to-person understandings, or amplifying existing cultural misunderstandings? Is the Web a space where physically disabled people can enjoy the freedom of virtual mobility, or a space biased toward the able-bodied, leaving the disabled to struggle for full access? Is online sexual content destroying relationships and degrading morals, or offering liberating knowledge? Are video games turning users into mindless virtual killers, or teaching valuable life skills? Is the Internet making us more knowledgeable, or just drowning us in a sea of trivia? Is the digital world one where we are more "connected," or one that steals our privacy, offers up way Too Much Information, and stunts the face-to-face interactions that alone can carry true human connection?

Clearly, a case can be made for each extreme side of each of these questions. But that doesn't mean that the truth is somewhere in the middle. It means that the "truth" of digital cultures is a set of ongoing processes, and will depend on the thinking and acting users do now, as well as on decisions we make, as citizens and as consumers, about the further development and use of new technologies in the near future. It will depend on the personal decisions we make, on the political work we do to shape social policy about technology, and on the lives we choose to pursue as participants of a rapidly digitizing age that is upon us, whether we like it or not.

So digital cultures are very much in progress, and no one really knows what the almost seven billion of us stranded on the third rock from the sun we call Earth will eventually make of this still relatively new set of technologies. We are dealing with two ongoing processes, the human development of digitizing technologies, and the human use of those technologies. They are not the same thing because humans do unexpected things with the tools we create. And that is what a technology is, a *tool*. The roots of the word technology are in the Greek name for practical things that extend our human capacities. Some of our more famous technologies, the wheel, the printing press, have changed the world and human identities in unimaginably diverse ways. So too will our digital tools, with an emphasis on the unimaginable part. The tools will only be as good as the imaginations of the people that put them to use.

While we are still learning to make sense of the new media explosion, there is little doubt that it represents a major transformation in human culture, what one scholar has called a "fourth revolution in the means of production of knowledge" (Harnad 1991), following the three prior revolutions of language, writing, and print. As with each of these previous "revolutions," much consternation has been generated by the arrival of the digital age. The Greeks worried that the invention of writing would fundamentally undermine the key human capacity of memory. The arrival of the printing press was viewed by some as a dangerous degradation of human communication. And so too have many lamented that digital media will bring the "end of world as we know it." The end of the world has been predicted since the beginning of *homo sapiens,* and this latest prediction is no doubt as wrong as all the others. But some things in the world certainly are changing. And the "as we know it" part of the phrase is undeniable. New media will not bring an end to the world, but they are deeply changing the way "we know it." New ways of knowing have in the past (like the printing press) not brought an end to the world, but they did bring an end to certain ways of knowing, while adding new ways of knowing, and new identities. And that is surely what is happening now; we are experiencing a (digital) revolution in how we come to know the world and ourselves.

Having raised the issue of knowledge, let me say a word about my approach to knowing about digital cultures. Objectivity is one of the great inventions of the modern world. It is a worthy ideal of the natural sciences and much scholarship in the social and human sciences. But, like all ideals, it is never fully attained. The idea of information and analysis presented without personal, cultural or political bias is a wonderful thing to strive for, because no one benefits from distorted information. Some think the way to achieve objectivity is to pretend to be a person without biases. Instead, I agree with scholars who argue that such a position just hides biases that all of us have. So my approach will not be to pretend to be neutral on all issues raised in this book (I will not, for example, give white supremacists equal credence with folks fighting racism online). Rather I'll make my own positions (read bias, if you wish) explicit when I have a strong point of view and trust that readers will factor my position into their responses. I believe all knowledge is *situated knowledge,* that it is produced and interpreted by humans always embedded in cultures, always able to see some things better, some things less well, from their particular place in the world (Haraway 2003 [1984]). This is not relativism, but rather a search for a *deeper level of objectivity,* one that acknowledges instead of denying our human fallibility. Having said that this is a book with more questions than answers, I will also share my ambivalences and uncertainties along the way.

Before moving too deeply into this revolutionary world of digitized cultures, it is important to note who is *not* part of those cultures, i.e., most of the people on earth. Of the roughly seven billion people on this planet, between four-and-a-half and five billion, 60 to 70 percent of us, have no access to the digital world at all. And millions of others have severely limited access compared with the taken-for-granted fast broadband access enjoyed by those of us with economic or social privilege. These *digital divides* in turn rest upon growing economic and social inequality in almost every country around the globe, and vast disparities of wealth between countries. In broad statistical terms, there are clearly great digital divides between the Global North, and the Global South, as represented by these percentages across continents: 79 percent of North Americans have access, 63 percent of Europeans, 49 percent of Middle Easterners, 42 percent of Latin Americans, 27 percent of Asians, and only 16 percent of Africans (Internet World Stats; International Telecommuncations Union). Access varies by country within continents of course, and by class, since even the poorest countries have economic elites. In the many countries with a dominant ethnic group and other minority ethnicities, minority ethnic groups almost invariably have poorer access, usually due to having lower incomes and fewer cultural benefits compared with the dominant ethnicity.

Why does this matter so much? Consider these statistics:

- 80 percent of people live in countries where the income gap is widening.

- The richest 20 percent of the population controls 75 percent of world wealth.

- 25,000 children die each day from poverty.

- Seven in a hundred people have a college education.

- A billion people in the world are illiterate.

- One in five people on earth has no clean drinking water.

- *One in five owns a digital device.*

(Statistic Brain n.d.; UNESCO Institute
for Statistics n.d.)

While statistics at the global level are subject to considerable variation depending on methods of measurement, a general pattern of
profound poverty alongside great concentrations of wealth is undeniable. And, with some local exceptions, it is clear that economic and
social inequalities in the world are currently being replicated, and
often exacerbated, by parallel inequalities in access to the Internet's
resources; this in turn means that the economic, political, social
and cultural benefits provided by digital access are distributed in
extremely unequal ways.

Scholars also recognize that digital divides are about more than
access to devices and software. There are also divides centering on language and culture (which languages and traditions are prominently
and fairly represented on the Web, and which are not), techno-literacy
(who does and who doesn't receive culturally relevant education in
using digital devices and resources), and censorship/openness (who
does and who does not have their access significantly limited by governmental or corporate forces). All these various digital divides are crucial to keep in mind if we are to approach a realistic appraisal of what
is going on in the online (and offline) worlds. (For more on digital
divides, see Chapter 9.)

With these issues of huge scale and widely varying contexts in
mind, let me be clear that I will not pretend to deal with all aspects
of new communications technologies. My focus will be on cultural
and social questions, on asking what can be done to make digital
communication technologies serve the cause of richer representation
for groups currently on the cultural margins, and how digital communication technology can be used to further economic and social
justice for all. Thus, the three keywords in my subtitle—*culture, power*
and *social change*. An emphasis on digital *culture* means focusing less
on the gadgets, more on the human interactive dimensions of digital
phenomena (though, as we will see, there is no way to fully separate
the technical and the cultural). Focusing on *power* means centering

TABLE 1.1 *Top 20 Countries with the Most Internet Users (by % of World Users), 2012*

Rank	Country	Population (2012 Estimate)	Internet Users	Internet Users (% of Population)	User % of World
1	China	1,343,239,923	538,000,000	40.1	22.4
2	United States	313,847,465	538,000,000	78.1	10.2
3	India	1,205,073,612	137,000,000	11.4	5.7
4	Japan	127,368,088	101,228,736	79.5	4.2
5	Brazil	193,946,886	88,494,756	45.6	3.7
6	Russia	142,517,670	67,982,547	47.7	2.8
7	Germany	81,305,856	67,483,860	83.0	2.8
8	Indonesia	248,645,008	55,000,000	22.1	2.3
9	United Kingdom	63,047,162	52,731,209	83.6	2.2
10	France	65,630,692	52,228,905	79.6	2.2
11	Nigeria	170,123,740	48,366,179	28.4	2.0
12	Mexico	114,975,406	42,000,000	36.5	1.7
13	Iran	78,868,711	42,000,000	53.3	1.7
14	Korea	48,860,500	40,329,660	82.5	1.7
15	Turkey	79,749,461	36,455,000	45.7	1.5
16	Italy	61,261,254	35,800,000	58.4	1.5
17	Philippines	103,775,002	33,600,000	32.4	1.4
18	Spain	47,042,984	31,606,233	67.2	1.3
19	Vietnam	91,519,289	31,034,900	33.9	1.3
20	Egypt	83,688,164	29,809,724	35.6	1.2

Source: Internet World Stats (internetworldstats.com), as of June 30, 2012

questions about who currently benefits from digital cultures and who doesn't. It means asking to what extent and in what ways the digitization of a large chunk of life on planet Earth has helped lessen or has deepened economic, social, political and cultural inequality. Focusing on *social change* means suggesting how these new media could be used to further progressive change. These are issues upon which the very survival of the planet itself may depend. Such a focus, however, does not mean that other issues about the impact of digital cultures will be ignored. Any book on the vast arena of digital cultures must be selective, limited. Focusing especially on issues of social justice is the selectiveness I have chosen, but the series of case studies I highlight can to a great extent be generalized to better understand much of the wider realm of digitally enabled communication.

⇥ DOES TECHNOLOGY MAKE US MORE THAN WE MAKE TECHNOLOGY? TECHNOLOGICAL DETERMINISM VS. TECHNOCULTURAL ANALYSIS

The metaphor of Web "surfing" that entered the vocabulary of Internet life during the early days and has stuck around for quite a while provides one way of imagining the power of digital technologies. Apart from the fact that I grew up in California, the surfing metaphor makes sense to me because it is an image of folks struggling to control, and even artfully use, a force much bigger than they are. Surfing is a highly individualized sport, but it can also be done in tandem (on one board) and in groups (though separated along the same wave). A wave is not a bad metaphor for the Web in that it is a massive, moving force beyond the full control of any individual human. Any user has at some point wondered how the wave took them far off the course they had plotted (for example, how did you start looking up information on Albert Einstein and end up surveying the microbrews at a tavern in Toronto; big hint, the tavern is called Ein Stein). (Sometimes the fault is purely with the computer, not the user, of course. As a reminder of how dumb computer algorithms can be, I recently searched "wiki-leaking" in Wikipedia commons and was asked, "Do you mean wife-leaving?" No, I did not.) Despite distractions and the dumb brilliance of algorithms, many individual users and groups of users can surf the waves of the Web with a high degree of precision. Web waves, like those in an ocean, are endless and each one unique. Nevertheless, patterns can be charted, and a certain amount can be predicted. Cyberskeptics will warn that information tsunamis will soon drown us all, while cyberhypers will focus only on the pure joy of those many varied waves each providing a rad ride. Somewhere between these extremes we can make sense of the ever-changing but readable relations that exist between people and technologies.

In less metaphorical terms, one of the most common ways of talking about the relationship between humans and the technical devices they invent is a theory called *technological determinism*. As the name suggests, this approach stresses the technological side of the technology–society relation. In its more extreme form, technological determinism argues that technologies are the single most important force driving human history, and that there is an almost automatic cause-and-effect relationship between the kind of technology a culture has and the essential qualities of that culture. Technological determinism grants technologies themselves independent causal power. Much of early discussion of cyberculture, for example, suggested that something inherent in the technology would lead inevitably to evil (dystopian) or highly positive (utopian) outcomes. Neither has happened because technology never acts alone. Critics of this deterministic approach argue that it exaggerates the extent to which social meanings and uses arise *automatically* from technological innovations. Most serious scholars now reject the extreme forms of technological determinism. However, much of the work that has been done to understand the impact of technological innovation across thousands of years of human history is immensely important, and makes clear that the society-shaping role of technologies should never be underestimated.

At the same time, it is clear that a central problem with techno-determinism is that it largely ignores the fact that technologies emerge from various social and culture groups, and that those groups play a profound role in how the technology is subsequently used. In other words, cultures create technologies, and the extent to which a given technology comes in time to alter culture is never a simple one of technology dictating to society. Technology is not a Frankenstein monster or the Terminator running amok. It is a series of devices and practices in the hands and minds of users. We are all Dr. Frankensteins, we all have Terminator power (aka smartphones) at our command, and it is up to us whether our monsters and cyborgs help us to make a culturally richer, politically more just world, or strangle the life out of us. In relation to how these technologies work in the world, I take a position stated succinctly many decades ago by one of the first thinkers to look closely at what communication media are doing to us and to the world, controversial media critic/prophet Marshall McLuhan who remarked, "We shape our tools, and afterwards our tools shape us" (McLuhan 1994 [1964] xxi).

McLuhan here is trying to avoid two kinds of mistakes in thinking about technologies of communication. On the one hand, he seeks to avoid technological determinism (though he was not always so careful to avoid this trap), and on the other hand, he seeks to acknowledge that each communication tool (from the pencil to the television) has certain likely uses built into it that can shape our actions in ways we may not intend or initially imagine. Keeping with the tool metaphor, think of the expression "to a hammer, the whole world looks like a nail." Hammers were designed to do certain specific things, and they are very good at those things. But they can't do everything because not everything in the world is a nail. And they can be put to ill uses not originally intended. They can, for example, like Maxwell's silver hammer in the Beatles song, be used as a weapon (so can a pencil, for that matter). So one key trick in thinking about any technology is to ask not only what can it do for us, but also what can it *not* do for us, what are its limits, and what do we *not want* the tool to do. If we don't ask these questions, new technologies might just metaphorically, or should I say virtually, bash our skulls in, or at least hammer away in destructive ways at lots of things that aren't nails.

All technologies have some uses built into them. It is hard to fly a car or float a plane (James Bond and sea planes notwithstanding). But technologies also always have unforeseen consequences. The Internet, to take a pertinent example, was designed with the needs of a small number of military personnel and scientists in mind. Hardly anyone in on the early development of what became the Internet conceived of it as the revolutionary medium of popular communication it has become. On the one hand, the technology had the potential use to which it is now being put built in, and so in some sense the technology has driven the development that became the modern Internet. But on the other hand, that development was a highly uneven, stop-and-start process that, while enabled by technical breakthroughs (especially the invention of the World Wide Web), was a thoroughly social and cultural phenomenon. Complex technological devices might be thought of as like a chessboard. Chess has many rules and restrictions; you cannot do just anything on a chessboard. But the number of particular outcomes that are possible on the platform, that simple board of squares, is virtually infinite. The military-scientific inventors of the Internet had no idea that it would one day be used to share videos of cats playing the piano (if they had, would they have had second thoughts?), but they did build in the possibility of doing so. Fortunately, as it turns out, the Net is big enough to contain *both* scientific brilliance and feline silliness.

What virtually all forms of critical digital culture analysis have in common is a rejection of pure technological determinism in favor of approaches that can be grouped under the rubric *technocultural*. As the term's blending and blurring of the words technology and culture suggests, technocultural approaches argue that technologies and cultures can never be neatly separated, because technical innovations are always created by individuals and groups deeply shaped by cultural assumptions and biases, and technologies are always used in particular cultural contexts which reshape them even as they reshape the cultural contexts.

Choices about which technologies are to be developed are always partly economic, partly political and partly social. In turn, choices about which technologies become popular are deeply social and cultural, as are the uses to which technologies are ultimately put. Decisions about which technologies get built and disseminated (and which do not) are shaped by economic systems, governmental action, social needs/desires and individual choices. The adoption and use of technologies is always a social process that is only partly predictable (as the makers of hi-tech devices that bombed on the market know all too well). Once created, technologies are subsequently adapted, changed or replaced through further sociocultural processes. None of this can be easily determined in advance. This means that whether we have a technological utopia coming our way, or a technological apocalypse, is not something looking at technologies alone can ever tell us. We must also look at the human contexts that shape and reshape those technologies.

Among the more useful and interesting frameworks for thinking about culture and technology are *actor–network theory,* and a parallel *feminist technoscience* approach. Actor–network theory is associated with figures like French philosopher of science Bruno Latour, and a similar feminist approach developed most fully by Donna Haraway. Actor–network theory views technological devices as actors (agents), with something resembling human agency (power to impact events), but with the caveat that like humans, technological actors are always caught up in larger networks of power and causality (Haraway 1997; Latour 1987). Technologies and humans are both entangled in economic relations, political relations, social relations and cultural relations. To further the metaphor, you could say that a given technical device, say the smartphone, is an actor in the world with a variety of identities (*personalizations* like color, size, shape, ring tones, language, etc.) and behaviors that vary widely, but all act within a set of wider social and technical systems (networks) that shape and limit their nature and uses. Uses of the cellphone are wide but not limitless, and certain uses are far more likely given the specific social contexts and networks of their users (business people are more likely to think of them as work tools, while teens are more likely to think of them as socializing tools, and so on).

Technocultural approaches to digital culture issues avoid the extremes of viewing technologies as running amok, out of human control, and the equally dangerous assumption that technologies have no likely social consequences, including unintended ones, built into them. The good news is that we are still early in the process of collectively determining what we will do with the (relatively) new digital devices and platforms that are the subject of this book. And, ironically, the devices themselves may provide us with some key tools we need to make good technocultural choices. At least until fully functioning AIs (artificial intelligences) come along that are as complex, subtle, creative and multifaceted as the human brain, it will still be fallible, culture-bound humans who, through individual and collective action, will determine the future path of technology (and culture). The best technocultural approaches offer a more dynamic way of thinking *with* our hi-tech tools, approaches that regard ever-changing cultural, political, economic, and social conditions as integral to, inseparable from, the media that help create those social conditions.

⊡ COMPONENTS OF DIGITAL CULTURE ANALYSIS

The complete study of digital cultures can be thought of as addressing four main components: *production analysis,* which looks at the wider political, economic and social contexts shaping a particular digital culture; *textual analysis,* which closely examines the content and form in digital spaces—words, images, sounds, etc.; *audience/user analysis,* which tries to get at precisely what actual users are doing with digital devices and what meanings they are making of digital texts; and *historical analysis,* which measures the unique qualities of digital cultures in relation to previous forms of communication and as they change over time.

Understanding the production process enabling digital cultures means asking who actually makes digital devices, and under what economic and social conditions. Who are the *electronic company executives* and what are their working lives like? Who are the *software designers* and what are their working conditions? Who are the *hardware designers/ engineers* and what are their working conditions? Who are the *assembly line workers* and what are their working conditions? These questions matter in regard to issues of just and unjust labor practices, and also because digital devices are never culturally neutral; they always have the particular cultural biases of their makers built in. Production analysis asks what cultural ideas are built into hardware, into software, into Web interfaces or the shapes of smartphones? What cultural ideas are built into various webpage genres, templates and styles? How do dominant cultural ideas influence design, and to what extent can folks from less socially powerful, more marginalized cultural positions influence the design and creation of our digital devices?

Textual analysis in its various forms (rhetorical, semiotic, psychoanalytic, and so forth) examines the verbal (written and spoken words), visual (colors, layout, still and moving images), and aural (voice, music, and other sounds) elements of websites, games and other digital spaces, as well as these qualities as manifested in digital devices like smartphones, game consoles or tablet computers. Much digital text analysis focuses on what we most often mean by text, the written word, examining the verbiage on a web page or the conversation in a chat room, doing the kind of close reading associated with literary analysis. But because digital cultures generally exist these days in multimedia form, textual analysis often also includes sounds and imagery, as well as words. Whatever its focus, textual analysis has to be extremely sensitive to differing cultural contexts. Color on a website or on an iPhone cover, for example, can convey very different things to people whose culturally derived associations with color symbolism differ. For example, in Brazil the color purple signifies mourning, in Asia luxury, in Britain royalty, and in the US frivolity. Subcultures likewise may offer signifiers that counter dominant ones.

In addition, as with literary textual analysis, textual studies of digital cultures pay attention to the forms and formats in which digitized texts appear. Each genre and platform, from a less-than-140-character microblog, to e-books running to hundreds of pages, from texts experienced on cellphones to ones read on a laptop to ones projected onto huge screens in classrooms or movie theaters, contain different implicit meanings and expectations and create differing experiences. Form deeply shapes content, which in turn shapes consciousness. Major debates in digital culture studies, for example, swirl around the issue of how the rapidly shifting, link-driven reading experience typical in online spaces may be shaping our ability to think linearly, or to pay attention to long narratives, or to follow complex, multilevel logical arguments.

Textual analyses are generally qualitative (involving close interpretative reading), rather than quantitative (based upon statistical data), but one sub-category of textual approaches, *content analysis,* takes a largely quantitative form, doing things like counting the occurrences of female Asian American characters in a particular genre of video games. Content analysis at the numerical level alone is generally not very illuminating, but when combined with cultural analysis these data can give a more solid statistical base to interpretations. Contrary to the adage, "the facts" never "speak for themselves"; even the purest quantitative data are subject to (always debatable) interpretation. However, interpretation is generally more believable when backed by one or another kind of empirical evidence, and much of the best interpretive work in the cultural study of technology remains grounded in one or another archive of data that combines qualitative and quantitative elements.

Audience or user analyses take a number of different forms and use a number of different methods. These can be ranged in degrees of breadth vis-à-vis depth. The broadest amount of information can be gained through *surveys* or *representative sampling,* which can involve hundreds if not thousands of respondents. The Web itself has contributed immensely to the field of social surveying in general, and it is obviously an even more perfect tool for gathering information about specifically online cultures. A second approach uses *focus groups,* a method long used to study *old* media. Focus groups survey a relatively small number of people, typically fewer than 20, interviewing them in more depth and more interactively than is possible through a poll survey. Finally, the anthropological and sociological approach called ethnography is being applied to digital culture (Escobar 1996; Hesse-Biber 2011).Traditional ethnography involves living among while studying a cultural group. *Cyber-ethnography* (aka online or virtual ethnography, netnography, webnography, computer-mediated ethnography, etc.) applies this approach to digital culture groups. Typically cyber-ethnography takes one of two forms. In one mode, scholars act as "lurkers," observing online activities surreptitiously by visiting cyberspaces (work spaces, play spaces, socializing spaces) unannounced. The second main mode of cyber-ethnography involves researchers engaging in *participant observation* by openly joining an online community (a chat room, or an MMORPG), in order to study the group's experience from both inside and out. One group of scholars, for example, joined World of Warcraft, the largest online game community (with reportedly over ten million players), playing for several months and then writing up, sharing, and publishing their analyses of the game and game experience from a variety of perspectives (Corneliussen and Rettberg 2008). There is much debate about whether honest disclosure that one is a participant-observer is preferable to lurking, since the presence of a researcher may skew the activity of other users, while lack of candor on this issue can raise charges of privacy invasion. Elaborate rules have been devised to mitigate some of these issues, but no clear consensus on the best approach has emerged.

User analysis tries to understand what *actually happens to people* as they utilize digital spaces and devices, both in the narrow sense of finding out what they are doing and the larger sense of uncovering what is being done to them. By the latter I mean trying to get at the personal and social impact of spending time using particular digital devices and platforms. How does a person's idea of geography change when they work primarily with mobile devices? What is the impact of digital surveillance on a worker whose every keyboard stroke is being read by the boss? What is the impact on one's sense of self, community and privacy of being in an always-connected state through a smartphone? And so on.

One particularly intense kind of audience, fans, has received a great deal of attention in relationship to digital culture. While fandom has a long history prior to the rise of the Net, the online world has exponentially increased the amount and depth of fan activity. And because much of this activity is publicly visible, researchers have been given a richer look into how audiences interpret a range of popular culture topics (movies, celebrities), as well as providing data on how online practices may be changing the nature of fans in regard to their objects of affection and interest.

Historical approaches in effect surround all these other methods, since without knowing the history of technocultures, the history of cultural texts, and the history of media audiences, it is impossible to really measure the specific impact of any element of new media production. Thinking historically, the alleged newness can be separated out into various degrees or levels across a continuum by addressing questions like these: 1) What does the new technology do that could not be done by earlier forms of communication? Prior to the Web and applications like Skype, visual conversations across great distances were only possible on "Star Trek"; 2) What does the new technology do more easily, more cheaply, or more effectively than earlier mediums? Downloading digitized music greatly increases access to a range of forms, and, even when done legally, generally reduces costs; 3) What does the new technology do that might be done as well or better by older mediums? When you see two friends walking down the street, each with a cellphone talking to other people, you may well ask whether they would be better off actually talking to each other via the ancient medium of face-to-face communication. These three questions certainly do not cover the full range of possible historical meanings and impacts of new media, but when kept in mind they can sort through a lot of hype and clarify a good deal about what is truly important and innovative in new communication technologies.

Few individual studies of digital culture substantially deal with all four elements, though they often combine two or more, but the richest view of the terrain of digital cultures emerges when all these elements are factored into the picture. I have tried to do that with the topics all-too-briefly surveyed in this book, but I urge those of you who wish to dig more deeply into any particular aspect of digital culture, starting perhaps with resources provided on the companion website, to keep this full array of factors in mind as you proceed.

⇨ IS THERE A VIRTUAL WORLD/ REAL-WORLD DIVIDE?

One of the most enduring terms used to describe the world created by the Internet and related digital domains is the term *cyberspace.* That term came into the English language via a science fiction novel, William Gibson's *Neuromancer* (1984). The book was prophetic in the sense that it described an online world that in some respects resembled the not yet online world we now know (though Gibson had never been on the then nascent Web when he wrote the novel). But more important than the prophetic element was the power of the word. Cyberspace quickly caught on as the name for the place created by electronic communication. It became a ubiquitous term (and therefore perhaps part of a *self-fulfilling* prophecy in some ways), but it has also been misleading in a number of ways. It is, after all, as its origin in a work of fiction should remind us, only a metaphor. In fact, Gibson points us in this direction by defining cyberspace as

> [a] consensual hallucination experienced daily by billions of legitimate operators, in every nation . . . A graphic representation of data abstracted from the banks of every computer in the human system. Unthinkable complexity. Lines of light ranged in the non-space of the mind, clusters and constellations of data. Like city lights, receding.
>
> (Gibson 1994 69)

Cyberspace doesn't exist in precisely the same way that Montreal or Melbourne or Mogadishu exist. The Net's physical existence has less visible relation to its imaginary existence. While cities and countries are also in a sense imagined places, we generally imagine their geographic location in a way that is more grounded, literally, than is our imagination of cyberspace. In the broadest sense, the geography of the Internet is three things at once: the place from which the user is accessing it, the user's experiences online in that space, and a largely invisible space of connected servers, data centers, and individual computers that enable the experience. We often forget the first of these spaces (lost in cyberspace), and seldom think much about the third space (because its materiality is also subsumed by our online experiences). This makes cyberspace a somewhat different kind of place, but it is still a place in the world. Or, better yet, it is many places, all of which are in the world (not the ether). Just as the word San Francisco calls up different images for each of us depending on our knowledge of that real, imagined city, there are as many cyberspaces as there are users of networked electronic communication devices. The difference is that few of us imagine cyberspace's geography in any physical way; its geographic grounding is weirdly dispersed and invisible, with most of us imagining it rather abstractly, if at all. Even a parallel media form, television, tends to evoke more material reality. We think of studios, sets, cameras, etc. that give some physical reality to TV. Cyberspace's base, the Net, on the other hand, is seldom more than an abstract image, often depicted as lines of light brilliantly traveling across the globe; few users who are not engineers know how the physical Internet looks or think of it in material terms.

As Andrew Blum puts it, we misleadingly tend to think more in terms of "ether" than "net" (Blum 2013). The seemingly placeless, ethereal world of the Web is not possible without millions of very earthbound terminals and CPUs, hundreds of thousands of miles of cords and fiber optic cables, thousands of wifi towers, hundreds of huge warehouses full of servers, millions of routers and switches, arrayed as a whole panoply of engineering esoterica like Dense Wavelength Division Multiplexing terminals and regen sites (see Figure 1.1). No matter how lost we may get imaginatively in cyberspaces, those seemingly virtual spaces are possible only because of a massive array of material objects anchored in geographically specific places. But, almost as if it were ashamed of the concrete reality behind the illusion of empty cyberspace, the industry deeply buries and places behind secret closed doors much of this infrastructure; for a glimpse inside, see the short documentary "Bundled, Buried and Behind Closed Doors" (Mendelsohn 2011) and visit Google's rather sanitized and aestheticized Data Centers Gallery (*Google* n.d.).

The concept of cyberspace has fallen out of favor with many scholars of digital culture, along with the prefix "cyber" in general. For a while everything seemed to be a cyber-this or cyber-that—cybercafes, cyberbullying, cyberdogs, etc. More recently, "e-ing" seems to be preferred such that we now have e-books, e-commerce, e-learning, e-waste (see Chapter 2) and so on. But even if the term cyber is being superseded among scholars, cyberspace is still widely used in popular discourse and a better alternative has yet to be coined (the most common other candidate, "virtual space," is equally problematic in some ways). A better (perhaps temporary) solution is to

FIGURE 1.1 *A bit of the material internet. (Courtesy of shutterstock.com.)*

pluralize, to speak of many cyberspaces, to remind users to distinguish among various different imagined spaces created by interacting
with different devices and media (the Web, console games, smartphones, etc.), for differing purposes (shopping, learning, working,
playing, voting, etc.), and through differing cultural lenses. So in the
context of this book, I will use the term cyberspaces in the plural,
along with other analogous terms, to help assure that we do not too

easily homogenize this complicated, imaginary terrain as one continuous space, place or thing.

As a product of culture-laden people, cyberspace is always very much attached to, indeed woven into, the rest of the world. As a space for the production of culture, it has evolved its own special forms, styles, rules, structures and identities, but these never stray far from offline connections. The line between cybercultures and wider cultures is never absolute or stable; the boundaries are being crossed all the time in both directions. Wider cultures always shape or spill into cyberspaces, and cyberspaces spill out to wider cultural fields in a myriad of ways. Given the ubiquity of posting these days, for many the entire "offline" world is just a text waiting to be tweeted, YouTubed or Facebooked, or Instagrammed (Jurgenson 2012). Not to mention that face-to-face interactions these days often revolve around "online" events. Still, surprisingly to some, most of the world most of the time is offline, and much still happens there that never gets online.

Increasingly, digital cultural contexts include other forms of mass media like television, film, radio, newspapers, magazines and so forth. This is part of the complex process known as *remediation,* taking one media form and transmitting/transforming it through another (e.g., "old media" television programs digitized and broadcast via a tablet or smartphone). This is a two-way process in that incorporating older media reshapes the new (websites that look like TV screens), while the old media adapt to the new (TV news shows that look like websites). In these and many other ways, there is no absolute split between virtual worlds and the so-called real world, new media and old, or between digital spaces and analog spaces. These "worlds" are actually always interwoven in complex ways. This does not mean that virtual, digital or cyberspaces cannot or should not be isolated to some extent for the purposes of cultural analysis, but it does mean that it is crucial to remember that such isolation is always somewhat artificial, always on another level incomplete.

This leads us into another set of commonly used (and abused) terms, the *real world* and the *virtual world.* While this distinction is in certain respects unavoidable, it can also be deeply misleading. It is misleading because no one and no thing ever exists only in the virtual, only in cyberspace. As suggested above, we are always somewhere in the Real World (even if we are moving through it with mobile smartphones in hand), using physical devices networked to other physical devices, whenever we imaginatively experience ourselves to be in a virtual world. Now, depending on the degree of *immersion* we feel, that sense of otherworldliness may be subtle or very strong. And it is important to take that illusion of virtuality seriously; it *is* to some degree a new kind of experience. But it is also not wholly new (whenever we read a novel we also enter a virtual world, just not a digitally delivered one). Part of studying virtual worlds should be to remind users that they are never just in a virtual world, but also always in the real one too. The founders of the widely used file-sharing site Pirate Bay (subject, like Napster before them, to a lawsuit regarding the issue of legal vs. illegal downloading) prefer the term "away from keyboard" life, noting that "the Internet is for real" (Klose 2013). For the purposes of this book, I will mostly use the term *online* to name these spaces, because it is the most commonly used term and is a somewhat more neutral term in that it merely designates connection to the Internet without unduly characterizing the nature of that connection. But when you read the word, please imagine "scare quotes" around it, because the notion of two worlds is ultimately a false one.

To a very large degree, the online world is a reflection of the offline world. But reflections are always distorting, whether it be as simple as showing things in reverse to the huge, deeply weird reflections of funhouse mirrors. The reflecting and refracting medium matters a great deal, but it is essentially the same world whether represented via a digital medium or face to face. If you don't like what you find on the Web, don't just blame the online world; blame the offline world out of which it came. There are many things unique to digital cultures; if there were not we wouldn't need this book. But that uniqueness is not otherworldly, it is this-worldly.

Much of the hype, or *cyberbole* (Woolgar 2003), surrounding digital cultures, especially games and virtual reality simulators, is that they are deeply immersive, engaging us in wholly new and deeper ways. The assumption here is that users/players lose themselves in virtual worlds as never before in human history. Yet from ancient story telling around campfires to novels to movies, virtual reality has always been a part of human experience. Might it be as, or perhaps more, immersive to enact scenes from a story where your own imagination fills in the details, rather than having them digitally simulated? Neuroscience may give us the answer to this question, but the research on the topic of immersion is immensely complex. The term turns out to have no stable meaning, and many different dimensions that are hard to measure (Madigan 2010). This again reminds us that claims of newness or uniqueness regarding digitized experiences need to be approached carefully.

As discussed above, when a technology is newly minted it often seems quite strange. In its early years, the Web was experienced as a very weird, almost miraculous space, or place. But over time (and in the case of new media the amount of time seems to be growing shorter and shorter), the new becomes ordinary, becomes taken for granted as just part of our world. This is part of what scholars call the *domestication of technology*, the process by which things that initially seem new and wild can quickly become familiar. All of us have had that experience, and at this point in the evolution of ICTs domestication has occurred far and wide. So-called *early adopters*, many of whom seek out truly new things to do with new technologies, give way over time to more and more conventional users who subsume the new into older patterns of interaction. Domestication refers in common parlance to the home, and that is a convenient way to think about this process: it is becoming "at home with" the technology. In this case, domestication included the literal movement of digital devices from schools and offices into the home (into domestic space) partly via smaller and smaller devices, from bulky to smaller desktop computers to laptops and smartphones. The ongoing domestication of technology is also very much a gendered process impacting men and women differently, given that home space has long been stereoptyped as feminine. Domestication is also an ongoing historical process, one that is repeated whenever a new group of users encounters a new technology, and whenever a group of existing users encounters a newer technology (as in the move from dumbphones to smartphones, where telephone-like communication was augmented by communication with the Web and other features of the Net).

Scholars of all things digital caution also against thinking of a particular device like the cellphone as one thing that has gone through changes and variations (symbolized by physical transformation from devices the size of a cat to ones that now fit into the palm of your hand). Lisa Gitelman, for example, in her book *Always Already New* (2006), argues that we should not think of the telephone or even the cellphone as one "thing" that has changed over time (in size, shape, and features), but rather as something like an evolving process. Much the same can be said about many other forms of digital technology. They make sense more as processes than as things, or at least as a series of things, not one thing. Specificity in time (history) and place (geography) and social context (culture) all matter greatly in talking about ICTs.

▣ TERMINAL CONFUSION?

Whenever a new field is devised to understand new social phenomena, that field generates new words to help define and clarify those phenomena. The nasty name for these new words is "jargon"; the more positive word is "terminology." To the uninitiated, these new terms often seem like unnecessary complications, if not downright gibberish. But to those in the field, they are helpful shorthand and absolutely crucial tools. The field of technology, and with it technology studies, is often criticized for generating particularly inscrutable jargons. Some of this criticism is no doubt deserved (the proliferation of acronyms and neologisms surrounding computer culture is truly baffling). But new terms also offer vitally necessary specificity and clarity. Every field has them; your plumber has a vocabulary every bit as esoteric as your computer technician, but we seldom criticize plumbers for a specialist vocabulary that runs from "adjusting links" to "zero soft" water because we know it helps them get the job done. Just as you would probably allow a plumber the right to call not for that shiny metal thing with a kind of c shape on the end, but rather specify a crescent wrench, I hope you will recognize that the specialist vocabulary introduced in this book is not designed to obscure but to clarify, to create a shorthand language that makes it easier to communicate complicated ideas. While mostly defined as used, fuller definitions of many of these keywords appear in the Glossary. I trust you will come to see most of them as useful tools rather than as attempts to colonize your brain.

One key duo of terms that obviously shapes everything discussed in this book is the Internet, and the World Wide Web. Technically speaking, the Internet is the physical basis that makes most cyberculture possible. It is the *network of linked computers* all over the world over which information, from e-mails to documents to websites, travels around the globe. The World Wide Web, on the other hand, is the most popular Internet interface; it is the system of codes (HTML and its variants) that make the information traveling along the Internet visible and accessible to users. Since the Internet is the more common, popular word used to talk about what is online, much of the time I will use it (and its shorthand, the Net) as a synonym for the World Wide Web (and its shorthand, the Web). There has in recent years been an argument made that the word internet should no longer be capitalized, that a small "i" should be used because we do not capitalize seemingly comparable words like television. This change has not yet been popularly adopted, so I will stick to capitalizing, but this trend itself is another sign of domestication of technology as the Internet, or internet, loses its aura of difference, becoming just another medium alongside others.

Another, hipper kind of domestication can be found in the many tongue-in-cheek variations on Internet and Web that have arisen over the years, including interwebs, Dub Dub Dub, Webternet, the tubes or intertubes, or, for the truly esoteric, 1n73rw3b (in Leet, a code language used by some digerati), and many more. Regardless of the name you prefer, it is helpful to keep in mind that the Internet is actually the material, physical basis that allows the so-called virtual worlds to appear via the Web and other interfaces.

⊡ WHAT'S IN A NAME? NEW MEDIA/CYBER/ DIGITAL CULTURE/ETC. STUDIES

Ironically, the field that has generated so many new terms to make sense of all this high-tech stuff has yet to agree on a term to name itself. Given that the field draws from the sciences (neuroscience, for example), the social sciences (psychology, anthropology and communications, for example), and the humanities (literary and cultural studies, for example), inability to agree on nomenclature is not surprising. Known variously as new media studies, cyberculture studies or digital culture studies, among others, the field that tries to make sense of recent trends in electronic communication is still debating what label best characterizes the field (Silver 2006). Fortunately, thinking about each of the most common names proposed for this area of study actually can be quite useful in revealing something about some key issues involved in thinking about communication technologies.

One major contender is the name new media studies. This particular name immediately takes us back to the problematic question: "new" compared with what? The quick and easy answer is new compared with "old media" like TV, radio, film, photography and print. But exactly when and how does a medium become new? When exactly does a new technology or a new medium cease to be new? The public version of the Internet is now close to three decades old. It is certainly not new to some people. Yet, new people are constantly being added to the user rolls. Does that make the medium new again? Doesn't the experience of newness change depending upon when one encounters the new? For new to be more than a marketing tool, it is crucial to always ask new compared with what, and new in what sense.

Emphasis on the media (the new devices and platforms) implied in the name can also bias study toward the "techno" side, and away from the "cultural" side of technocultural analysis. A related issue with the term new media is its entanglement with commercialism. Under modern consumer capitalism, "new" is always good, always better. How many ads use the phrase "new and improved," with the latter word hardly needed? So there is a certain prejudice in the term new media that tends automatically to connote progress, rather than leaving open the question of whether the particular newness in question is for better or worse. And overall, as discussed in Chapter 2, the endless search for newness is having devastating ecological consequences (Slade 2007).

Another way to talk about the newness of new media is to speak of their impact on "old media." The rise of the broadband, broadcast dimension of the Web, for example, has been accompanied by the declining popularity of the old medium of television among young (under 25) users. When young people do access TV programming, they increasing do so via digital devices. The impact of digital music production and digital downloading on the old media of the CD is well known (from the Napster controversy to rise of services like iTunes), and the old medium of radio has been given a new but different life on the Internet. Likewise, digital technology has taken over the old medium of film in a variety of ways, from the digitization of much Hollywood "filmmaking" to digital cameras used increasingly in independent films to video capabilities on smartphones. How does viewing movies on computers, tablets or phones change the experience? (Some studies of digital remediation compare this with earlier issues like how watching movies on TV differs from seeing them in public theaters.) In each of these cases, old media have undergone remediation into new media, have been reworked through a new medium. They have not disappeared (yet), but have in various ways and in varying degrees been transformed by newer, digitally based media. How different is the experience of watching TV programs on your smartphone from watching them on a television set? Scholars debate how much and in what ways transferring content into a new medium changes the experience, but they agree that the medium matters to the message. So, while the term new can be misleading, and overemphasis on media form over the content can be a problem at time, the name new media studies points to a variety of key questions about (relative) new*ness,* and to what is or is not truly new about cultures reshaped by digital media.

A second term, cyberculture studies, was popular for quite a while to name the field, but fell into some disrepute in the 2010s. On the one hand, the term rightly points to one of the key aspects of (much but not all) new media, the fact that it favors cybernetic systems, that is systems in which non-human devices or processes do things previously only done by humans. Robots are an extreme example of this; search engines like Google are a more mundane, currently common form. The term raises two main problems. First, it tends to call up images of things beyond our control, of technology running on its own. And second, because cyber as a modifier partly arose from and remains associated with speculative/science fiction (cyberspace, cyberpunk, cyborgs, etc.), the prefix cyber often calls up associations with s/f that suggests futurity and strangeness, or suggests that these processes are part of an inevitable future. But cyber is still a popular prefix and continues to shape how people think about all things digital. And public perceptions or fantasies are themselves an important part of digital culture, part of what is sometimes called the technological imaginary (our imagined relations to technologies, as interwoven with what we actually do with them and through them).

The third common term for the field is digital culture studies. It, too, is both useful and somewhat problematic. Making something digital technically refers to a process by which information (verbal, visual, aural) is turned into a particular kind of mathematical code, the binary code of 0s and 1s. The ability to turn information into digital code is the technological breakthrough that enables computers and computer programs, the Internet, the Web, smartphones, video games, e-readers and most other forms of new media to exist. This is crucial to remember because taking a digital form, as often contrasted with an analog one, does entail certain possibilities and certain limitations. One famous example is the debate about the differing sound quality between digitized music and earlier analog forms like vinyl records. Keen listeners may disagree as to preference, but they agree that there is a difference. The down side of the term digital is that in privileging this code language, we may be engaging in a subtle form of technological determinism as we suggest that this coding process is the essence of what we are studying, rather than the cultural processes *shaped by* but not *determined by* the mathematical coding that underlies various uses of digitized cultural phenomena. In other words, that something is digitized inherently tells us only some things; what is made of those digitized things depends on much more than the fact that 0s and 1s underlie it.

A slightly different approach is to talk about new media/digital/cybercultures is to see them as the essence of an information society (or sometimes networked society or, as in my subtitle, the Internet era) (Castells 2000; Fuchs 2008; Webster 2006). This term makes the broadest claim of all, suggesting that these new digital communication technologies and the cultures they help enable have become so important that they have redefined the entire social world. Now, the good news is that "society" plays a prominent role in that description, in a way that terms just privileging the technology do not. But the modifier "information" largely erases that benefit. First, when was there ever a society where information was not of central importance? Of course, those who use this term intend to indicate something more than what we traditionally mean by information. They especially mean digitized information, and/or information carried on computer networks like the Internet and mobile phones. But beyond this they mean to suggest that somehow the circulation of information has become *more* important than ever before. The phrase also credits (perhaps over-credits) information technology as a key force enabling the current form of neoliberal globalization. While it is true that the movement of ideas, money, products and labor transnationally would not be possible without the Internet and related communication technologies, there is nothing in the technology, for example, that determined it would be used, under revived "free market" ideologies, to increase economic inequality around the globe.

Those using the term "information society" also suggest that information has become a more central economic resource, a commodity, one that accounts for a greater amount of economic activity than ever before (accompanied by a corresponding decline in the importance of manufacturing). They suggest that with the greater importance of information comes greater social and cultural power for those with access to or control over the flow of information. There is certainly truth in this, and battles over the power of information are clearly central today. But at the same time, it is important to realize that material production, including the production of digital devices themselves, is still very much with us and very much part of societies around the globe. As we will see, to forget that the electronics industry is indeed an *industry* is to obscure, among other things, its environmental impact and its impact on workers. It is therefore probably more apt to talk about the significant growth of the information sector of contemporary societies rather than using the term information society to characterize the current world system overall.

While perhaps a bit frustrating, the fact that each of the most common terms used to describe this emerging field is problematic should not cause despair. Rather it indicates a certain healthy openness. Each term keys us into important aspects of the terrain, as do other variants including Internet studies, networked culture studies, computer-mediated communication studies, Web studies, etc. Each of these terms proves partial, in both the sense of incomplete and biased, in relation to the overall dynamic experience of our digitizing world. "New media" points us to the forms and devices—the Web, video games, smartphones, virtual reality suits, etc. "Digital" points us to the common, underlying and enabling mathematical coding process that animates all these devices. And "cyber" points us toward the way popular culture *imagines* these emergent communication developments.

In this book, it is the *culture surrounding and embedded in these devices and processes* that will be the main focus. But it is impossible to think clearly about these cultural formations without thinking about the devices, processes and encodings that intertwine with them. There is no way to abstract the cultural content from the new digital cybernetic media that enable them, nor should they be separated from the broader historical forces that create and recreate them. One obvious way history matters in all this is, again, highlighted by use of the word new. Much of the hype around new media emphasizes this new side over the media part. But anthropologists of communication point out that the most common uses of "new" technologies may be to do "old" things. That is to say, new devices may most often just reinforce the same old existing patterns of communication and interaction. One of the most comprehensive studies of the impact of the landline telephone, for example, concluded that during the period of its "newness" in the United States, defined as from 1900 to 1940, "the telephone did not radically alter American ways of life; rather, Americans used it to more vigorously pursue their characteristic ways of life" (Fischer 1992 5). Could this be true of our latest batch of ICTs? Are they far less new than we think? Are they merely reinforcing old ways of being, rather than, as so much of the hype suggests, radically changing our way of life? If the answer were simply Yes, this book would probably not be necessary. So, for the sake of my publishers, among others, let me say that the answer is more complicated than a simple Yes or No can offer.

While the field-without-a-name is full of intense debates, not only over what to call itself, but also over many other more substantive issues, most of the best questions and best answers about the social and cultural impact of digitizing our lives do come from this variously named academic discipline (though journalists and other non-academic analysts have also contributed significantly to our understanding). Knowledge in all academic fields is incomplete and imperfect, and all fields worth being called scholarly are rich in debate. There is a growing amount of very useful research that is crucial to sort through if we care about what digital cultures mean now and are likely to mean in the future. Knowledge starts with information (facts, basic data) but knowledge is something more; it is making sense of the information. It involves finding the right analytic framework to put data into meaningful and useful patterns that can lead to intelligent action. What, for example, do we make of this fact: when I spoke the word "facts" into my dictation program as I was writing/speaking the previous sentence, the program initially wrote, "FAQs"? What does that tell us? That my laptop is trying to take over writing my book? Probably not, though in the not-so-distant future we will have to deal increasingly with artificial intelligences that blur the line between humans and techno-devices (my dictation program was at least smart enough to "choose" FAQs over FAX as closer in relevance). No, the less paranoid knowledge we could take from this incident is the reminder that this book is inside the very thing it is trying to look at from the outside, that these technologies are very deeply embedded in our everyday lives in ways from which we can only partly distance ourselves, even when we try very hard. Is it possible, for example, that my decision to write this book in relatively short chapters was, unconsciously, in part determined by my knowledge that many observers claim our attention spans have been shortened by spending time in the distracting world of hypertext links and microblogged tweets?

Since each of the names for the field of study upon which this book draws is illuminating, but incomplete and somewhat misleading, as well as for the sake of variety, I will use each of these modifiers—new media, digital, cyber—interchangeably when naming the field of cultural study. At other times, I use the terms with their more precise meanings to indicate devices (new media), the technical form underlying the devices (digital), or the human/non-human control elements (cybernetics) of these devices and processes.

Many topics covered in this book are immensely complex, and we will just be scratching the surface of them. This inevitably means simplifying, but I try to avoid *over*simplifying by pointing to complicating factors and suggesting through the companion website where readers can go to dig more deeply into each topic. That there are few definitive answers stems partly from the fact that these new media are evolving rapidly, and that means their meanings are still up for grabs. We the users continue to remake these devices just as quickly as designers and workers make them. Devices, apps, platforms come and go. Some ones I mention in this book will already seem quaintly historical by the time you read this. But these ephemeral devices and apps represent deeper cultural processes. By drawing from the rich existing scholarship on new(er) media using the range of scientific, social scientific and humanities-based approaches sketched above, it is possible to gain insight into these deeper processes that particular digital devices or programs embody (for a time), processes that continue beyond the passing moment of particular pieces of hardware and software.

2

How is the Digital World Made?

The Dreamers/Workers/ Users Production Cycle

Most of the time for most users, the Internet simply magically appears through a click on a smartphone, tablet, or laptop. Most of the time we don't think about how this magic is made possible, do not think about the complex production process behind that pretty little screen and the Internet that seems to hold all the world's knowledge. Before taking up questions about *what* goes on in digital cultures, it is important to think about *how* digital cultures are possible at all, to look at the history and present of the production process that enables an online world to exist in the first place.

⊡ THE INTERNET'S WEIRD HISTORY

The technocultural history of the Internet is a fascinating one that offers a rich example of the interplay of conscious design, unpredicted consequences and ongoing human adaptations. But first we might ask, is there really only one Internet that has been in existence since the 1970 or '80s, as most histories tell it? Or is it more accurate to think of a series of Internets, because the nature, scope, uses and meaning of the Internet(s) have changed so much over time? The Internet is more like a process than a thing. At the very least the Internet we know today has evolved through several very different phases, and will go through more radical changes in the future.

Though there are many possible ways to characterize the phases or versions of the Internet(s), I think the following labels provide a shorthand pointing to most of the key stages or transformations, and they will provide the scaffolding for my version of this history: 1) the military/academic internet (in the 1970s and '80s); 2) the scientific/academic internet (of the 1980s); 3) the avant-garde countercultural internet (of the early '90s); 4) an emergent public internet (in the mid-'90s); 5) the commercial internet (in the late '90s); 6) the domesticated internet (growing increasingly since the last decade of twentieth century); and 7) Web 2.0/interactive internet (beginning in the early 2000s). Each of these stages or versions overlaps with and partly incorporates elements of the earlier stages, and the boundaries between the phases are porous and somewhat arbitrary. But however one chooses to name it/them, the history of the Internet(s) is a culturally complicated one that continues to evolve in only partly predictable ways. It is also a history that is more than a little bit strange.

The cultural history of the Internet is strange in large part because what has come to be the defining media form for our age evolved largely through a series of unexpected, unplanned transformations quite far from the original intentions of its creators. While a technological system as immensely complicated as the Internet has many and varied origins, it is clear that its initial uses were military and scientific. What has become the most public, extensive communications network in the history of the world was originally a top-secret, highly restricted communication system built by and for the United States military with support from mostly university-based scientists and engineers. The Defense Advanced Research Projects Agency (DARPA) of the US government created ARPANET to facilitate communication among military personnel and scientists working in or for the military. With the rare exception of one key figure in this developmental process, J. C. R. Licker of MIT and DARPA, who as early as 1962 spoke of a "galactic network" that sounds quite a bit like the Internet that was to emerge decades later, the people responsible for what became a worldwide network of users had a very restricted idea of what their project would entail. This networked computer system was first referred to as the Internet in 1974 ("A Brief History of the Internet"; Edwards 1996).

The Internet began life as a top-secret secure network designed to allow the United States military command and control to survive a nuclear attack. The dispersed, decentralized nature of the Net that gives it such a powerfully democratic potential today was initially intended to allow communication to continue if vast areas of the network were destroyed in war. The transformation of this system into the largest most open, public network of communication in history could be characterized as, in a very quirky way, technologically determined, in the sense that the technology overran its intended uses. But there was nothing predetermined about the various phases the Internet has passed through. Those have very much been determined by sociocultural, not solely technical, factors, though the technical breakthrough of a more user-friendly way to access the Net was inarguably a key in the transformation.

The path by which the Internet has come increasingly to be a major medium of popular communication is a winding one with many unexpected turns. Another key step forward occurred in 1991 when the National Science Foundation in the US received permission from the military to link to the ARPANET, permission granted largely because of a close connection between many scientists and the military. While hardly a general opening to the public, this move proved crucial in expanding the Net beyond the military and more deeply into academia such that universities soon became an important force in the further expansion out into public space. The scientific/academic Net gradually drew in more and more users in more and more scholarly fields (and continues to do so), moving from the sciences to the social sciences to the arts and humanities. As the number of academic entry points grew, knowledge about this new online world began to slip outside of colleges and universities.

But no doubt the strangest-seeming detour along the route to the current Internet passes through the "hippie" counterculture. Among the first folks outside the military and scientific communities to take an active interest in the new communication possibilities deriving from networks of linked computers were some refugees from the 1960s counterculture (popularly known as hippies). The San Francisco Bay Area was famously one of the major meccas of hippie culture in the 1960s and '70s, and that area was just adjacent to what became the symbolic center of digital innovation, Silicon Valley, just south of San Francisco. The proximity of those two communities, along with nearby centers of academic computer research like Stanford and the University of California, Berkeley, were a matrix for the next stage of development of the Net. Counterculture-shaped figures like Stewart Brand began to envision the Internet as a potential cyberutopia embodying the values of "peace, love and understanding" at the heart of hippie ideology. The Bay Area has a long history of bohemian communities (not only the hippies, but in the 1950s it was one of the centers of Beat culture and others before that), a site with a more openly progressive political orientation than many other parts of the US. Those communities developed a serious social critique of America's obsession with wealth, war and selfish forms of excessive individualism (Turner 2006). Folks who had helped end racial segregation in the US and protested the disastrous Vietnam War, and who felt the soul of America to be lost in a sea of excessive consumerism believed a free, open new form of communication beyond the control of corporations and the government could radically change the country and the world for the better.

The combination of "freaks" (as counterculturalists preferred to call themselves) and "geeks" (as the technosavvy were beginning to be called) proved a potent mix for imagining and building early popular cyberspaces. It is important to keep in mind that this phase was still largely a written text phase; some sound, and images were present but in nowhere near the levels we now take for granted. Much of the early utopian thought about cyberspace (the term came into wide usage at this point) that spoke of it being beyond gender, beyond race, beyond disability stemmed from the fact that many online communicators were invisible and inaudible to each other at this stage. All you had to go on were words not noticeably connected to particular human bodies. In two of the most influential early books on digital culture, Howard Rheingold (2000 [1994]) touted the possibilities of a virtual community that transcended all social and geographic borders, and social psychologist Sherry Turkle (2012 [1995]) speculated that online communication would enhance self-exploration by allowing us to engage in masquerade, to play with identities not our own. Both of these books offer cautions as well as optimism in regard to computer cultures, but they were largely received as part of a wave of praise for the possibilities of life on screen. They represent a wave that pictured the Web as a place not just for scientists or computer "geeks" (before geeks became chic), but for anyone seeking an exciting new space to explore, create and change the world.

The counterculture origins of much early digital culture work have had a lasting impact. This history in part accounts for a strong anti-establishment, anti-authoritarian streak in much "geek culture," ranging from the libertarian efforts of the open-source movement to political hackers and wiki-leakers. But where these early adopters touted the utopian possibilities of virtual communities and the exciting new kinds of identities possible via the Web, others, partly in response to this optimism, saw only dystopian possibilities. Critics expressed fears that humans would all become mindless drones lost in computer screens with little sense of the real world and little connection to others. In subsequent years and with wider use of the technologies, this two-sided exaggeration has largely given way to more modest assertions about the cultural impact of digital cultures. But it is not hard to this day to find cyberutopian and cyberdystopian screeds on the bookshelves or Amazon.com.

The countercultural, avant-garde Web slowly opened up into wider circles over the course of the early 1990s. In order for digital culture to become a significant phenomenon, two key technical things had to happen to make the Net more user friendly. The first huge step in this direction has been mentioned, the creation in 1990–1991 of the World Wide Web. When British physicist Tim Berners-Lee invented the interface that he dubbed the World Wide Web in 1989, he had little idea he was creating the means for billions of people to communicate. He was responding to a very practical problem that had developed in his place of work, CERN (originally Conseil Européen pour la Recherche Nucléaire), the foremost physics laboratory in the world (home to the fastest and most sophisticated atom-smashing particle accelerator, among other things). Berners-Lee wanted to find a better way for scientists at the lab to communicate, and feeling, as he put it, rather "desperate," he pulled together a bunch of software and networked hardware (using a NeXt computer created by Steve Jobs shortly after he was unceremoniously kicked out of his own company, Apple Computers), and out of that messy matrix emerged the World Wide Web (Berners-Lee 1999).

At the time, the name World Wide Web was a ridiculously ambitious one, but it has proven to be a prophetic one. Berners-Lee has consistently been one of the most important promoters of the idea that the Internet should in fact be world-wide, that access to it is nothing less than a "human right," and that it should be regulated only technically with no censoring interference by governments or corporations (see "net neutrality" in the Glossary). The crude browser that Berners-Lee and his younger French colleague, Robert Cailliau, came up with, was the great-great-great-grandparent of Chrome, Firefox, Safari, Opera and Internet Explorer, and all the others that came to be the main entry points to the Internet. Due in part perhaps to the accident of its naming, the World Wide Web started on a self-fulfilling prophecy of becoming an ever-expanding network of computers moving first slowly, then at breakneck pace, beyond the confines of the military and the scientific community. With hindsight, such a development seems inevitable, but it was far from obvious to anyone, including Berners-Lee, that the Web would gain anything even remotely resembling its current ubiquity.

The second key development, the point at which the Web truly became the hub of popular digital cultures, came in the mid-1990s with the invention of truly easy-to-use browsers. First Mosaic in 1993 broke the ground, and then two years later Netscape produced the first truly user-friendly and widely adopted browser. Ever more user-friendly web browsers emerged in rapid succession. Where early navigation of the Net had required a fair amount of technical knowledge, new browsers made cyberspaces far more accessible. By 1996, close to 90 percent of web traffic occurred through Netscape, with the other 10 percent mostly taken up by Microsoft's browser, Internet Explorer. But that year, Microsoft started including Internet Explorer as part of its basic software package, and the first of several browser wars was under way. While the details of who won and who lost in this and subsequent browser battles is of little consequence, the wars signaled recognition that the public Internet was a phenomenon here to stay (as late as 1995 Bill Gates had dismissed it as a passing fad), including as a space where corporate profits could be made.

Indeed, corporate profits define the next major stage of Internet growth, the commercialization or monetizing (making a profit) moment. Put bluntly, a sector of the corporate world, first in the US, then in pockets around the globe, realized that the Internet could be used not just for business communication, but for business period. Some had recognized the commercial potential of the Net from the beginning, but full commercialization evolved slowly until the mid-'90s. Then came the phase first glorified, then vilified, as the dotcom boom. Just as the utopian phase of the early, avant-garde Net proved to be overly optimistic, so too the commercial phase proved overly ambitious in its claims, and the dotcom boom eventually came to seem like a dot*con* job when the dotcom bubble burst. But this phase set in motion the development of the Web as a site of commerce that has of course continued to grow. After recovering from the dotcom bust, e-commerce has steadily increased its presence in the world, becoming a very significant part of the Internet. Slowly but steadily companies like Amazon and eBay began to prove that the Net could be a profitable place for business. But even after the dotcom boom-and-bust cycle ended, the commercialization of the Net has been something of a rollercoaster ride. Initially, many major media corporations believed that they could turn the Web into a pay-per-use broadcast medium like television. What they did not realize was that a significant portion of the population that had grown up on the free, open and frontier-like Internet was not willing to relinquish that freedom for corporate control. The anti-authoritarian component of the digital world was soon at war with the commercial version, and that war continues in a variety of ways today.

There is no doubt that giant media corporations control a great deal of the content of the Web. Initially, the Time Warner/AOL merger seemed to promise a transformation of the Net into just another form of corporate media. But just as the Web slipped out of the hands of the military, and then of scientists, and then of avant-gardists, it has eluded complete takeover by media moguls as well. A kind of uneasy truce, mixed with occasionally open warfare, characterizes the relation between the free Web and the monetized Web. And between the giant media corporations and the advocates of a wholly free Web, there are mixtures, including small businesses able to compete more easily with larger ones because of this cheap communication medium, and sites like Google and YouTube that provide free search and upload spaces, respectively, but along with heavy injections of advertising.

The free Web spirit also continues to limit commercial uses of the Net in other ways. When television networks came to realize that charging for their shows on the Web would be widely resisted, they used digital space to intensify the popularity of their shows through overt and covert Net advertising, including encouraging development of fan sites that, thanks to new media capabilities, were far more intense and extensive than fan communities of the past (previously confined primarily to print and snail mail). Likewise, old media like newspapers found that they had to offer at least some content on their new websites for free if they were to lure users into a relationship for which they would later pay. Search engines, the lifeblood of the Net, also had to find a medium ground. Initially attempts by Google, by far the world's most widely used search engine, to put advertising on their site met with a great deal of resistance, especially when advertising seemed to merge with pure search responses. Eventually they compromised by more clearly delineating paid from unpaid search responses, and lost credibility whenever it was rumored that search rankings could be manipulated for a price.

The next major phase of the Net, generally referred to as Web 2.0, intensified debate about control and commercialization of digital spaces. First used by Darcy diNucci, and popularized by Tim O'Reilly, the term is meant to designate a more interactive set of networked relationships. The Web has long been the center of most digital culture, but the features designated by the phrase Web 2.0 represent the fact that has it become even more central. The main devices associated with digital culture—desktop, laptop and tablet computers, cell phones and video game consoles—now all have the capacity to be networked via the Web. That greater interconnection is in fact part of the definition of Web 2.0, along with claims of greater personal and collective interactivity via things like social media sites (Facebook, Pinterest), blogs and microblogs (Wordpress, Twitter, Tumblr), wikis, electronic self-publishing, video sharing sites (You Tube, Vimeo), mashups, crowdsourcing, and so on. Clearly many of these things were available before the phase called Web 2.0, and to the extent that the term represents a new phase of the Net at all it is one more of degree than absolute transformation (Tim Berners-Lee rejects the term as misleading jargon). But for the purposes of this book, the term is useful shorthand for ways in which the Web as a site of cultural production and exchange has expanded and intensified in recent years making questions about just what digital cultures are all about all the more important. And it is a term that has shaped how people think about the Web and digital culture, has shaped what some call the "technological imaginary", our collective images of what a given technology is and can be.

Each stage of the evolution of the Net has left its mark. Each new phase has incorporated rather than fully supplanting the previous phase, and each of these phases or moments in the history of the Internet(s) has left some impression that can be uncovered with a little archeological digging. Successive versions never fully erase previous iterations, and clearly the history of the Interwebs is still very much in progress.

⇲ FROM DREAMERS TO REALITY: PRODUCING DIGITAL STUFF

When we unwrap and pick up a shiny new high-tech device—a laptop, a smartphone, a game console—we don't have to think much about how it came to be there in our hands. But understanding the process of production is as much a part of digital culture as analyzing the conversations generated by a blog post. Dozens of technical design decisions, intentional and accidental, enable and shape digital cultures. Technical decisions are always also social, political, economic and cultural decisions. The material objects—tablet computers, digital music players—are the result of many non-technical decisions that are laden with cultural import. Why did those decisions get made the way they did? What business pressures were involved? What social and political policy decisions shaped the technology? What cultural values were built into or left out of the design? Who participated or was consulted in the design decisions, and who was not?

We know the names and think we know the digital dreamers who founded electronic corporations in their garages or brilliantly invented digital products that shook the world. We know names like Steve Jobs, the zen genius of Apple Computers, Bill Gates the once maligned, now heroically philanthropic genius behind Microsoft, Larry Page and Sergey Brin the "do no evil" geniuses behind Google, and, of course, Mark Zuckerberg, the Harvard geek genius turned billionaire head of the Facebook empire. The media pays a lot of attention to the dreamers and digital stars, but far less is paid to the thousands of workers who make the visions of these "geniuses" become reality. Moving from the shiny new box containing the latest video game or tablet computer back in time to that object's creation reveals some far less shiny realities.

At the very top of the labor chain, there are some folks who no doubt embody the popular image of digital brainiacs sitting on sunny decks atop sleek steel and glass buildings sipping lattes and thinking up new digital gadgets and games. These are the heroes (and fewer heroines) of the industry, the ones every tech-savvy kid dreams of becoming the way every kid with basketball talent dreams of being an NBA star. But, as with the tiny elite of players who make it to the big leagues, this stratum of digital workers is a tiny group. Most of the rest of the workers who create the digital stuff wealthier folks love to consume face far different, considerably less pleasant work conditions.

While creating videos games or hot new tech devices is the dream job of millions of young people, the realities of most production in the electronics industry are often more like a nightmare. Most of the second-tier production of computers, cellphones, apps and digital game software is done by hundreds of microserfs (Coupland 1995) in tiny cubicles working on some tiny part of a project of which many only have a tiny understanding. Few of these folks get to have substantial creative input into the products. Given the rapid obsolescence of much digital hardware and software, these workers also often face long hours to meet tight deadlines, while the relative glamour of a new industry only briefly compensates for often mediocre wages.

The largest, third tier are the assembly-line manual laborers who produce the microchips and other hardware components, or package (and package and package) the digital devices. Most of this labor force is terribly underpaid, overworked and often handling or breathing toxic materials without proper protective gear. While some of this work is still done in the Global North, the vast majority is done by women, men and children in the Global South. Some of this work, involving staring for hours into microscopes to check for irregularities in microchips, has led workers to severe eye injury or blindness. Ironically, and contrary to images of robots in electronic industry advertising (watch, for example, 2011 Droid commercials on YouTube), most of these hi-tech devices require old-fashioned, painstaking hands-on assembly. While the two upper tiers continue to be dominated by males, this third tier is mostly composed of Third World women who are often stereotyped as more obedient employees (Margolis and Fisher 2006; Pellow and Park 2002).

The occasional exception to this production process often gets more attention than the truth of the daily grind. Just as in the film industry, occasionally a low-budget, independent film will strike gold and make a huge profit, so too independent game or app designers who now and then have a big hit that once again animates the myth of the lone genius or the do-it-yourself entrepreneur striking it rich through imagination and perseverance. But the overwhelming reality of the electronic culture industry, like that of the mainstream Hollywood film industry with which it increasingly competes, is the story of few major mega-conglomerate media corporations (in this case mostly console makers Nintendo, Sony and Microsoft) controlling the work produced by a handful of major "content providers" like EA, Konami, Ubisoft, THQ and Activision. These larger companies tap into and absorb smaller game design studios, frequently siphoning off the most talented designers and bringing them into the conglomerated world. The impact of this process might be compared to how the mainstream music industry works. In order to keep selling music, the music industry must tap into emerging independent music trends. But it does so not to create real innovation, but only to turn real innovation into a more mundane mass marketable commodity for sale to pop audiences with less demanding tastes, but a desire for the thrill of the seemingly new. Just like the way punk or rap developed toned-down mainstream versions, but even more quickly, many significant innovations in game design are absorbed by game corp giants who generally dumb them down (Dyer-Witheford and de Peuter 2009).

This lowest level of the digital production world is, not surprisingly, the most invisible one. The world's increasing income inequality, a process accelerated by the economic and cultural forces that go by the name "globalization," is written all over the realms of digital production. Those actually producing what hip designers imagine often work for poverty wages in dangerous conditions. Many live crowded into dormitories in situations approaching slave conditions, often working 16-hour days, and, when production deadlines loom, non-stop for several days. Apart from the occasional scandal when workers in a computer assembly factory in China or Bangladesh commit suicide or die in a fire because they were literally locked into the factory, these workers do not get much attention. And when scandals bring them to public attention, their work conditions are dismissed as aberrations and swept from popular memory as easily as the mind cleansing in films like "Eternal Sunshine of the Spotless Mind" or "Men in Black."

China Watch (2013) reports that "Apple has zero tolerance for lapses in the quality of its products. If a quality issue arises, Apple will do everything it can to have it corrected immediately. But a lower level of urgency apparently applies in responding to labor rights abuses. Despite its professed high standards for the treatment of Apple workers, serious labor violations have persisted year after year." China Watch and other labor rights organizations find it difficult to believe claims by electronics corporations that they are unaware of working conditions in the factories of their subcontractors. Corporate executives often deploy a tactic made famous by corrupt politicians: plausible deniability. CEOs for giant electronics corporations like IBM, Apple, Microsoft, Intel and the like generally express outrage, briefly, and assert they do not know what goes in their company's supply chain. Creating some distance between the corporation and its actual producers is quite deliberate, done for both legal and public relations protection, given the inevitability that awful conditions will be exposed at some point. When challenged to clean things up, electronics corporations invariably spin out some story about more careful monitoring, better conditions and so forth, while at the same time, again plausibly but ultimately dishonestly, claiming that because other companies do it too they can only improve things a small amount without being driven out of business (Pellow and Park 2002; Smith, Pellow and Sonnenfeld 2006).

Critics admit that a concern with competitiveness is a real thing, but counter that this means the industry as a whole must be targeted, rather than periodically singling out one electronics corporation for momentary public shaming. Some who uncritically praise global markets argue that these underpaid, overworked, often endangered laborers are nevertheless better off than before when many of them were penniless peasants. There is surely a grain of truth in this regarding some workers in the high-tech economy. But critics ask the next question: Are worse and slightly better but still horrendous the only options? Can we do no better as makers of a global economy? These processes not only exploit workers in the Global South, but they also come home to roost in privileged places like North America and Europe where the wages of workers are driven down by employers threatening to outsource jobs to the cheaper labor markets of Bangladesh, Malaysia, Mexico or Ghana (Gabry 2011; Pellow and Park 2002; Smith et al. 2006).

A similar question about workers in both the less industrialized, less technologized Global South, and the overdeveloped, over-teched Global North is why, if certain jobs are really so bad, so many people fight to get them? Again, critics respond, the answer is fairly simple, given the choice of starving with no job or taking a bad job, anyone in need is going to opt for the bad job. The less simple follow-up question is, how is it that the world economy has produced so many dangerous jobs and such vast income inequalities, and, more important, how might various forces, including technological forces, be marshaled to improve worker conditions and economic fairness around the globe? How do you justify a wage ratio in which CEOs in the US make 355 times more than laborers, 105 times more in Sweden, or in Japan a "mere" 55 times as much? The disparity among countries alone reveals that there is nothing natural or inevitable about this degree of inequality.

The electronics industry is by no means the only one relying upon exploitative labor practices, but electronics is in many respects the leading contemporary industry and thus reform of its practices would reverberate through the entire global economy. There are hundreds of groups and thousands of people working to provide more humane alternatives to current conditions. Politicians and government workers, educational institutions, unions and other worker solidarity organizations, and social protest movements in every part of the globe are working diligently to create a more equitable economy. But they are up against immensely powerful, highly mobile corporations, often supported by governments, with vast resources to fight against any reform that represents even the smallest threat to their profits. In yet another twist of the Internet plot, however, those very devices and processes created by high-tech corporations have provided more economical, accessible and communicatively richer means to organize to resist corporate exploitation. It is quite possible to appreciate the designers of hi-tech gadgets, cool apps, and hot video games without ignoring the human costs of putting those designs into existence. What is important to keep in mind is that valuing the hip entrepreneurs of digital production more than those who materially produce the things that make cybercultures possible is a political choice with political consequences for millions of people. Pressure to reform by providing better pay, and more humane, safer work environments can only work when pressed upon the entire realm of electronic production. And that pressure will have to come from many quarters, social movement activists, unions (local and transnational), governments, non-governmental organizations (NGOs), and consumers unwilling to buy devices produced by near-slave labor. Ironically and fortunately, the technology at the heart of all this process, the Internet, is a near perfect tool to organize and publicize such efforts to change the system.

PRODUCING THROUGH CONSUMING? PROSUMERS AND INTERACTIVE IDENTITY

A fourth tier or category of digital culture production includes non-professional producers. One of the most common claims about new media compared with old is that they are highly interactive and participatory. Indeed, interactive and participatory are generally cited as among the key components distinguishing Web 2.0 from the earlier Web. User-generated content has always been part of the Net, but new technologies and broadband capabilities greatly expanded that potential. One critic coined the term "prosuming" to name the process by which culture consumers have become culture producers via the WWW. User-uploaded videos, iReports for major media outlets like cable news networks, thousands of online product reviews and a host of other consumer-generated content represent what some see as a far more democratically produced cultural content. Undoubtedly digital cultures offer exciting new forms of interaction. An ordinary individual can be an I-Witness reporter, alerting the world to breaking news of a natural disaster or a political crisis. A layperson can be a scientist or scholar participating in a crowdsourced research project. An amateur Sherlock can go online to help detectives solve real-world crimes. Certainly these forms of digital participation are popular and have impact in enriching lives and in diversifying the overall content of the Web. YouTube users generate more video content daily than all of network television in its entire history. Sheer volume, again, makes it very hard to characterize the nature and impact of prosuming and participatory culture production.

What we can say, however, is that much free pro- or con-sumer-created content underwrites immense profits for major corporations, not only ones like YouTube but also for companies whose products are endorsed, sometimes through manipulation, via things like Facebook "likes." Some have critiqued this as merely the next step in product branding wherein companies, having already turned consumers into walking billboard advertisements through ubiquitous logos on clothes, are now going a step further by turning them into an unpaid labor force of content producers. Consumer endorsements, real and fictionalized, have long been a part of advertising, but the Web has turned this form into a much larger phenomenon, though one lacking the compensation given to more formal endorsers (Karaganis 2007; Schäfer 2011).

No one denies that there can be something quite empowering in uploading cultural material of one's own creation onto the Web. But it is important to realize that as of yet all the participatory culture on the Web has not seriously challenged the content dominance of the main culture industries (the major media corporations), and in many ways they have benefitted from these products of free labor incorporated into their sites and platforms. The traditional giant culture-producing corporations have moved quickly to incorporate and profit from user-generated content. As Tobias Schäfer summarizes, so far it is "evident the new [media] enterprises emerge and gain control over cultural production and intellectual property in a manner very similar to the monopolistic media corporations of the 20th century" (Schäfer 2011). This is hardly surprising since some of those "new" monopolistic media enterprises are the same old ones: Time Warner, Bertelsmann, NewsCorp/Wall Street Journal (owner now of Tumblr) and once idealistic new media corps like Google seem to have forgotten their promise to "do no evil" (Hillis, Petit and Jarrett 2013; Jarrett 2008; McChesney 2013; Schäfer 2011; Vaidhyanathan 2011).

The myth of egalitarian interactivity needs to be scrutinized on a number of levels. Most importantly, it is key to recognize that new, alternative cultural forms are always up against deeply entrenched, fabulously well-funded existing cultural production monopolies. The old adage that the only people with true freedom of the press are the people who own presses is equally true in a slightly different way regarding digital culture; while in some sense, all users *own* the Web, the power of an individual not working for a large media corporation to disseminate cultural offerings to the Net's audience pales alongside Viacom's ability to do so. The occasional exception to the rule—the blog comment or video that goes viral—serves mostly to keep alive the fantasy of a level playing field, rather like the way that lotteries keep alive the highly unlikely possibility that tomorrow you may be a multi-millionaire. A far more level playing field is indeed a potential within the capabilities of the Net, but it is an as yet unfulfilled potential that will take collective social action, not just individual luck, to create.

▣ CLEAN ROOMS OR "DARK SATANIC MILLS"? TOXIC PRODUCTION, E-WASTE AND ENVIRONMENTAL JUSTICE

Perhaps the biggest lie told about the electronics industry is that it is a "clean" business (companies widely circulate images of clean rooms where workers in white suits carefully handle precious circuit boards). While when looking at corporate headquarters, the industry *looks* clean—sleek white buildings, no smoke stacks billowing pollution up into the air—in fact both the manufacture and the disposal of electronic devices involve serious dangers to people and the environment. Looked at more closely, the electronics industry is not that far from what the poet William Blake called the "dark satanic mills" of nineteenth-century industrial production. It is no coincidence that large chunks of major electronic production sites are among the most polluted places on the planet. In the Silicon Valley alone, birthplace of the electronics industry, there are 30 "superfund sites," representing the US Environmental Protection Agency's highest level of toxic contamination (*Silicon Valley Toxics Coalition* n.d.). With digital devices now outnumbering humans on the planet, the situation is worsening.

In fact, at every stage—mining for components, assembly, use, disassembly—electronics has proven to be an extremely environmentally damaging industry. Mining for key minerals, and toxic assembly and disassembly processes, endanger the lives of workers, and toxic e-waste (electronic waste) presents major health issues for people and the environment all around the globe. In addition, the extensive use of electricity-hogging digital devices has a very high cost in energy resources, thus contributing to global climate change.

Computers, monitors, game consoles, cellphones, printers, cables and most other e-devices and peripherals contain significant amounts of toxic, often carcinogenic, elements. These include arsenic, barium, beryllium, bromated flame retardants like polybromated biphenyl, cadmium, chlorofluorocarbons, chromium, copper, dioxins and furans, lead, mercury, phthalates, polychlorinated biphenyls (PCBs), polyvinyl chloride (PVC) which when burned create hydrogen chloride gas, and selenium, to name a few. A list of the hundreds of dangerous elements in hi-tech devices, along with specific health hazards attached to each, would take up much of the rest of this book. Some of these toxins affect the workers who assemble devices, some can impact users, all impact those who disassemble devices (especially when components are burned), and all of us, though hardly equally, are impacted by landfills piling up obsolete e-devices that can leach into local water supplies and agricultural lands, as well as incinerators that send this material into the air where they can potentially drift over any community (Grossman 2007).

There is also danger in some of the mining that unearths the minerals used in digital devices. The case of one of these minerals is comparable to the "blood diamond" controversy in South Africa, with genocidal war in the Congo surrounding the mining of coltan (used in the capacitors found in almost every kind of digital device) (Snow n.d.). Thousands, including many children, have died in the coltan wars, and ultimately those lives are lives lost to our electronic pleasure. After extraction, the assembly process of electronic devices likewise often takes place under horrendous conditions. Among the most troubling of those conditions is failure to protect workers from exposure to dangerous chemicals. Conditions in Silicon Valley have historically been deeply inadequate, and conditions in other parts of the world are even worse (Pellow and Park 2002). Pictures of regimented rows of Chinese workers wearing medical gowns while assembling digital devices might suggest they are being protected, but in fact the gowns are to protect the chips and circuit boards from contamination by humans. In Europe, there are strong regulations on the books that putatively protect workers from exposure, but evidence makes clear those rules have frequently been bent or broken by less than scrupulous producers, and US rules are far more lax. And when those regulations become even mildly financially burdensome to electronic corporations, they generally export assembly jobs to countries with far more lax, or non-existent, protections for workers and the environment. This production process has been critically examined in satiric game form by Molleindustria's Phone Story (*Phone Story* 2011). Its game was removed by Apple after three days in its App Store, no doubt causing more controversy and bad publicity for the company than the game itself. But there is no reason to put the blame just on Apple Computers; the entire industry contributes to these horrendously hazardous work conditions and environmental impacts.

While the appearance in recent years of electronic recycling depots is generally a good thing, they may give a false sense that e-waste is being dealt with seriously. In fact, the rapid obsolescence that digital products undergo (the average user life of a cellphone is

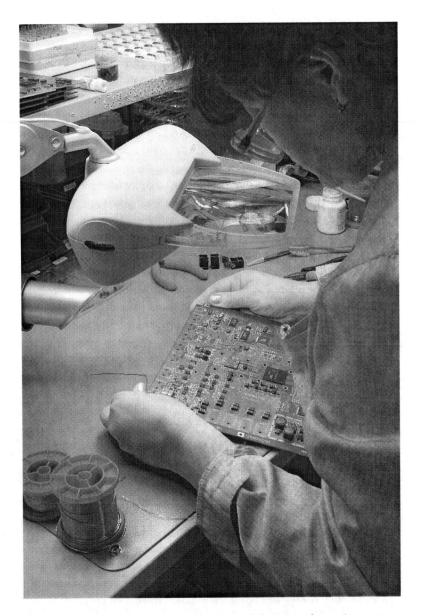

FIGURE 2.1 *High tech, handmade. (Courtesy of shutterstock.com.)*

less than 18 months, a laptop two years) has led to massive amounts of toxic waste, and a variety of failures to deal responsibly with that waste has compounded the problem. Overall, 50 million tons of electronic waste was produced in 2012, and over 70 million tons a year is expected by 2014. Less than 15 percent of that waste is recycled and a large percentage that is recycled is done so inadequately, in terms of handling the toxic materials and/or location of disposal sites. The US is the only industrialized country that has not ratified the Basel Convention, the international agreement that makes it illegal to export toxic waste. The US alone has over 50,000,000 obsolete computers, and US consumers toss away over 1,000,000 cellphones every year. Similar figures exist for Europe, Australia (30 million computers a year), UK (900,000 tons annually of e-waste), Japan, China (70 million cellphones a year) and other major users of technology have proportionately comparable amounts of e-waste. E-waste is the fastest growing contributor to municipal landfill toxicity worldwide. And all these figures are growing at a rate of between 4 percent and 10 percent per annum. The rapid economic development of India and China, two nations far from the saturation point in terms of digital devices, will greatly deepen the problem.

As with all other aspects of digital culture, the e-waste problem shifts with changes in digital design and marketing. While playing a positive role in expanding Net access to previously digitally deprived populations, the spread of smartphones around the entire globe threatens to increase the e-waste problem exponentially. The fact that the electronics industry has honed to an art form the practice of planned obsolescence (the purposeful creation of products that go out of date quickly to assure new sales) likewise compounds the problem (Slade 2007). The fast rate of obsolescence not only impacts the volume of electronic waste, but also decreases its chances of being recycled. For example, for several years recycling glass from computer monitors and TV sets was sufficiently lucrative to be a viable business. But the arrival of LCD, plasma and other flat screen technologies decimated that particular terrain of recycling, such that many former recyclers are now illegally dumping their old toxic TVs (Urbina 2013).

Electronics recycling and reuse efforts have a considerably mixed history. Much recycling has been done illegally, with few safeguards for those handling the materials. Reuse of devices by passing them down the line to less privileged users has grown over the years. But reuse is a mixed blessing environmentally in that older devices sent to less technologically developed countries or poorer areas of developed countries (with good intentions by charitable organizations) are generally more toxic than newer ones currently in use among wealthier consumers. This becomes yet another way in which the e-waste problem falls unevenly on poorer populations in the world.

As with so much of the world's pollution, the burden of e-waste falls upon the less developed world, while the vast majority of the waste results from use in the overdeveloped world, especially North

FIGURE 2.2 *A pile of circuit boards for recycling. (Courtesy of shutterstock.com.)*

America, Japan and Europe. The issue is therefore not only an environmental issue, but very much an environmental justice issue. Environmental justice is the branch of environmentalism that documents and fights against the fact that environmental hazards are far more prevalent in working-class neighborhoods and neighborhoods with high concentrations of people of color in the Global North, and in the poorest communities of the Global South. The vast majority of workers endangered by e-waste around the global are the poor, women and people of color, because they do most of the toxic assembly and because, as noted, most of the e-waste is exported from the developed world and dumped on the Global South where protections for disassemblers are largely non-existent. Most of the toxic waste from electronic devices ends up leaching into the land, air and water in the poorest parts of Africa, India, China, and other parts of the less industrialized world. Go to YouTube and punch in "e-waste" and you will come face-to-face with countless images of young children, pregnant women and all other manner of human beings breathing toxic fumes, handling dangerous chemicals and generally being subjected to the deadly impact of the digitized lives of others they will never meet.

The Global North is not free of these problems either, though once again the greater burden falls on people of color there too. Many factories in Europe and the US employ immigrants at extremely low wages and often do not provide safety materials in all languages spoken by workers. Some disassembly work in the US is done under seriously unprotected conditions by free or nominally paid prison labor, a labor force that is disproportionately non-white given deep racial inequities in the American economy and justice system. In the US, most incinerators used to burn toxic waste are in poor, mostly African American and Latino neighborhoods, or on Native American reservations. In parts of India, China and Africa incineration takes place not in facilities designed for that purpose, but in open fires in cities and villages where toxic smoke drifts through the streets (Pellow and Park 2002). It is far from unusual for pregnant women and very young children to be working near these toxic fumes for hours at a time. Birth defects, neurological disorders and a host of other diseases result from this process of recovering precious metals from digital devices.

In addition to electronic waste, vast amounts of electricity are consumed by various proliferating forms of computing, mobile phoning and gaming. For example, Nicholas Carr points out that in

> *Second Life*—whose parallel universe, though free at the most basic level, is populated by the avatars of Europeans, North American, and Japanese with annual real life incomes of $45,000 or more—the average [virtual] resident uses about 1,752 kilowatts of electricity a year, as much as an average Brazilian, and generates CO_2 emissions equivalent to a 2,300 mile journey in an SUV.
> (Carr 2006)

And that is just for one, admittedly fairly extensive, online territory. Multiply that by multiuser online game sites, console games, and the rest of the Web, and we are talking about a vast increase in the amount of directly and indirectly polluting energy used in a world deeply threatened by global climate change.

Many people—from engineers to artists to activists—are working on these issues. Important green computing or sustainable IT efforts are under way, due in large part to increasingly bad publicity that has in turn led to pressure from consumers (Hilty 2008; Tomlinson 2010). It is already possible to build digital devices that have far fewer toxic components, and are more truly recyclable. Green computer research is also attempting to make devices more energy efficient, and more broadly digital technologies like *smart grids* and *green grids* have the potential to make energy use overall more efficient (*The Green Grid* n.d.). But efforts to shift to less toxic materials for digital devices can be expensive, and few large electronics firms are willing to bear the costs. Perhaps they underestimate the environmental consciousness of consumers, who if made aware of the environmental costs, might well be willing to pay a bit more for their e-devices until mass production brings the costs of green digital technologies in line closer to the costs of currently toxic ones.

Artists have brought attention to the issues in a variety of ways, from artworks made from recycled computer parts, to aesthetic clean-up art that creatively restores environments damaged by e-waste. Some artists have made e-waste a theme of their work, as for example in the photography of Chris Jordan who has produced images that seem initially quite beautiful but upon closer inspection reveal the massive problem of e-waste dumping (Jordan n.d.). Use of recycled electronic components by artists like Marion Martinez can both raise awareness of the e-waste problem, and suggest the need for creative solutions. Martinez, by using e-waste like recycled circuit boards to create *chicana futurist techna arte* related to her Latina and Native heritage, evokes environmental stewardship as a spiritual value (Martinez n.d.). Some artists reshape the environment more directly through *environmental restoration artworks,* some of which, like the Gardening Superfund Sites project in Silicon Valley, have incorporated e-waste (*Gardening Superfund Sites* n.d.). Activists have also shown creativity through things like *eco-toxic tours,* a somewhat satiric variation on eco-tourism that points up environmental hazards like e-waste present around the globe.

Numerous non-governmental environmental organizations and environmental justice movement groups include e-waste in their work (Gabry 2011; Pellow and Park 2002). They continue to pressure governments for better waste regulations, more effective recycling programs, greater protection for assembly and disassembly workers, and less toxic, more efficient devices, among other issues. In yet another ironic twist of the digital world, much of this work is carried out via the World Wide Web and using various kinds of digital devices. Environmentalisms in general, and environmental justice efforts in particular, have a significant online presence. These efforts show great promise, but as with so many environmental issues time seems to be running out, and much more is needed as unsustainable electronic production expands, threatening thousands of lives, rendering many environments uninhabitable, and contributing significantly to overall environmental degradation and global climate change.

3

Who Are We Online?

Digital Masquerade, Privacy, Anonymity, Community and Cyborg Dis/Embodiment

One of the most talked-about and studied questions about digital culture is how similar or dissimilar our "online" identities are to our "offline" ones. In this chapter I want to take up from a number of different angles key linked issues surrounding efforts to make sense of the relation between real life (RL) and digitized or virtual life (VL). These issues include people *disguising their identities on*line, *changing ideas of personal privacy* brought about by a surveillance culture and revelatory social media, similarities and differences between *virtual communities* and traditional offline ones, *online anonymity* as it shapes how we talk to each other, and questions around whether or not we are becoming more like *posthuman cyborgs* (part person, part machine) as we become more deeply entangled with digital devices.

→ Is Life Online a Masquerade?

→ Has the Internet Killed Privacy?

→ Are We Becoming Posthuman Cyborgs?

→ Anonymity, Disinhibition and Trolls, Oh My!

→ Are Virtual Communities for Real?

→ How Much Online Life is Good for Us?

→ Hegemony, Cultural Imperialism and/or Digital Diversity?

While as noted strict real world/virtual world splits do not hold up under scrutiny, being online can *feel* quite different from being offline, and there is little doubt that online experiences can change people in many different ways. There are a variety of ways that these changes have manifested, and great debate about how extensive these changes really are. Fundamental to most of these discussions is some sense that cultural identities in our postmodern era are less stable, more malleable than they have been historically, and that ICTs are playing a role in that destabilization. There is a general claim that the complexities of contemporary life are weakening traditional kinds of social identities. The sheer amount of information about other cultures and other ways of being (much of it provided by digital media) can be deeply confusing and challenging to one's identity, especially among those in the still formative years of youth. Some celebrate this condition as liberating us from overly rigid roles and lifestyles, while others see this as a dangerous development whose flip side is people desperately turning to religious or ideological fundamentalisms, or disintegrating into aimlessness and moral confusion. Social scientists (sociologists, cultural anthropologists, psychologists) are deeply divided about the validity of such claims. Some are quite skeptical that stable identities are less common today than in earlier eras, and some doubt that stable identities are necessary. What's the truth? How much do real lives and virtual lives differ? In what ways are digital cultures changing who we are as individuals and as communities?

⊡ IS LIFE ONLINE A MASQUERADE?

An influential body of work from the early days of cyberculture studies that continues to prove relevant today is typified by Brenda Danet's 1995 essay, "Text as Mask: Gender, Play and Performance on the Internet," a work fascinated with the fact that the Web seems designed for infinite play with identity (Danet 1998). Particularly in the period when the Web was primarily a word medium, no one on the other end of a digital encounter necessarily knew who you were or what you looked like. Danet found that close to 80 percent of Web users she surveyed admitted to pretending to be a different gender, race or sexual orientation than they were in "real life." This number is no doubt inflated by the fact that at the time of her survey the Intertubes were largely populated by adventurous early adopters of an avant-garde and countercultural bent. In any event, this notion of an anonymous space open to identity play was soon taken up by advertisers who famously began to talk about the Web as a place beyond race, class and gender (as if the virtual world had fully replaced the real one). Almost immediately the misleading nature of that claim was parodied in a famous cartoon in the *New Yorker* from 1993 featuring a dog at a keyboard, telling a canine pal, "On the Internet, nobody knows you're a dog" (Steiner 1993). Soon there was a whole industry of further parodies: "On the Internet nobody knows you're _____" ("a space alien," "a cat," "a pickle"; you name it).

Exaggerating the breadth and depth of these identity-bending phenomena was part of a wider tendency in early cybercultures to exaggerate the gap between RL and VL. Again, this was partly due to the fact that the medium was still new, primarily textual and still inhabited largely by extremely adventurous folks not representative of wider populations. But beneath the exaggerated claims that people could be wholly someone else online, and that who we were offline would be unknown and irrelevant, there were very interesting questions being raised about the impact of cybercultures on identity.

Significant instances of identity-shifting phenomena, under concepts like racial cross-dressing and identity tourism (Nakamura 2002), continue and are actively studied. From relatively trivial forms like cyber fibbing about one's looks or job or age on online dating sites, to more serious, even criminal, acts of impersonation, it is clear that engaging with digital cultures can have an impact on self-image. But as the term identity tourism suggests, merely touring an identity is very different from profoundly inhabiting a body that is frequently subjected to discrimination. Developing the deep cultural competence to understand another person's subject position (subject position as the way your race, gender, language, class, etc. position you in the world and unwittingly shape your world view) when it differs significantly from your own in terms of ethnicity, class, gender and so forth is not achieved by casual surfing or digital masquerading.

These early insights about identity in cyberspaces continue to be very important, though in less hyperbolic form. Identity cross-dressing remains a significant phenomenon in chat rooms, social media and dating sites, and other online spaces. Rise of the slang term catfish to describe someone who systematically lies about who they are online testifies to this ongoing process. The popularity of the documentary film "Catfish" (2010), and the spin-off reality TV docudrama "Catfish: The TV Show" (2012+) in which participants uncover falsified identities, has revived interest in the question of how much identity trickery goes on online.

The claim that identities may be more fluid online than off-continues to be approached from a number of other angles as well. Two scholars, for example, have written about the phenomenon they call "wikidentities," claiming that social networking sites like Facebook and MySpace have led young people especially to take a very malleable view of their identities. The study suggests that young people often work collaboratively with online friends in fabricating their self-images, just as a wiki works to collaborate on a common project (Mallan and Giardina

2009). This is not an unprecedented phenomenon. There is a rich literature on the performance of identities over the centuries, and there have been eras in the past where the crafting of identity was a far more active, conscious and collective project than what goes on in social media today. So-called individual identities have always been socially constructed and managed. But online identity formation needs to be looked at on its specific terms, and does seem to bring something new into the world, at least in comparison with recent generations.

Talk about the fluidity and malleability of identity in certain arenas of digital culture must always also be counterbalanced with two other truths. First, it is very difficult to leave behind identities formed by history and deep processes of socialization. Even digital natives are subject to offline forces, particularly the influence of the folks who raise them, and the teachers who teach them, people who in turn have been deeply impacted by a host of forces far wider than any putatively world-wide Web. And second, our identities have always been performative, collective and variable. We are not the same people with our bosses as with our families, with our parents as with our peer age friends. And our identities have always been formed by complex interactions with others, not in some isolated identity chamber. Online worlds certainly provide rich grounds for experimentation with identity, and falsification is not uncommon; 25 percent of teen boys and 30 percent of teen girls say they have posted false information about themselves online, most commonly their age (Madden 2013). But we should not exaggerate how many people partake of serious experiments in identity masquerade, nor over-emphasize the depth of transformation such actions entail in reshaping fundamental social identities. We simply don't know yet how deeply identities are being reshaped by online masquerade, digital cross-dressing and other forms of identity gaming.

A greater impact on identity online may come from the formulaic packages that increasingly make up Web genres. As longtime Silicon Valley digital presence and one of the early creators of virtual reality, Jaron Lanier, demonstrates at length, users are in danger of becoming mere "gadgets" if they do not become more aware of ways in which design decisions, templates, and other technical operations not visible on the surface of the Web subtly and not-so-subtly shape who we are and how we think (Lanier 2010). Technical configurations, out of concern for cost, laziness, and sheer inertia tend to "lock in" many design elements that fundamentally limit human creativity in digital spaces. Minor forms of personalization on social media sites, for example, belie the fact that identity parameters are defined very narrowly by a set of categories that exist partly because they make sense to engineers, regardless of how well they represent the range of human emotion and thought. Lanier urges far greater degrees of involvement of everyday users in design decisions because his experience as an engineer has taught him that, by and large, technicians at best represent a small, rather socially narrow portion of humanity. They tend to do things because they have technical logic, but that logic is not always human logic. He further expresses concern that while crowdsourcing and wikis can have great value, there is in the ethos surrounding them a danger of downplaying the uniqueness of the individual voice, and disrespecting hard-earned forms of knowledge expertise that cannot and should not be replaced by a "hive mind." Though he doesn't use the phrase, what he is in effect describing is a move toward the crowdsourcing of identity. Lanier's book is something of a screed (he subtitles it a manifesto) that misses as often as it hits on what's wrong with digital cultures, but it is full of insights about the dangers of identity loss in cyberspaces that need to be brought out into the public arena for discussion and debate.

⊡ HAS THE INTERNET KILLED PRIVACY?

Well, to kill is a pretty strong verb. But it is undeniably the case that the Net, in conjunction with other digital technologies, has given privacy a severe blow. True, privacy itself is a relatively modern concept. In the villages and small towns that have historically been the home of much of humanity, privacy has been (and still is) hard to come by. In the modern world (i.e., since the sixteenth century or so), however, we have become accustomed to a fairly high degree of personal privacy. Yet with remarkable rapidity the digital era has severely eroded spaces of privacy. Wikipedia offers a useful general definition of privacy: "the ability of an individual or group to seclude themselves or information about themselves and thereby reveal themselves selectively." The dual emphasis in this definition on the *individual* and on *groups* is important here. Thinking about privacy means thinking about both *personal privacy* and what might be call civic or *political privacy*.

While particular notions of what should or should not be private vary from culture to culture and person to person, the key issue here is the second half of the definition, "reveal themselves selectively." Privacy is about controlling what information about yourself or groups to which you belong is made available to others. By that definition, and regardless of what it is a particular person wishes to keep private, privacy has been deeply eroded through the use of digital technologies. This is an issue because privacy is a key element in shaping your identity and presenting yourself to the world, and because privacy is also a key element of political freedom, especially freedom of speech, freedom of assembly and the right to protest.

In the digital era, ideas about what constitutes privacy seem to be changing, and differing notions of privacy may be one of the largest gaps between digital natives and digital immigrants. Younger people do not seem for the most part to share the same concerns about the loss of certain kinds of privacy that their parents do. People under 30 are generally much more open to sharing intimate details of their once private lives on social media sites and other forms of public media. Sometimes it seems as if the kind of private thoughts once reserved for locked diaries have now become fodder for public exposure. In a 2012 survey, Pew researchers found that while 81 percent of parents had concerns about online privacy, fewer than 10 percent of their teenage children shared that concern, though a significant number of youth had taken at least some action to remove or not upload certain kinds of information they wished to keep private (Madden 2013 59–60). Nevertheless, betrayal of personal information is a major complaint of many younger social media users. This is not necessarily a contradiction. It seems to be that while young people in general share far more intimate details of their lives publicly (online) than did their parents' generation, they still care deeply about certain people revealing certain things (e.g., a "friend" betraying a confidence about a person's attraction to another individual).

It is hardly a secret that the Web is a site of much excessive self-disclosure, intentional and otherwise. But few realize the full costs such disclosure may entail. Every day hundreds of people lose jobs or fail to get jobs, are denied admission to a college, lose custody rights, have their marriages compromised, or become victims of harassment or crime because of information gathered from their social networking sites. Cops use information from social media pages to trap criminals, while robbers use postings about vacations to figure out when to target homes for break-ins. The "privacy" settings on social media sites falsely lull people into thinking that their identities or photos or browsing history or other information are far more protected than they in fact are. Every time you "like" something on FB, for example, you are opening yourself up to invasive scrutiny by the producers of the product you have "liked."

Often this is the result of failure to remember just how easy it is for any bit of online communication to spiral (or viral) out of control. Take the case, for example, of the American "sorority girl" who sent an obscenity-laced e-mail to her "sisters" at the University of Maryland urging them to be more sociable, and by clear implication more sexually available, to members of their partner fraternity. Within hours the e-mail hit the blogosphere, went viral, caused an international sensation and led to dozens of parodies. She was praised in some quarters for the creativity of her profanity, though usually with a wink of irony (and what was thought to be her most original phrase, one in which a type of football kick was rhymed and paired with a slang term for female genitalia, proved to be not hers but a term already in circulation, alas). The public exposure of the young woman's name spiraled into a hacking of her Twitter account, where her unsisterly rant paled compared to racist remarks she had tweeted. Not only did the hapless (though hardly innocent) young woman suffer personally, including getting booted out of her sorority, but she confirmed the worst stereotypes about her peers to millions of people. Clearly, going viral is not always a good thing, though in another weird twist in the story, her ranting apparently also led to some job offers (Gross 2013). There are hundreds of examples of this kind of unintended public exposure, sometimes leading to far worse outcomes, including job loss and even suicide.

There are in addition equally disturbing, far more systematic and less invisible ways in which the Net slashes through privacy. Not enough users know, for example, that their social media sites are routinely combed by data miners who sell to corporations information about their likes, dislikes and habits. The amount of information search engines, websites, social networking sites and other digital spaces have gathered on individuals is truly staggering, enough to make James Bond blush or the MI6 or FBI jealous (except, of course, that they now, legally and illegally, use this very information to spy on us).

Most people in the industrial/electronic world now live, sometimes knowingly but often without fully realizing it, in an age of unprecedentedly intense surveillance. While modem bureaucracies have long gathered excessive amounts of information on citizens, the Internet has brought an exponential growth in the amount and kind of information available. The average person living in a modern city is photographed or videotaped dozens of times every day. Surveillance cameras are everywhere, and when they are not present, numerous other kinds of intense, intrusive digitally driven scrutiny is present (Andrews 2012). Whatever you imagine to be the surveillance capacity of modern technology, the truth is far worse than you imagine. Younger people who grew up amidst this age of surveillance tend to see it as normal, rather than as a radical break with the democratic tradition.

Should it trouble us that Amazon and Google know more about us than our mothers or best friends? Should it worry us that every cellphone conversation we have can be monitored by government officials? Should it worry young people that potential employers, school admissions offices *and* their mothers are mining Facebook pages for information that may cause them big trouble? Most users know about cookies, but fewer know about zombie cookies, cookies that may be installed on a web browser that has opted to not receive cookies, can invisibly track your every site visit across all your browsers, and cannot be eliminated by typical cookie deleting processes. Most people know governments can listen in on cellphone conversations, but fewer know they can turn cellphone microphones on remotely to listen in on ambient conversations even when the phones are not turned on (McCullagh and Broache 2006).

Digital technologies have brought privacy invasion to unprecedented levels. Digital networks track our every credit card use. Our every online move, in some cases our every keystroke, is recorded and enters one or more data banks about which we know little or nothing, and over which we have very little, if any, control. While it may seem like a nice thing that Amazon is able to predict what new books you will like, that knowledge used by less scrupulous folks could mean a deep violation of your rights to read what you want without anyone else knowing. Cybercrimes like identity theft are only the most dramatic and visible layer of the many layers of illegal or legally dubious use to which data about our life information is being put. But equally concerning to many are the non-criminal (as of yet) uses to which corporations are putting the immense amounts of data gathered about us each day. In democratic countries, this threatens a tradition of privacy, and in non-democratic societies it can be a deadly threat to forces seeking to expand democracy and freedom. The problem exists at the heart of the Web on most of the widely used resources like Google, Amazon and Facebook. These and similar sites have brought the phenomenon known as dataveillance to a whole new level (Vaidhyanathan 2013). And as with so many other things, practices that had been banned in previous cultural situations have been given second life online. One of these is "weblining," the digital variation on a long illegal practice known as "redlining." Redlining was (and in some areas still is) a practice that prevented residents of neighborhoods with high levels of people of color from receiving mortgage loans, persuaded retailers to establish their businesses in more affluent areas and encouraged the denial of employment, insurance, health care and other essential services to individuals and families based on location in inner-city neighborhoods. Weblining, also known as data profiling, uses information gathered online to stereotype users and pitch only certain products and services to them. It is the prejudiced flip-side of the pleasure you may feel when Amazon's algorithms correctly identify a book you would like to buy.

The temptation to go beyond necessary data gathering appears to be hard for tech companies to resist. For example, the "do no evil" digital media corporation, Google, has been shown to be doing some privacy invading that looks a lot like evil. In 2012, Google was forced to dump huge amounts of data it gathered while updating its maps application, information that had no relevance to the mapping project but could be sold to third-party advertisers. As Google employees went about photographing and charting buildings in the creation of Google Street View (as part of an update to their widely used Google Maps app), thousands of people were photographed without their knowledge, sometimes in compromising or endangering situations. Some of these employees also surreptitiously gathered other kinds of personal information, including the e-mail addresses and passwords of millions of people in the UK. This information was in no way relevant to the mapping process. It was later revealed that after apologizing and claiming to have erased this data, Google had in fact retained much of it due, it claimed, to "human error." Even before these revelations, Privacy International, a UK-based organization aimed at protecting privacy rights of all kinds around the globe, gave Google a rating of "hostile to privacy," its worst ranking.

Similar controversies surround Facebook and other social networking sites. Facebook gathers massive amounts of information and gives members the false impression that privacy controls protect this information. But in fact many FB users have found that their right to privacy by withholding sharing options has been violated by their employers. Demotions, denial of insurance, job losses, broken relationships and even suicides have resulted from sharing of information thought private. Facebook execs have responded with highly publicized efforts to tighten certain controls over information entry points, but not to the satisfaction of all users. The paradoxical openness built into the Net comes to the fore here again—a system originally designed to control top-secret information was actually an inherently porous, multi-entry system where secrecy is nearly impossible to maintain. And if today the most sophisticated corporations, governments and militaries have difficulty maintaining secrecy because of the Internet (e.g. cyber-crime, cyberwar and wiki-leaks), think how much more vulnerable ordinary citizens are.

There is a basic contradiction or structural condition that pits social media site managers against social media site users. In effect, your privacy is the product these sites sell. FB, Twitter, Pinterest et alia make money *by selling you* (or more precisely your name, age, gender, race, sexual orientation, and myriad of personal preferences) to corporations. So long as this is the case, social media companies have a vested interest in pushing their invasion of your privacy as far as users will let them. And since most of their data gathering goes on behind the scenes, and is largely unaffected by privacy settings, few users resist, and without large numbers objecting, resistance is futile (as the Borg would say). Most of us are unwittingly complicit in the multiple violations of our privacy that occur every day. While most of this activity is hidden, it is not difficult to make it unhidden once you are aware of the problem. For example, to get some idea of just what your personal data is worth, and who gets it, there are browser apps (like Privacyfix) that can assist in getting behind the digital Wizard's curtain.

The Internet is known for many things, but too few know it as the greatest surveillance device ever invented. Revelations in the summer of 2013 of massive, invasive and illegal use of the Net for information gathering by the US National Security Administration reveals just how fully the privacy of average citizens has been compromised. Those revelations include the fact that major tech and telecom corporations like AT&T, Verizon, Microsoft, Apple, Skype, Yahoo, YouTube, Google and Facebook were actually paid with tax payer money to turn over data on citizens with no clear connection to any criminal or suspect behavior. A conservative estimate suggests that at least 75 percent of all Internet metadata has been made accessible, as gathered from chat room conversations, e-mails, browser history, voice over Internet phone (VoIP) calls, putting millions of ordinary user/citizens under unprecedented surveillance. Critics across the political spectrum point to this kind of data gathering as absolutely incompatible with democratic freedoms.

While much of this is now beyond individual control (though some anti-tracking software can limit surveillance), critics argue that there is a great deal that can be done collectively. A medium that prides itself on interactivity is vulnerable to charges that it is not responding to its interacting users when they protest in significant numbers. Increasing numbers of people are becoming aware of the seriousness of issues surrounding surveillance. The major electronic corporations that are responsible for making private information available to friends, family and enemies, as well as to corporate advertisers, insurance companies and employers are also the key link in making private data available to government. Thus far the Googles and Facebooks when challenged have largely fended off significant change by making minor, largely cosmetic alterations in privacy policies. Privacy advocates argue that without pressure from their customers, these corporations will continue to trample the right of individuals and groups to control what information becomes public. The other side of this coin, the right of citizens to know what their governments are up to, the right to democratic transparency, is addressed in Chapter 6.

A second area of focus for those fighting privacy erosion focuses on strengthening current government policies (legal guidelines) and enforcing government practices (which have often violated legal guidelines with impunity). Even in the countries where privacy laws exist, they are very weak with regard to new media. Lawyer and law professor Lori Andrews offers a host of disturbing examples of how Google, Facebook and other tech corporations are abetting a massive invasion of privacy: insurance companies checking up on your health habits, credit card services checking your marital status, lawyers checking out what kind of a juror you would make, law enforcement gathering evidence on you without a warrant, and a thousand other forms of data scraping are possible in the new media world (Andrews 2012). The phrase "guilt by association" has taken on a whole new power in the world of social media "friending." As Andrews and others have elaborated, laws simply have not kept up with new media, and new laws are needed to specifically protect privacy in cyberspaces. Andrews herself has offered one interesting version of what a new Internet privacy rights document might look like (Table 3.1). Whether or not her particular "constitution" is the perfect mechanism, it is clear that privacy laws in most parts of the world need to be significantly altered to keep up with innovations in ICTs, and new legislation will be needed if some semblance of personal and political privacy is to be kept alive in a rapidly digitizing world.

TABLE 3.1 *The Social Network Constitution.* © *Lori Andrews,* I Know Who You Are and I Saw What You Did: Social Networks and the Death of Privacy *(Simon and Schuster, 2013)*

We the people of Facebook Nation, in order to form a more Perfect Internet, to protect our fundamental rights and freedoms, to explore our identities, dreams, and relationships, to safeguard the sanctity of our digital selves, to ensure equal access to technology, to lessen discrimination and disparities, and to promote democratic principles and the general welfare, declare these truths to be self-evident:

1. The Right to Connect

The right to connect is essential for individual growth, political discourse, and social interchange. No government shall abridge the right to connect, nor shall a government monitor exchanges over the internet or code them as to sources or content.

2. The Right to Free Speech and Freedom of Expression

The right to free speech and freedom of expression shall not be abridged (and an individual shall have the freedom to use a pseudonym), as long as the speech does not incite serious, imminent harm nor defame a private individual. Employers and schools shall be prohibited from accessing social network pages or taking adverse actions against people based on what they express or disclose on a social network, except in cases of imminent harm to another individual.

3. The Right to Privacy of Place and Information

The right to privacy in one's social networking profiles, accounts, related activities, and data derived therefrom shall not be abridged. The right to privacy includes the right to security of information and security of place. Regardless of active security settings or an individual's efforts to guard his or her digital self, social networks are private places.

4. The Right to Privacy of Thoughts, Emotions and Sentiments

Social networks provide a place for individuals to express themselves and to grow. A person's thoughts, emotions, and sentiments—and his or her characterization by others—shall not be used against him or her by social institutions, governments, schools, employers, insurers, or courts.

5. The Right to Control One's Image

Each individual shall have control over his or her image from a social network, including over the image created by data aggregation. A person's image may not be used outside a social network for commercial or other purposes without his or her consent, nor shall it be used online for commercial or other gain without his or her consent.

6. The Right to Fair Trial

Evidence from social networks may only be collected for introduction in a criminal trial if there is probable cause and a warrant has been issued. Evidence from social network sites may not be collected for or introduced in civil cases unless the activity at issue occurred on social networks (such as defamation, extortion, invasion of privacy, or jury tampering). Evidence from social networks may only be introduced at trial if it is directly relevant to the crime or civil action charged and the probative value outweighs the prejudicial value, the evidence is relevant, the evidence is properly authenticated, and the evidence otherwise complies with all rules of civil and criminal procedure. In custody cases, social network information should be admitted only if it provides direct evidence of potential harm to the child.

TABLE 3.1 *(Continued)*

7. The Right to an Untainted Jury

Jurors shall decide cases based on the evidence presented in court and not information or inferences acquired from social networks, search queries, or other sources.

8. The Right to Due Process of Law and the Right to Notice

An individual is entitled to due process, which consists of advance notice and the ability to control, correct, and delete the individual's online information. No information shall be collected or analyzed without advance notification of the individual. That notification shall include an explanation of the specific use and purpose of the collection and analysis of that information. There shall be a warning about possible repercussions of giving consent for the collection of that particular information. Access to a social network shall not be denied based on a decision not to consent to the collection, analysis, or dissemination of information. An individual shall have the right to know what entities are in possession of or are using that individual's information and he or she shall have a right to gain access to and obtain a copy of all the information regarding him or her.

9. Freedom from Discrimination

No person shall be discriminated against based on his or her social network activities or profile, nor shall an individual be discriminated against based on group data aggregation rather than on characteristics of that particular individual, unless the social network activities provide direct evidence of a crime or tort.

10. Freedom of Association

People shall have freedom of association on social networks and the right to keep their associations private.

▣ ARE WE BECOMING POSTHUMAN CYBORGS?

One of the strong claims that have been made about cyberspace(s) is that they are places of disembodiment, places where our RL bodies no longer exist. But as I've been noting, no one is ever just in cyberspace. A user is always also somewhere in material, geographic space. Even if you are currently reading the e-book version of my words, you are doing so from some place, in some time zone. You may be lost in reverie as you follow my brilliant threads of thought (or not), but this is true when you read a book as well. People often talk about being swept up into new worlds by a book, especially fiction works. Yet no one thinks of "bookspaces" as somehow outside the real world. Or, if they do, they always talk about these spaces as spaces of imagination, not as if they were parallel universes. In the same way, it is important to remember that cyberspaces are imaginary. We imagine ourselves into cyberspace, but we remain physically anchored in material worlds. Just as our bodies remain in particular places, so too we need to remember that visible cyberspaces that seem to appear magically on our screens are always dependent upon hardware that has an equally material reality, as well as traces of a history of production by human bodies.

Another very important body of work speaks of bodies in cyberspaces as cyborgs. A key founding text here is Donna Haraway's "A Manifesto for Cyborgs." This brilliant essay brought to the foreground questions about how we are being transformed by the experience of increasingly becoming hybrids of machines and humans, becoming cyborgs (*cyb*ernetic *org*anism) (Gray 2002; Haraway 2003 [1984]). In the hands of careful, innovative scholars like Haraway, Chela Sandoval and Chris Hables Gray, cyborg theory has illuminated a number of important issues regarding how the notion of a human–machine hybrid can be used to break down sexist, racist and homophobic claims of "human nature." Unfortunately, in the hands of less careful thinkers, cyborg theory has also led to a great deal of nonsense and exaggeration of how deeply current generations of humans are being reshaped by digital technologies. Humans have been giving over certain amounts of power to machines for hundreds of years, but digital technologies have brought control by non-human entities (e.g.,. robots and AIs) to a new level and with that has come heightened anxiety about them. Popular culture images of cyborgs are roughly split between malevolent and benevolent varieties. For every Terminator, Darth Vader or vengeful replicant (*Blade Runner*), there is a Six Million Dollar Man, a Molly Millions (*Neuromancer*) or a Geordi LaForge ("Star Trek TNG"). This is no doubt as it should be, since no one, not even Jean-Luc Picard (Figure 3.1) quite knows what becoming more cyborg-like will do to us, as the best of the cyborg theorists make clear.

We should not overstate the novelty since we have been extending our human capacities via technologies since our first ancestors built spears to hunt game, and sharpened sticks to dig for root foods. Each new technological development changed us, and thereby changed the nature of humanity to some degree. As Jason Farman has pointed out, the first writing on paper (papyrus) transformed our relationship to space in ways not dissimilar to the first mobile phone. Having words that were previously bound on immovable stone tablets be able to travel with us in the form of paper documents changed our sense of space just as surely as being able to take vocal communication with us as we travel has done. Prior to the cellphone, answering the phone and being asked, "Where are you?" would have led you to question the

FIGURE 3.1 *Captain Picard as Borg.*

sanity of the caller. "Where am I? What do you mean? *You* called me. I am here at home on the phone. Have you been drinking?" (Farman 2011). (Having raised the question of sanity, this is perhaps the place to mention that many people have jokingly observed that the biggest danger from cellphones may be that it is no longer always possible on the street to tell a potentially harmful mentally ill person from an exuberant mobile phone user.)

A number of writers, sometimes referred to as posthumanists, have argued that new technologies, cyborgization and other aspects of contemporary society have so radically transformed human qualities and capabilities that we need to speak of a new posthuman species. Scholars of posthumanism come in a variety of styles, from brilliant, thoughtful ones like N. Katherine Hayles who examine the pros and cons of the various versions of this concept (1999), to uncritical enthusiasts like the transhumanists who believe we can overcome death by downloading our brains. What all posthumanists have in common is the sense that computers are prosthetics, and like the prosthetic devices used by amputees, they give us capabilities we would otherwise lack. But where prosthetic devices for people with disabilities generally seek to restore lost functions, posthuman prostheses aim to create new capabilities, capabilities that take us beyond the merely human qualities of our bodies. It is the issue of the body, or embodiment, that largely separates the wise from the foolish posthumanists. For critic Hayles, the separation of mind from body has been a theoretical error for both humanists and posthumanists. For the more problematic posthumanists, bodies are largely seen as impediments to be overcome. For them, being post-human generally means to leave the body behind, or to so alter it as to be unrecognizable as *homo sapiens*. The already doubtful idea that we can somehow leave our bodies behind and live only in mind is being rendered even more suspect by recent work in neuroscience and consciousness studies. This work suggests that consciousness is distributed throughout the body, not restricted to the brain (see Damasio 2010). Moreover, while neuroscience is discovering fasci-nating things about the mind, one of the things it is revealing is that consciousness is far more complex than we ever imagined. While we have more knowledge than ever about how the human mind works, that knowledge tells us that we are still in the very early stages of exploring the vastly complicated terrain of the many differing kinds of intelligence that make up human thought and emotion, and drive human behavior. In that context, a modest approach, rather than wild speculation, is the far better way to explore the complex ques-tion of what makes us human.

On the other hand, the wise thinkers about our increasingly cyborg natures, and the variety of ways in which we are becoming if not posthuman, then at least posthumanist, have much to teach. There is no doubt that digital technologies are going to continue and deepen human interactions with machines. To take one small example, digital games now involve greater degrees of cyborgiza-tion through things like WonderBook, dance mats, wii remotes, and Kinect that increasingly mimic and utilize more and more body parts as part of the interaction. Once much hyped, then largely for-gotten because of excessive expense, virtual reality devices that can deepen a sense of dislocation are also poised to make a large impact as more economical forms are made available. Wearable computers (like Google Glasses), direct brain–machine interfaces (controlling devices with our brain waves) and implanted computers are already in use and as they develop further will intensify these intimate connections.

The best of work in a posthuman vein avoids claims that the human–computer relationship is an utterly unprecedented experience.

What they are really talking about is being post*humanist,* getting beyond a certain limited definition of what constitutes humanness that has been around since at least the Renaissance. This definition of human essence now seems deeply biased towards a limiting white, male, Western idea of the self that has sought to impose itself on the rest of the world, by force of intellect at best, by war and colonial domination at worst. In relation to this dominating definition of the human, becoming posthuman is an excellent idea. In a larger time frame, one of the prime characteristics defining *homo sapiens* is that we are tool users. And another name for tools is *technology.* Technology has always extended our bodies and identities into new spaces and forms, as it has also for our non-human relatives. Research on tool use by macaques, for example, shows that even something as simple as a rake becomes integrated into its mental self-image with repeated use (Maravita and Ikiri 2008). Even the putatively bird-brained, crows for example, use tools. Somewhat larger human brains incorporate our technological protheses in complicated ways, but such incorporation could be viewed as part of the essence of what makes us human, rather than as something that makes us *post*human. A pencil or pen is no less a technology than is a laptop. And the use of the pen (or writing implements more generally) transformed human beings more profoundly than any previous technological development, outside perhaps of the domestication of agriculture. Likewise for the invention to which the computer is often compared in terms of social impact—the printing press. The printing press brought profound changes to the social world that continue to reverberate even as we move closer and closer to a post-print world. However, the printing press did not make us posthuman in relation to the pre-print *homo sapiens,* and it is far from clear that digital technology has made us posthuman in relation to print-imprinted humans.

There are very good questions currently being asked about how digital devices are reshaping our relation to the world and each other, but they are very much variations on a theme, not utterly unprecedented. As noted, mobile communication is likely changing our relationship to social space. Jason Farman points out that the pocketwatch is in many ways a comparable tool to the smartphone. Just as the watch redefined our relation to time, regularizing it and making us more intensely aware of time passing, digital mobile devices may be changing our relation to space, shrinking our sense of distance. The world comes *to* us via mobile media far more than in the past when we went to the world. Similarly technologies are no doubt changing our sense of connection to the world and to each other. A state of always being connected, made possible by ubiquitous smartphones, may give us a stronger sense of being in more than one place at a time. The smartphone takes us away from our immediate environments, or at the very least doubles that environment. Is this a cyborg doubling?

Cyborg theorists, and even some of the whackier among posthumanists, are putting before us key questions about how to think about our increasingly intimate relationship with digital technologies. At stake in these questions is nothing less than human nature. As technologies allow us to change our bodies through surgery, extend our physical and mental capabilities in a host of new interactions with digital devices, and even modify ourselves at the level of our DNA, we will be increasingly creating "designer humans." The history of such attempts contains enough horror stories (Frankenstein's monster, the eugenics movement, Nazi medical experiments) to raise flags of caution. Once again, the best questions will not be what are technologies going to do to us, but rather which technologies should we develop (and which not), and to whose benefit will those technologies be directed. The exciting thing about the cyborg metaphor is that it frees us from many confining notions of human nature. The frightening thing about the cyborg metaphor is that it frees us from many confining notions of human nature, leaving us to collectively struggle with the daunting issues of what we really are and what we want to be as human or posthuman beings.

Still, even granting the power to provoke thought that the term offers, posthuman sounds to me a little too close to posthumous, the state of being dead. So for the moment, I suggest that, while thinking through the important issue of what constitutes humanness in the face of new technologies, we should not neglect things like nuclear warfare or global climate change that may render us posthumous, and thereby render the world posthuman in a very literal sense.

⊡ ANONYMITY, DISINHIBITION AND TROLLS, OH MY!

If disembodiment has been overstated, there is another dis, disinhibition, that is much more prevalent and relevant. Much of the early discussion of technology touted the benefits that online anonymity provided. Psychologists talk about disinhibition as a factor shaped by anonymity. The most famous forces of disinhibition are alcohol and drugs. Anyone who has ever attended a party where alcohol enlivened the event can testify that disinhibition can be a good thing. (For those of you who have never been in a situation in which alcohol or other drugs have been consumed, think of things you might have said in confidence to your closest friends or family members but would never say in public.) At the same time, anyone who has attended a party where alcohol consumption led someone (surely not you!) to make an absolute fool of themselves, or say or do something deeply offensive, knows that disinhibition can have highly negative consequences. The same pattern can be seen regarding the disinhibition provided by online anonymity in digital culture. Studies have shown clearly that people say things online when their identities are protected that they would never say if they were known and could be held accountable for their words. Anonymity has, for example, provided a cover for vast amounts of online hate speech. One form of hateful speech that has proven especially destructive is cyberbullying. Bullying is hardly a new phenomenon in the world, but the anonymity provided by digital spaces has added a new dimension that has made bullying easier. Eighty percent of young people interviewed about bullying said they were more likely to bully online than offline. Evidence suggests that cyberbullying has been increasing, though fortunately that increase has brought greater attention to this issue such that there are now more resources (including online ones) than ever before to deal with all forms of bullying (*Cyberbullying Research Center* n.d.).

In thinking about online anonymity, it is important to realize that while online disinhibition is real, anonymity ultimately is not. Anonymity is a temporary condition that can almost always be turned into identification with the right investigative tools. Given that even some of the most sophisticated hackers seeking to remain anonymous, for obvious reasons if their activity has been defined as criminal, have been tracked down, what chance do the rest of us have of remaining anonymous if someone really wants to discover who made that comment, posted that image, did that cyberbullying? Putting too much faith in the anonymity of cyberspaces inevitably leads to perilous consequences, as a number of politicians, celebrities, hackers and ordinary folks have too often discovered. It seems better to assume that there is no such thing as absolutely anonymous cyberspace.

The more positive side of disinhibition is that it may be provoking certain more honest conversations. While the Roman adage *in vino veritas* (in wine is truth) is at best a half-truth, the freedom to speak without self-censorship has its virtues. The seemingly anonymous spaces on the WWW have revealed a great many things about current social thought and emotion. Much of it is far from flattering to our sense of humans as a rational, compassionate species, but generally speaking it is better to have those expressions out in the open than repressed. The half-truth side of things is that our unbridled *Ids* are no more the whole truth about us than is the more controlled expressions of our *Egos* (to use the convenient Freudian metaphors). Vino-induced and web anonymity both reveal as many lies as they do truths. As always, we humans are stuck with the interpretive task of sorting out the more true from the less true from the totally false.

We can also talk about the impact of what might be called *political anonymity*. Exposure of political anonymity can have very severe consequences when states invoke national security (a catchall term that is valid in some cases but has often proven to be a cover for not wanting to divulge embarrassing or illegal activities). The case of US Army private Bradley Manning (now Chelsea Manning), who provided the website WikiLeaks with the largest cache of confidential military and diplomatic documents ever published, makes clear the costs when anonymity is lost. Manning's arrest, abuse by US captors, and eventual multiyear prison sentence has sparked intense debate about what information the public has a right to know (*I Am Bradley Manning* n.d.; *WikiLeaks* n.d.). Clearly powerful governments around the globe will seek to make the kind of anonymity provided by digital dissidents like those at WikiLeaks impossible to sustain. But it remains to be seen if they can succeed. As their name suggests, the political hacker group known as Anonymous understands anonymity to be central to its ability to expose corruption and deception in governmental and corporate rule (*Anonymous* n.d.). While some alleged members of Anonymous have been arrested, the anonymous face of the group (a Guy Fawkes mask modeled on the graphic novel/film *V for Vendetta:* see Figure 3.2) has meant that others immediately step in to replace those who are rendered no longer anonymous. This kind of anonymity is designed to remind people of the fact that without political privacy, without a space to confidentially discuss political ideas, democracy cannot flourish. And that without governmental transparency, we cannot know if democratic will is being exercised. At the same time, there is another dimension of political anonymity that we will discuss in Chapter 6, the fact that anonymity seems to facilitate social and political dogmatism that may undermine, rather than encourage, serious citizen discourse.

Anonymity and disinhibition are clearly complicated issues, but in general, having through the vast apparatus of the Net a fuller range of human expression and public knowledge available than ever before, hate speech and dim-witted troll provocateurs notwithstanding, must be accounted a social good.

FIGURE 3.2 *Pride Day Protest for Bradley/Chelsea Manning. (Courtesy: Koby Dagan/Shutterstock.com.)*

☐ ARE VIRTUAL COMMUNITIES FOR REAL?

From the earliest days of the public Internet, the possibilities of virtual communities have been much touted and much derided. While the utopian hopes for such communities have faded somewhat over the years, there is no doubt that new communities have formed online that would not be possible, or at least not as easily possible, offline. Some of these communities that simply could not exist at all are ones of particular importance to people who are place bound or who live in geographically isolated places. The Internet, for example, has deeply changed life for many immigrants, making it much easier to maintain connection to homeland countries. Diasporas (voluntary or forced exile communities) have much richer possibilities for communication across great distances. At the same time, given that many of these migrants are forced to move for economic reasons, digital divides mean that these communication possibilities are often severely limited for these communities that need them most.

Many other kinds of online communities built across previously unbridgeable distances of time, space and cost have been formed around politics, leisure and recreation, and virtually every other aspect of life. The importance of these kinds of online community connections is undeniable. They certainly represent an enhancement of possibilities for those who take advantage of them. To see them as less real than other kinds of group connections is clearly a mistake from the point of view of those involved in them, and it would seem little more than prejudice against the new to see them as somehow less than other kinds of community. Especially given the availability now of visual communication apps and devices that provide a kind of face-to-face interaction, it is difficult to see what is lost in online communication.

More ambiguous are communities formed around people who could in fact meet in non-cyber spaces. Most critiques of virtual communities argue that some authentic human relation is lost when people connect only through online media. Sociologist Robert Putnam, in his widely read book *Bowling Alone: The Collapse and Revival of American Community* (2000), lamented the alleged decline if not death of community and civic culture under contemporary social conditions, before the emergence of the Internet as a significant public space. While focused on the US, this analysis has been said to fit the situation in many other democratic societies. Putnam's claims have been challenged on many grounds, but it is interesting to note that his critique arose just as the Internet was taking off. It seems plausible that either much civil life was already in the process of moving online, or that a perceived deficit in community was quickly taken up by folks online.

Those who refuse to take virtual communities seriously would do well to consider this possibility that the Net is in some ways reviving civic culture. The claim that online communities are somehow less real also ignores the fact that, with the fairly rare exception of those communities mentioned above that can *only* exist in digital spaces, few members of virtual communities limit themselves exclusively to online interaction. Hardcore video gamers, for example, often parodied as living excessive, obsessive online lives, love to get together face to face in spaces ranging from living rooms to giant arenas at gamer conferences. There is ample testimony (far beyond dating sites) of relationships beginning online and spilling out into various offline worlds of work and play. Much prejudice against virtual communities seems based on either fear of the new or nostalgia for some supposedly perfectly unmediated world that never existed.

⧉ HOW MUCH ONLINE LIFE IS GOOD FOR US?

The kind of questions raised above about privacy, surveillance, trolls, and dehumanization have led to questions of just how good for us is online life, or at least how much online life is good for us. Some of those of a technological determinist bent fear new media are robbing us of an essential humanness that can only be conveyed face to face. This claim, however, doesn't deal with the fact that no one spends all their time solely in cyberspaces, and usually exaggerates the digital dualism of online/offline. More importantly, communication theorists point out that *all* human interaction occurs through media. Every communication we engage in is mediated. The single most important communication medium humans have is verbal language. And like all media, language is imperfect at conveying thoughts and feelings; language separates us even as it connects us. Anyone who knows more than one language knows that there are things that can be said and thought in one language that simply cannot be translated into another. As any literature professor will remind you, form does matter, form does impact meaning. Each linguistic medium creates a particular world. Visual languages (images of various sorts) communicate some things words cannot (though the claim that a picture is worth a thousand words has not yet been statistically proven, to my knowledge). But in truth they are just two equally imperfect media of communication. The point here is that all communication between humans is shaped both positively and negatively by mediation; digital mediation is just a variation on this wider set of processes (Kember and Zylinska 2012). There is no completely neutral medium, no medium that does not shape or privilege certain kinds of interaction, and limit other communicative possibilities. But this is a far cry from the famous, much misunderstood, claim by Marshall McLuhan (1994 [1964]) that "the medium is the message." Yes, the medium profoundly shapes the message, but it does not become the message, does not fully take over the message.

The form of communication most often spoken of as most real, authentic or unconstrained, is face-to-face conversation. But not only is face-to-face communication shaped by choice of language and by visual cues (body language), both of which are deeply culturally shaped, any face-to-face moment is filled by thoughts and feelings shaped by all the other media we use (and that use us)—newspapers, books, television, telephones, radio, film, photography, music, painting, and now the WWW, e-mail, blogs, microblogs and vlogs, mobile phones, video games, DVDs, social media platforms and so on. Some or all of those forces of mediation are now with us when we meet face to face, so there is no inherent reason to privilege face-to-face communication as somehow more real, more immediate. Nothing is *im (not)* -mediate; we are always already in a multimedia state when we talk face to face. This is not to downplay the importance of face-to-face interaction; it has unique qualities that cannot be replicated, as does each medium. Rather it is to remind us that we are never in a pure state of communication; all communication in technologically rich cultures is shaped by not only the medium we are using (including the human voice using the medium of one of many human languages), but also by all the other media that have shaped the person who enters into so-called face-to-face communication. Social media is a particularly inappropriate name for sites like Facebook, since all media are social. Conversely, even when we are in conversation face to face we may well be having what might be more accurately called a face-to-Facebook communication, given the way that experiences with digital media are now woven into our other modes of communicating.

Nevertheless, it would be a serious mistake to assume that there are no differences between digitally mediated life, and other experiences. Pioneering digital culture theorist Sherry Turkle, for example, is far less sanguine about the technological world than in her earlier work. She believes ubiquitous computing, constant connection via mobile devices, and the evolution of more and more human-seeming robots (from toys to talking smartphones) have rendered many people better able to relate to digital devices than to people. Perhaps intentionally echoing Putnam's title, Turkle writes in *Alone Together* (2012) that as we expect more from technology, we expect less from each other. She suggests that computer users are losing the capacity to be alone, and at the same time, are not really together; she believes that the kind of virtual intimacy we have with electronic devices is not a full substitute for complex human interactions. While she sees technologies getting better and better at mimicking human speech, mimicry is by definition only an imitation for something richer, or dare we say, more real. The danger Turkle is pointing to is that digital natives, growing up on this form of digitized intimacy before they have an opportunity to develop deeper forms of intimacy with fellow humans, will never learn the difference, will never know that they have lost a vital part of personhood.

Nathan Jurgenson has countered Turkle by suggesting that, paradoxically, because many of us are spending so much time online, we have come to value offline family time, solitude and general disconnection more than ever, that these times have become more precious than ever before precisely because we think we are losing them. Jurgenson points out that many people have come, in a kind of reverse digital snobbery, to brag about how much they resist being online. "People boast about their self-control over not checking their device [during restaurant dining]," he writes, "and the table usually reaches a self-congratulatory consensus that we should all just keep it in our pants. The pinnacle of such abstinence-only smartphone education is a game that is popular to talk about (though I've never actually seen it played) wherein the first person at the dinner table to pull out their device has to pay the tab" (Jurgenson 2012).

As Jurgenson argues explicitly and as Turkle too knows well, the offline/online division ("digital dualism," Jurgenson calls it) is an overly simplified, false one. Yet, Jurgenson doesn't address the fact that the vast majority of the world's population still has never been online at all, or discuss the vast range in degrees of onlineness that individuals experience. Conversely, Turkle doesn't sufficiently acknowledge that once one has been online, the online world is part of one's "real life." Each author may have part of the truth here, and only the future will tell how users come to balance (more) digitized and (less) digitized realms of experience. Increasing desire for such a balanced approach has led to a Slow Technology Movement (Ascharya 2012; "Slow Technology Movement" n.d.). Not against technology, and including many tech industry professionals, the movement argues for more careful and thoughtful engagement with digital spaces and cultures, recognizing that time away from digitized life can be essential to a richer, more complete life.

⊡ HEGEMONY, CULTURAL IMPERIALISM AND/OR DIGITAL DIVERSITY?

While the range of human thought, opinion and emotional expression available online is truly staggering, that does not mean that the digital terrain presents an even playing field. The road blocks to a truly democratic, egalitarian set of digital cultures and virtual communities include a host of inequalities best understood through the concept of cultural hegemony. Hegemony in this context is *cultural domination without overt force or coercion*. Hegemony is a process by which groups with greater economic, political and/or cultural power lead those with lesser power to adopt or at least consent to their dominant ideas as common sense, even when those ideas work against fairness, justice or the self-interest of the dominated group. In this way, we come to consent to our own oppression, under the illusion that it is the only way or the natural way for things to be. Another important fact about hegemonies is that they often come wrapped in pleasure, like a deadly pill inside a delicious piece of candy. The prime vehicle for pleasurable hegemony in the contemporary world is popular culture, including popular cyberculture. In ICT terms, hegemony has meant greater power to shape cybercultures in the hands of certain social groups (white, male, affluent), based largely upon their initially greater access to the technological and cultural tools essential to take part in digital cultures, as well as their continuing to have greater economic and social resources.

A couple of examples of cultural hegemony might be useful. Take the music industry. It is now possible, thanks to the Internet, to access a huge variety of music from all over the world. Nevertheless, when you look at data like the Billboard Top 100, it is clear that a very narrow segment of the music world gets promoted by powerful economic interests that push most innovative music to the margins. Again, this is hegemony at work. No one forces you to listen to bad pop music, but it is so much easier to find bad pop music in the world due to the hegemonic corporate power of the music industry (though certainly digital technologies have poked some pretty big holes into this arena of cultural hegemony).

Or take the case of the magazine publishing industry. If you go to a supermarket or a news shop and look at the magazine rack you will find dozens of "women's magazines," most of which function primarily to make women feel insecure enough to buy the clothes and beauty products whose advertisers bring profit to the magazine. (Do my clothes make me look thin enough? Is my skin blotchy? Am I giving my man the sex he needs?). By contrast to the overwhelming array of dozens of women's magazines, there are usually at most one or two other magazines that are critical of the many oppressing elements of "women's magazines." Hegemony works not by censoring these more female-equality-oriented or feminist magazines, but rather by overwhelming them in a sea of this other kind of women's magazine. Feminist magazines, like *Ms.* and *Bust* that more fully support the non-consumerist empowerment of women, can then be pointed to as evidence of the generous free speech available in democratic societies. In such claims, the vastly greater resources available to the conservative capitalist publishing industry are discounted, and instead the illusion of "free choice" by consumers is lauded. That is cultural hegemony turned against women. Choice under cultural hegemony is like the request to pick a card, pick any card, offered by a magician. Looked at more carefully, you will find that the deck is a trick one, that your choice was not free at all.

In terms of digital cultures, much hegemony works primarily through corporate websites, search engines and portals that tend to dominate the content and narrow the range of viewpoints to which most users are exposed. Again, no one forces you to follow Reddit's or Yahoo's or Baidu's (China's largest portal) links, but evidence makes clear that for most people it is far easier to accept their portal's view of the Web rather than personally exploring the far wider range of cultural viewpoints available in the global network.

Hegemony is often a subtle process. Many different features of the Net play a role in favoring the already powerful, and making it more difficult for alternative voices to be heard. Take the example of search engines. As Siva Vaidhyanathan observes,

> If Google is the dominant way we navigate the Internet, and thus the primary lens through which we experience both the local and the global, then it has remarkable power to set agendas and alter perceptions. Its biases (valuing popularity over accuracy, established sites over new, and rough rankings over more fluid or multidimensional models of preservation) are built into algorithms. And those biases affect how we value things, perceive things, and navigate the worlds of culture and ideas.
>
> (Vaidhyanathan 2011 7)

A related dimension of this is the process known as cultural imperialism. Cultural imperialism is hegemonic influence over cultural production (movies, TV, music, etc.) by one culture over others. The culture subject to cultural imperialism is overwhelmed and overridden by the cultural products of dominant culture, by cultural texts from outside such that local traditions are lost or transformed beyond recognition. Cultural imperialism as a phenomenon long predates the invention of the Web, but particularly as Web 2.0 integrates other media (film, TV, radio, etc.) into itself, it has become a major purveyor of cultural imperialism.

The US and to a lesser degree Europe have been the cultures most often accused of cultural imperialism vis-à-vis most of the rest of the world. These nations have had the wealth and popular culture production capacity to overwhelm the rest of the world with their products. In a similar vein, Japan has been accused of cultural imperialism with regard to the rest of Asia (and sometimes with regard to the US). But there are also smaller-scale cultural imperialisms that occur within countries, especially between ethnically and linguistically dominant cultures in relation to minority cultures, or between dominant cultures and politically oppositional subcultures. While the Web has the potential to create a more even flow of culture from many places around the globe, in fact Europe, Japan, and North American overwhelm the rest of the world in digital production as they do in other media (film, TV, etc.).

The Web and other dimensions of digital culture have reinvigorated the cultural hegemony and cultural imperialism debates because they have the *potential* to break up this pattern. Far more than film and television, digital popular culture has the potential to be interactive and far more open to do-it-yourself cultural production. The potential to, in relatively inexpensive ways, create pathways of cultural exchange from almost any cultural or subcultural location to almost any other is very real. It is already being done, though not yet on a scale that competes with corporate media in any significant way. The potential for a truly democratic cultural production and cultural exists, but that will not happen automatically. It is not technologically determined. Rather it will depend on a host of political, economic and cultural decisions. There are certainly powerful economic and political interests who would prefer to have the Web become more of a broadcast, rather than an interactive, medium through which they can push their commercial products and political ideas. As the chapters that follow will suggest, only action—through critical digital culture analyses, social protest activism and political lobbying—will make the wider democratic potential of digital cultures a reality.

This process of making digital cultures more open, democratic and broadly representative entails hard work on the part of people across the range of subject positions. Gaining depth of understanding of subject positions and cultures other than one's own is difficult, but far from impossible. This process involves gaining greater degrees of cultural competency. While we develop a more or less automatic depth of understanding of the cultures into which we are born and socialized, achieving something like that depth of understanding of other subject positions and other cultures is far more difficult. Again, difficult but not impossible, and it is usually done best by a combination of self-education and immersion in cultural situations outside of one's own. Virtually every country on earth is becoming more multicultural, but few if any have achieved substantive equality across their multiple demographic groups. Fortunately, digital cultural spaces provide a staggering array of resources to make the task of developing new cultural competencies, deeper understandings of other subject positions, easier than ever before. They cannot substitute for on-the-ground experiences with other cultures (again an online/offline balance is crucial), but they can significantly augment them. Since the future of the planet may well depend on how well we can overcome the barriers to communication across social differences, partaking in meaningful online efforts to address the underlying economic and political barriers to substantial cross-cultural understanding is vital. The Net cannot be the only tool in this process, but it is a very powerful one that can do some key things no other medium can.

4

Is Everybody Equal Online?

Digitizing Gender, Ethnicity and Dis/Ability

There is no race. There is no gender. There is no age. There are no infirmities. There are only minds. Utopia? No, the Internet.

("Anthem," MCI WorldCom, 1997)

While few claims about the Internet have been as deeply challenged as the sentiment in this MCI advertisement from 1997, belief in the socially equalizing nature of digital culture continues to be quite strong. Not all such claims are wholly wrong, but they need to be made more carefully and in context-specific ways, because the Web also is being used to promote and deepen inequalities.

Claims about the race-less, gender-less, etcetera-less nature of the Net arose initially out of the era when online communication was primarily through written words. But even when digital spaces were just words, the claims made little sense because they vastly underestimated the depth of socialization we humans inevitably undergo. Years of learning our place(s) in the world cannot be washed away magically by going into online places. While certain freedoms are indeed opened up by anonymity and some other features of some online spaces, countless studies make clear that we inevitably drag the heavy weight of who we are offline with us online. Moreover, no one seemed to ask the next question: if we are truly in a post-racial, post-sexist era, why would one *want* to disguise one's race or gender?

▤ THE DEFAULT SUBJECT POSITION?

To understand the social and cultural factors in online communication (as well as technology creation, dissemination and adoption), it is vital to understand the key variables in social identity formation. Sociologists have long identified what those key variables are, and digital culture interpreters have shown them to be interwoven into all levels of digital cultures. Typically, the list of key socialization/ identity formation factors include: class; gender; race/ethnicity/ nationality; sexual identity; age; language; education level; religion; and geographic location (urban/suburban/rural, etc.). To this list cyberculture analysts would add technological knowledge or techno-literacy, a factor typically very much shaped by all the other factors, especially class.

Together and in various combinations, these variables make up a person's *subject position*. If you think of identity as how you think about yourself, subject position is where *social structures beyond yourself place you in the world*. Some elements of subject position can change over time, but they remain extremely good predictors of belief and action. This is particularly so when people do not reflect on how their position was constructed, but just assume it to be the natural state of the world. Subject position deeply shapes personal identity, but especially in the Western world with its unusually strong emphasis on individualism, people tend to view their identities more as personally chosen than broadly shaped by cultural factors. As a teacher in North American universities, I notice this when assigning biographical essays; students invariably stress their personal uniqueness in their essays. Yet in comparing them it is abundantly clear how similar their tastes, styles, ideas, and values are in relation to their class, gender, ethnicity, age, sexuality and regional subject position.

In cyberculture studies, scholars speak of the *default subject position* (and default identity) in digital culture. This refers to the process by which straight, white, middle-class, Euro-American male cultural assumptions, values and ideas were/are unintentionally built into hardware, software and digital cultures. This default subject position emerged from those who were the early creators of digital technology and cybercultures. White men played the key role in developing much of this culture, and were largely unaware that they were building from a particular, limited viewpoint on the world. One classic example famously illuminated in an article by Cynthia and Richard Selfe (1994) is the choice of the metaphor of the *desktop* to name the *interface* between users and computers. The metaphor was designed to make computers more user friendly. But why that metaphor? Why not other possible metaphors like workbench, or kitchen counter, art canvas, or playground, etc., each of which would have been more user friendly to other sets of users? Clearly because it was one familiar to the mostly white male desk-bound designers. With no intention to be culturally limited, these kinds of unconscious assumptions were built into hardware and software at every level. As the use of digital devices and the making of digital cultures has expanded to new groups it is no longer possible to ignore the cultural limitations built into hardware, software and other aspects of the digital realm; more people, though still far from enough, who do not fit the default subject position are now involved in or desiring to be involved in digital cultures. A desire to expand the market probably drives change in this area more than a deep corporate commitment to cultural diversity per se, but the default subject position is no longer assumed as much as it once was.

And some areas of the digital world openly acknowledge and struggle with the problems of the default subject position. For example, in an admirably self-reflective piece on "Wikipedia: Systemic Bias," Wikipedia notes,

> Women are underrepresented on Wikipedia, making up less than 15 percent of contributors. . . . The gender gap has not been closing over time and, on average, female editors leave Wikipedia earlier than male editors. Research suggests that the gender gap has a detrimental effect on content coverage . . . Women typically perceive Wikipedia to be of lower quality than men do.
>
> Access to the Internet is required to contribute to Wikipedia. Groups who statistically have less access to the Internet, including people in developing nations, the poor in industrialized nations, the disabled, and the elderly, are underrepresented on Wikipedia. In most countries, minority demographic groups have disproportionately less access to information and education than majority groups. This includes African Americans and Latinos in the U.S., the First Nations of Canada, the Aborigines of Australia, and the poorer populations of India, among others. . . . Wikipedians are likely to be more technically inclined than average. . . . Despite the many contributions of Wikipedians writing in English as a

non-native language, the English Wikipedia is dominated by native English-speaking . . . These Anglophone countries tend to be in the global North, thereby accentuating the encyclopedia's bias to contributions from First World countries.

("Systemic Bias," accessed 16 October 2013)

Few online communities are as clear and honest as the Wikipedians about the systematic bias built in from the default subject position, but the vast majority of online services and communities could be analyzed in quite similar terms.

In default subject position terms, the English language is, for example, also a key component of online cultural bias across the board. As of 2013, more than half of the content of the Web was available only in English, despite native speakers of English being only 6 percent of the world's population and people with some secondary knowledge of the language making up only another 12 percent. No other language represents more than 10 percent of Web content, though Chinese is gaining rapidly. In addition much of the program language available for software creation was built on the linguistic logic of English such that even non-English-speaking programmers had to use a character set known as ASCII, an acronym whose full name, American Standard Code for Information Interchange, suggests its cultural origin and bias. Pressures from other language groups are slowly expanding the use of languages other than English both for content and programming, but the Web remains a place far more friendly to English speakers than to anyone else. While no one is forced to visit English language sites—there is content in many other languages, though far less of it—there is so much more available in English that it tends to drown out other languages. This is a problem of ethnocentrism, but it is also clearly a class issue, since in most parts of the world it is only the children of wealthier classes who are taught English as a second language. This is one of many ways in which the structure of the Web reinforces economic inequalities (Warschauer 2003 95–99).

Let me be clear that there is no conspiracy to exclude here; no ill will was required for things to end up this way. Rather, it is cultural hegemony at work. It is the historical result of those in the privileged position to create and disseminate much of digital culture being overwhelmingly middle-class, English-language-only speakers, limited by a particular set of cultural ideas and values. Nevertheless, the result of the limits of the default subject position from which much of the Internet and other components of digital culture have been designed and implemented has rendered digital spaces as deeply culturally biased. And the country most responsible for the early development of the Net, the US (my home country), is arguably more ethnocentric than most because, partly by virtue of being the world's only Superpower (for now), it tends to produce citizens who see little need to think much about the rest of the world (or learn other languages). When that mind-set went into the Internet-making process, the results were predictably narrow.

However just as it is possible to change the default settings on most programs, it is possible to move beyond the default identity initially built into much digital culture in order to open up digital spaces more fully to many other subject positions. And that work has been under way for many years now. But just as default settings often remain invisible to most computer users and don't get changed, *default identities have to be intentionally changed.* Much of the work of critical digital culture studies has been and continues to be to ferret out the places where default identity dominates cyberspaces, and to suggest ways to open up those spaces in ways supportive of a more diverse array of subject positions.

Clearly, the most effective way to overcome these cultural biases has been to bring greater gender, class and ethnic/racial diversity into the design and implementation of digital devices and processes, and to involve a more diverse population in the active creation of digital cultures. The electronic communication industry remains exceed-ingly white and male; in the US as of 2013 women make up less than 20 percent of the ITC work force, and those numbers fall rapidly when talking about the higher echelon jobs in the field. In Silicon Valley, fewer than 8 percent of tech start-ups are led by women, and in a region where Latinos make up close to 25 percent of the popula-tion, there are fewer than 5 percent Latino employees in Valley tech companies. All non-white ethnicities are seriously underrepresented. Similar statistics can be found in Europe, and the gender gap is even greater in Japan. Progress is further slowed by the fact that even when corporations see it as in their economic self-interest to hire a more diverse workforce, historical and ongoing discrimination in the offline world has meant that there are often not enough members of many marginalized groups in a position to learn about, let alone pay to be educated for, these jobs (*WISAT* n.d.).

The second most effective technique has been to extend the cul-tural competencies of those from the default subject position through various kinds of training. Historically, much of this training has been superficial, but corporations increasingly realize that without diverse cultural competencies they cannot extend their markets, and nothing motivates corporations like market growth. Both of these processes are well under way, but there is clearly a long way to go before digital cultures come close to reflecting the world's cultural diversity.

◉ IS THE INTERNET A GUY? ENGENDERING CYBERSPACES

There are a variety of different ways to think about digital cultures and cyberspaces as gendered, as favoring equality or inequality in gender relations. I will briefly trace five of the approaches: 1) gender imbalance in the ICT workforce; 2) the gendering of the design of ICT devices, spaces and applications; 3) forms of gender harassment and discrimination in online environments; 4) representations of gender in online media and digital games; and 5) the use of cyberspaces and digital devices in pursuit of gender equity. These are far from the only ways to talk about gender in cyberspaces, but I believe these approaches can suggest the structures that contribute to most other aspects of sexism online as well. Some other dimensions of gender online are dealt with in other chapters of this book, including pornography and the traffic in women in Chapter 5, and more on gender in digital games in Chapter 7.

At base, it is crucial to realize that as with all other aspects of life online, offline conditions deeply shape gender relations in cyberspaces. In North America, for example, women still earn on average less than 75 percent of the income earned by men. Associated issues of bank loans and credit, inherited wealth favoring males, and other economic factors place women at a disadvantage in most developed countries, and the situation is often equally or more biased in the developing world. These structural conditions, along with continuing forms of cultural sanctions (religious and secular) that deter or lessen the force of women in the public sphere, all shape the possibilities for life online too. Feminist movements worldwide have improved conditions greatly over the last few decades, but full equity is still far from being achieved. Access to online information and interaction has often proved vital to women around the globe, and women and men continue to work on the gender gap in cyberspaces.

We have already noted the fact that there are deep imbalances in the ITC workforce, with all but a handful of prominent women missing from the upper echelons, relatively few women at mid-levels except in pink-collar secretarial and graphic design positions, leaving women concentrated on the lowest, least well-paid and most hazardous levels of assembly and disassembly. Given continuing extreme gender imbalances in enrollments in engineering and tech schools around the world (fewer than 10 percent in most countries), that situation is going to change slowly, at best. This is doubly unfortunate because a number of the other forms of gender discrimination would no doubt be lessened by a greater presence of women in the decision-making levels of the ICT workforce. This situation in turn shapes things like the fact that women are less likely to contribute in certain areas of online knowledge production (as suggested by the figure cited above that only 15 percent of Wikipedia entries are by women).

The *representations* of women and men in digital media like web pages and video games are arguably the most disheartening. Digital media have set back gender representations decades. Where media activist and watchdog groups have done much to improve gender representation in traditional media (TV, film, etc.), though there is clearly much to improve, new media have frequently fallen back on stereotypes and representations that should have fallen into the dustbin of history. This is due to several factors, some technical, some cultural. The virtual, non-realistic nature of new media allow for a plasticity of representation that may lend itself to the exaggeration on which stereotyping thrives (bulging muscles on males, bulging busts on females). It doesn't take much effort to find e-games riddled with anatomically impossible cyberbabes, or websites that degrade women in every imaginable way. To test this hypothesis, try typing the words "Asian women" into Google or Yahoo. If you are lucky, or happen to be a long-time researcher on Asian demographics, you may find predominantly academic information. But more often, as when I just retried this experiment after typing that sentence, more than half of the first page of entries retrieved were sites that, one way or another, stereotyped or exploited Asian women. Here the issue is both cultural and technical. The ability for virtually anyone with a modicum of technical skill to upload content onto the Web has meant that the sexism rampant in the real world has found a media outlet it did not have before. Where film and television production consists of a relatively small community that can be addressed by critics of gender (or racial) stereotyping, the community of Web producers is almost infinitely extensive and far more difficult to reach.

Questions of how *offline gender issues* like sexual harassment, stalking, violence against women, and sexual trafficking have migrated onto and been impacted by digital technologies and digital culture once again remind us that allegedly virtual worlds and real worlds are never really disconnected. The anonymity of cyberspaces has unleashed new, though hardly unprecedented, levels of sexist discourse, as well as new forms of cyberbullying, cyber sexual harassment and cyberstalking, among other problems. While not all cyberbullying is gender related, an extremely high percentage of it is directed at girls or at boys considered insufficiently masculine. (Some experts argue that when harassment is directed at children under the age of 18, it should be classified as cyberbullying, and when directed at those over 18, as cyberstalking, but that seems to me a somewhat arbitrary division and one not sensitive enough to varieties of harassment.)

Cyber sexual harassment has become ubiquitous on the Web; in the US alone an estimated 850,000 cases of cyber sexual harassment occur each year, and similar patterns exist in countries around the world ("Cyber Sexual Harassment Statistics" n.d.). One survey found that 80 percent of gamers, male and female, believed sexism was prevalent in online gaming communities, and statistical evidence supports their beliefs. Women gamers, for example, receive three times as much "trash talk" as males, regardless of skill level, much of it directed in sexual terms. Sexist commentary is rampant in game chat, with anonymity often unleashing a torrent of truly misogynistic remarks. sixty-five percent of women reported being harassed, compared with 15 percent of men (and the 15 percent of men were often harassed by being called female derogatory or homophobic names—bitch, fag, etc.) (Dill, Brown and Collins 2008; Matthew 2012; Melendez 2012; Yao, Mahood and Linz 2009). While male gamers sometimes say abuse comes because of the incompetence of girl and women gamers, the statistics show the same level of harassing remarks even at the highest skill levels for female players.

The testimony of one female gamer is typical of many other reported incidents:

> [M]y boyfriend who is an avid player [of Modern Warfare] convinced me one night [to play]. Once the opposing team realized I was a woman, they acted out a virtual "gangbang" and kept pushing my avatar against structures in the game, crowding around me and saying the most vile things I've ever heard. This actually frightened me even though it was happening in a virtual reality rather than in "real" life. I can only imagine what people of color and different cultures must go through just to play a video game. And the fear they must have about just opening their mouth to speak . . . unbelievable.

> (*The Road Less Taken* n.d.)

In this case, the woman was identified by her voice, a reminder that not only visual but aural "outing" of women (and people of color with ethnically coded accents), a phenomenon also known as vocal profiling, has often replaced text-based anonymity in multimedia online spaces.

The reputation of male gamers has been helped along by men like Sam Killerman who founded Gamers Against Bigotry, a site that works against not only sexism and homophobia, but racial, ethnic and religious bigotry in games as well. A different approach to the issue has been taken at the site "Fat, Ugly or Slutty." The site collects and posts sexist and other derogatory comments by gamers with the goal of laughing the perpetrators into embarrassed silence. In a sense, this is the opposite of censorship (as can occur through "muting" or "reporting" abusers) and has the added advantage of publicizing what is often dismissed as harmless or exaggerated behavior ("Fat, Ugly or Slutty" n.d.). While the game world certainly offer vivid examples, similar kinds of sexist harassment can be found on many, many other Web spaces; indeed, on practically any site that allows comments.

Cyberstalking is a deeper level of harassment, one that doesn't always end at the edge of cyberspaces. While men and boys suffer harassment too, the vast majority of victims are girls and women. Cyberstalking has been used to track women into their homes, far too often leading to sexual assaults. While the Internet has provided lifelines and safe spaces for women facing violence, perpetrators of domestic violence are increasingly using ICTs like spyware and key-stroke logging software to track their partners' behavior. Fake ads have also been used to endanger domestic partners, as in the case of Jebediah Stipe who was sentenced to a term of 60 years to life for posting a fraudulent ad in Craigslist that resulted in the rape of his former girlfriend. The ad read, "Need an aggressive man with no concern or regard for women. If interested, contact Sarah" (Winfrey 2010). Stipe set up several "rape dates" for Sarah from the pool of 161 men who responded (Winfrey 2010). Cyberstalking is every bit as serious as offline stalking; in fact one study found that it is actually experienced by many women as more traumatic than offline stalking (Gutierrez 2013).

The Stipe case is just one particularly well publicized example of the massive, world-wide problem of violence against women. Cyber tools have been implicated in both the carrying out of domestic violence, and its resistance. Given that violence against women affects every culture, ethnic group and class around the globe, this is one more reason that being tech savvy can be vital to women and girls.

Violence against women has generated a substantial network of online organizations seeking solutions to this global problem (Fascendini and Fialova; Kee 2005; Southworth 2005). The UN's Unite to End Violence Against Women project and website is one of many clearing houses for these vital efforts. Some of these campaigns specifically target digital culture itself. For example, a successful petition campaign was launched in 2013 against Facebook for accepting ads characterized as degrading to women, especially images of domestic violence and rape fantasies (Kleinman 2013).

While overt and spectacular forms of sexism like trafficking rightly get most attention, sexism in a variety of less dramatic ways is the everyday experience for millions of women around the globe. The digital world is being used to make this apparent, and to counter it. One such effort describes its mission as follows:

> "The Everyday Sexism Project" aims to harness the power of social media to raise awareness of the ways in which gender discrimination impacts women on a day-to-day basis. It collects reports of daily experiences of sexual harassment, job discrimination, and other sexist treatment from women around the world via email and Twitter.
>
> (*Everyday Sexism Project* n.d.)

In the first year of operation, the site received over 30,000 separate incident reports (Gardiner 2013). Responses also included pornographic imagery, rape threats and death threats, directed at the site's host. Another such project specifically targets street harassment. "Hollaback!" encourages women to "out" street harassers and let other women know of harassing spaces. Active in 64 cities in 22 countries, the site uses the locative possibilities of digital media to pinpoint harassers' whereabouts. Their mission statement notes that

> The real motive of street harassment is intimidation. To make its target scared or uncomfortable, and to make the harasser feel powerful. But what if there was a simple way to take that power away by exposing it? You can now use your smartphone to do just that by documenting, mapping, and sharing incidents of street harassment.
>
> (*Hollaback!* n.d.)

In addition to the examples cited above in which advocates for gender equality have used technology to deal with each of these key issues, I want to end this section with a brief discussion of a different but related form of gender equity activism online, one centered on challenging gender identities themselves. Many argue that digital cultures, despite decidedly sexist origins, have great potential to shake up ideas about gender. At the base of these struggles are efforts to achieve rough parity for women as participants in all forms of digital culture. While the digital world to a large extent remains a "man's world," major developments in the amount and quality of women's involvement in the creation and use of cyberspaces are challenging this state. Women and girls, for example, have now achieved rough parity with men and boys in the overall number of digital game players, though there is still gender imbalance in some games genres, with some still implicitly coded as "male" (racing and war games, for example), and others as implicitly female (often stereotypically packaged in pink).

A key element in terms of this gender work is the rise of cyberfeminisms. Coined in the 1990s, the term is shorthand for a set of arguments for women to embrace and use technology in the service of gender equality and personal liberation. Cyberfeminisms of various stripes urge women to make their presence known in every type of digital space, and to use digital spaces to advocate for greater economic, political, social and cultural equality between the genders. Many cyberfeminists acknowledge inspiration from the brilliant arguments of feminist cultural theorist Donna Haraway in her "A Manifesto for Cyborgs" (Haraway 2003 [1984]). In particular they draw upon Haraway's claim that the breaking down of the human–machine boundary can be used to undermine historically oppressive claims that gender inequality is a "natural," biological thing. Haraway argued at the dawn of the digital era that the human–computer interface can serve to challenge assumptions about naturalized female and male roles and identities, and advocated embracing the "cyborg" as a symbol of this boundary crossing work. Haraway argues that because in patriarchal cultures men have long been identified with the mind and women with body, the cyborg—a creature part human, part electronic machine—can disrupt the notion of the "natural" body, and therefore can be utilized to challenge the assumption that there are natural roles into which women and men must fit.

Haraway not only offered a highly nuanced analysis of the positive possibilities of cyborg identities in liberating women from historical forms of sexism, but also pointed up the many digital dangers facing women, especially women from the Global South who as noted above do much of the most painstaking labor in constructing digital products. Their "integration into the printed circuits of capitalism" exemplifies one of many downsides to the cyborg. Haraway also reminds readers that cyborgs were in origin the "illegitimate offspring" of militaristic science and corporate exploitation, and that the prime popular culture examples of cyborgs were mindless killing machines like those in the "Terminator" movie series (though note, a tough female protagonist, Sarah Conner, is the Terminator's nemesis). Unfortunately, some less astute cyberfeminists have hyped the plus side of the cyborg metaphor, without equally attending to the ways digital cultures can perpetuate and even deepen some dimensions of sexism. It is necessary to talk of cyberfeminisms in the plural, to acknowledge several strands of this work, with varying degrees of complexity and effectiveness in using cyberspaces to further the cause of gender equity. For example, Zoe Sofia has argued that cyberspace is often coded as female, through terms like the Matrix (derived from the Latin for mother), and subsequently "penetrated" by hard-bodied male cyborgs and monsters apparently threatened by women's power, including the power to reproduce the species. She suggests that the fascination of many male scientists and sci-fi writers with self-replicating cyborgs seems a lot like "womb envy," an attempt to colonize one of the few social functions reserved exclusively to women, human reproduction, giving birth (Sofia 1984).

Whether they identify with the term cyberfeminist or not, there are hundreds of gender equity websites, from blogs to NGOs to official government sites to educational institution sites to social movement activist groups, that are using the Web and other digital culture spaces to fight against domestic violence, sex trafficking, discrimination in the workforce, and numerous other gender issues, and to fight for economic, political and cultural equality for all women. Feminism is an extraordinarily diverse set of ideas, and all the strands of feminist movements are represented by numerous sites on the Web, including ones targeting particular age groups, classes, nationalities and ethnicities, sexual preferences, and pretty much every other imaginable grouping, from feminist ballerinas to feminist teamsters, from feminist quilters to feminist rappers, from feminist gamers to feminist politicians, from feminist anarchists to feminist business people.

While the default subject position of the Web, gaming platforms and most other digital spaces remains biased toward white males (as clearly does the offline world), women are making major incursions into every type of cyberspace. One ambiguous sign of this was referenced in Chapter 1 as the domestication of technology. In the modern West and much of the rest of the world, domestic spaces have been defined as traditionally feminine spaces, ones limited in contrast with public spaces coded more as masculine. Thus the increasingly central role of domestic spaces and domesticating processes as sites of digital culture have to a degree taken away some of the male bravado of keyboard cowboys in earlier cybercultures. But such discourses and processes will prove truly liberating for women and girls only when domestic space and public space are gendered equally, or not at all, when equality of power exists in all private and public realms; a condition we are obviously still far from realizing.

⊟ IS THE INTERNET COLORBLIND? E-RACIALIZATIONS

The rise of the popular Internet coincided with the rise of conservatives' claims that racism had ended, that we were entering a "post-racial" or "colorblind" era of history. A variation on the famous *New Yorker* cartoon of the dog going online, pictures a be-robed, cone-hatted person clearly meant to represent a member of the infamous American white supremacist group, the Ku Klux Klan, again sitting in front of a screen typing on a keyboard. The caption in this version reads, "On the Internet nobody knows you're a racist." Even more forcefully than the original, this cartoon highlights and challenges the claim that online opportunities exist to communicate outside of socially defined roles and identities by side-stepping or actively masking ascribed identities, or by actively projecting a social position not one's own.

The concept of "race" and the practice of racism were invented simultaneously. Or, more precisely, "race" was invented to justify racism. Few social forces have done more damage to the world over the last 500 years than racism (and its close relative, ethnocentrism). While new media are indeed new in many ways, they too often fall into quite old patterns when dealing with issues of race and ethnicity. New media have reinforced old racisms, and created some novel virtual racisms. Fortunately, they have also provided new ways to combat these forces.

For several hundred years, science played a significant role in bolstering white supremacy. Scientific racisms, purporting to offer empirical evidence of the natural, biological superiority of the "caucasian race," lasted well into the late twentieth century (Duster 2006; Gould 1981; Kuhl 1994). But about the same time as the emergence of the popular Internet, journalists, social scientists and social movement activists began bringing forth the news that scientists had largely discredited the idea of race. Biologists showed that race made no sense as a genetic category. Race is literally only skin deep. Visible differences in skin color, facial features and the like are not a sound basis for biological categorization because the range of characteristics among people categorized as within the same "race" are as great as the differences between "races."

As my scare quotes suggest, "race" ceases to be a biological category at all for these more contemporary scientists. At the same time that scientists were showing the biologically meaningless nature of race, historians were documenting that the categories of races have varied immensely over time within the same country (the Irish, Italians and Jews did not become "white" in the US until the twentieth century, for example) and across geographic space (what constitutes a "race" and how the society divvies up races varies greatly from Brazil to South Africa to Australia to Canada, and so on). Similarities across so-called races, and differences within so-called races, made clear that the human race is one, not several. This confirmed what some social scientists and cultural theorists were increasingly arguing, that "race" is a socially constructed category, rather than a natural fact. The fact that racial categories themselves have changed over time, and differed from nation to nation thus reinforced the scientific breakdown of the category. But while race as a concept is hopefully being tossed into the dustbin of history where it belongs, historically created racial categories, socially embedded racist structures and racist cultural representations remain very much alive and continue to do great damage. We are in the ironic position of needing to use racial categories to challenge the idea of race because those categories have ongoing impact in present lives. New media have great potential to challenge racism and racialization (the process of creating racial categories), and in some areas they are doing so. But much digital culture instead continues to reinforce racial and ethnic stereotypes.

There are a number of different ways in which the Web has re-created, reinforced, or generated new spaces for racisms to flourish. These processes and representations are collectively known as forms of e-racialization. As was the case with women, the relative absence of so-called non-whites in the upper echelons of the ICTs is partly responsible for much of this racism going unchallenged before being disseminated into cyberspace. E-racialization, or the digitization of race, includes things ranging from (overtly or covertly) racialized avatars in virtual worlds and chat rooms, racialized characters in games (see Chapter 7), racial representations on websites, racial discourse among users of the Web, racially defined portals, social media cyber-ghettos and a variety of other manifestations.

The story of race in digital culture begins, as race always has, in the imagination. For many years, and still often today, when most people imagine the online world it tends to call up images of European (or sometimes Asian) males in glasses and white short-sleeved dress shirts with pocket protectors full of pens. This is the ubiquitous popular cultural image sent around the world of the "nerd" or "geek" only comfortable speaking computerese, and uncomfortable with most other human interaction. While on one level a rather harmless image, especially as it evolved over time into a somewhat heroic phase in which "geek chic" modified the rather unattractive stereotype, by subtle implication it leaves other people, other ethno-racial groups, out of the world of digital creation. Other racial stereotypes of folks producing and inhabiting digital spaces are in part dependent upon the nerd/geek white male stereotype. The Other races imagined to make and inhabit digital worlds fall into two broad stereotypes, the hyper-hyper-linked Asian, and the digitally-challenged racial under-classes. In the US, Asians have long been stereotyped as the "model minority," the good minorities who work hard and don't complain about silly things like racial oppression. This "positive" stereotype has long been used to denigrate by contrast the not-so-model minorities (black and brown people) who allegedly don't work hard, don't have the right values, and constantly protest about discrimination that supposedly ended long ago. This vicious American division of the world, and a modified version prevalent in Europe, migrated very easily into the imagery of cyberspaces. The extension of the WWW into more parts of the globe has of necessity complicated this imagery, but it has far from eliminated it from what remains the center of the digital universe in terms of cultural power, the default subject position of the European or European American male.

In addition, these ethno-racial stereotypes have been extended from the realm of the imagined user to a proliferation of ethnic and racial stereotypes in Web spaces and in video games. Digital studies scholar Lisa Nakamura refers to these new versions of old representations of race/ethnicity as cybertypes, virtual stereotypes (Nakamura 2002). In addition to recycling old stereotypes, many design features of new media, especially Photoshop and homemade animation, lend themselves to the kind of physical exaggeration of features that have historically been an integral part of much stereotyping (for example, cartoons have long been a favored genre for racial stereotyping because the exaggeration of physical features used in much racist representation is easier to do in non-realist graphic media). Cybertypes can be found across a range of digital spaces, devices, and forms, from virtual world icons, avatars and game characters, to websites to racist audio-chat in gaming spaces. The most outrageous forms of racial denigration have taken place in digital genres that permit a high degree of anonymity. W. James Au, author of the book *The Making of Second Life* (2008), notes that online games and forums where participants are anonymous seem to be slowly being replaced by popular networks like Facebook which more often match users to their offline identities. When anonymity disappears, people are generally more civil. "The shift to real identities online helps get rid of racism," Au suggests. Perhaps, but this is debatable on a couple of levels. First, one might ask whether false civility is always preferable to honest expression of prejudice in rooting out racism. Racism made overt is perhaps easier to attack. And second, as Nakamura has argued, visual profiling (identifying race by visual cues) and vocal profiling (identifying race or ethnicity by accent) has in other areas *increased* racial harassment online and in gaming (*GAMBIT: Hate Speech Project* n.d.; Nakamura 2009).

The irony in much of this is that just as stereotypes have moved closer to eradication in old media like TV and film due to extensive efforts by media anti-discrimination groups, new media have allowed old stereotypes to re-emerge (and invented new ones). As with the issue of sexist representation, this is due both to use of stereotypes in the industry (video games most obviously) and to the often uncritically celebrated amateur, DIY, participatory nature of the Web that now includes vast amounts of viciously racist imagery. This is a sobering reminder that not all of the "participation" championed by Web 2.0 enthusiasts leads to happy outcomes.

In addition, the Web has proven to be a fertile medium for white supremacists who benefit from the low cost and anonymity of cyberspaces to find like-minded individuals through which to spread their hate messages. A world-wide web of hate groups has been enabled by the Net, and many of these groups have utilized vicious cybertyping to good effect. As with all other forms of e-racism, these groups have not gone unchallenged, of course, since the Web has simultaneously allowed anti-racism groups to counter continuing manifestations of racism in both overt and less visible forms, including the deep structural inequalities that keep racisms alive around the globe.

While many talk about the (very real) new kinds of cross-cultural links possible via the Web and other digital technologies, it is important to also realize that digital cultures have often created cyberghettos that replicate existing informal forms of social segregation. One scholarly study, for example, found that many young white kids in the US fled from MySpace to Facebook because they believed that MySpace had become "too ghetto," a move that resembles the "white flight" of the 1970s and '80s when Euro-Americans left racially mixed cities for predominantly white suburbs (Boyd 2012; Hargittai 2012). Some have argued that ethnic portals aimed at particular racially or ethnically defined communities, while very useful for intragroup connections, may also be replicating damaging forms of essentialism and group self-ghettoization. Proponents argue that such sites offer important networks for groups facing continued discrimination and marginalization, while opponents argue that such sites perpetuate marginalization and reinforce the archaic notion that race is a natural, rather than a cultural, phenomenon. Still others argue that some ethnic portals exist primarily as marketing tools for corporations with little regard for social issues surrounding racism. Each of these perspectives represents part of the truth. Some ethnic, gender or sexuality-based portals are clearly designed substantially as tools for marketing to particular demographics (Lee and Wong 2003). Others clearly are concerned substantially with empowering the group in question (Women Watch; Gender Equality Evaluation portal of the UN, for example).

Many other affinity portals defined by gender, sexual orientation or other key markers of subject position also exist online. When one group, whether defined by race, class, gender, language, religion or other primary social factor, has been dominated, overlooked, harassed or discriminated against in some other way, joining together as a group can be essential to heath and survival. However, over time such groups may become insular. The trick for socially marginalized populations seems to be to find a way to utilize the benefits of group solidarity while also connecting with the world of the dominant group in order to assert their group's equality and rights. The Web is clearly one key place where these issues are being redefined.

Not all groups on the Web claiming marginalization are convincing. Digital culture theorist Tara McPherson, for example, offers a reading of the cultural symbols through which the neo-Confederate website Dixie-Net seeks to construct a white (implicitly male) identity in opposition to contemporary US multiculturalism. Confederate flags, use of the phrase the "war between the states," ubiquitous snippets of the song "Dixie," maps showing the South as a separate nation and so on reinforce a sense of rebel opposition to the United States with its stars and stripes, the Civil War, the national anthem, and 50-state map (McPherson 2000).

Another less obvious arena where digital technologies are reshaping race is the field of biotechnology. As noted above, by erasing the category from biology, science has over the last few decades been reversing its long and ugly history of underwriting racism. However, since the turn of the twenty-first century, the popular use and abuse of genetics have once again confused the issue of the biological reality of race. As a number of scholars have pointed out, genetic testing (itself made possible largely by developments in digital technology) has created an obsession with ancestry that has often been miscoded in simplistic racial terms (Chow-White 2012; Nelkin and Lindee 2004; Nelson and Hwang 2012). Ironically, this search for the pride of ancestry may resurrect the past illusion that race is a meaningful biological category, rather than a social construction serving to justify oppression.

Contrary to claims that we are in a post-racial, color-blind world, our newest social spaces, the digitized ones, make clear that online and offline life remains deeply marked by racism, and ethnic prejudice in a myriad of forms. The election of Barack Obama as US president, for example, set off a storm of online activity that revealed deep racial divides on a number of levels (Everett 2012). The promise that the Web can bring people closer together and closer to mutual understanding is not a wholly false one, though the promise is clearly undercut by so much racist and ethnocentric imagery and discourse also found there. And even if all racially offensive imagery were removed from digital spaces, it would not remove the inequalities stemming from hundreds of years of racial injustice. Indeed, some positive forms of egalitarian media imagery act as a cover-up ("How can there be racism, look how many black lawyers and doctors there are on TV"). This is the media-centered variation on the theme of how can the US or UK be racist societies when they have a black president and East Asian MPs, respectively.

While the vast amount of racism and ethnocentrism in digital cultures is deeply disturbing and discouraging, the digital world, by exposing the continued existence of racisms and ethnocentrisms many have claimed we have left behind, enables a critical mapping of these social blights, as well as providing new technical tools for fighting them. Beyond the important task of fighting for richer, more varied representations of the full range of ethnic cultures online and in other media, critics make clear that the end of racism will also require deep changes in the economic processes and social institutions whose structures carry the impact of historic and ongoing racisms. The immensely liberating potential of digital spaces will not be realized without considerable work offline and on to eradicate structural conditions that continue to favor some racial and ethnic groups over others, often in ways that are a matter of life and death.

▣ WHO IS DIS/ABLED BY CYBERSPACES? ENABLING AND DISABLING TECHNOLOGIES

The relation of people with disabilities to digital cultures is clearly a complex and contradictory one. On the one hand, new digital technologies have created a host of assistive devices that greatly enhance the lives of millions of people who lack sight, hearing, the ability to use their hands or legs, or a host of other limiting physical and psychological conditions. An array of "digital assistive devices" and digitized therapies are opening up amazing new possibilities for persons with disabilities. This is an area where becoming cyborgs has few detractors. Digital technologies have done astonishing things in enabling greater sight and hearing, in facilitating physical rehabilitation and movement, and in extending possibilities for folks with cognitive/psychological/social conditions such as autism, stroke or PTSD, among others. On the other hand, access to the wonders of digital culture in online environments continues to be limited by corporations, governments and others who fail to make the Net fully accessible to folks with particular physical limitations defined as disabling.

Both the positive potential and the current limitations of digital culture in relation to people with disabilities have been aptly summed up by Mark Warschauer.

> ICT is particularly important for the social inclusion of those who are marginalized for other reasons. For example, the disabled can make especially good use of ICT to help overcome problems caused by lack of mobility, physical limitations, or societal discrimination. Using ICT, a blind person can access documents by downloading them from the Internet and converting text to speech; a quadraplegic can pursue a college degree without leaving home; a child suffering with AIDS can communicate with other children around the world. Sadly, though, disabled people, because of poverty, lack of social support, or other reasons, frequently lack the means to get online. In the United States, for example only 21.6% of people with disabilities have home access

to the Internet, compared with 42.1% of the non-disabled population. This disproportionately low rate of Internet connectiv-
ity for people who in many senses most need it, and in one of
the world's most technologically advanced countries, is evidence
that market mechanisms alone are not sufficient for achieving
equitable ICT access.

(Warschauer 2003 28–29)

On average people with disabilities spend twice as much time online
as folks without disabilities, suggesting a deep disparity between
desire or need, and degree and quality of access (Chambers 2004;
Goggin and Newell 2003).

It is disheartening that in the second decade of the twenty-first
century, 60 percent of websites remain inaccessible to people with
disabilities (90 percent were inaccessible in 2001). This is largely an
issue of website design. Virtually all new computers now come with
"screen readers" that can translate text into sound. Unfortunately,
these devices are only effective on websites that enable their use, and
only a small percentage of websites do so. This too is partly an issue
of economics, since the costs of re-tooling old websites, or building
new ones with this extra feature, can be considerable.

Access for folks with disabilities is both a social issue, since it
excludes many extraordinarily creative people from digital cultures,
and a legal issue, since laws meant to ensure access do exist in many
parts of the world. In the US, the Americans with Disabilities Act
(1990) established "access" to all public spaces and public services
as a right, not a privilege or luxury, for persons with disabilities.
In this context, access to the "public space" of the Internet also
became a right. But it remains a right still routinely and massively
violated. On an international scale, these rights have been embodied in the World Wide Web Accessibility Initiative (WAI 1997) of
the World Wide Web Consortium or W3C (the organization, led
by Web creator Tim Berners-Lee that has tried to set standards for
web practices). Inspired by various national laws and the Accessibility Initiative, disability rights groups around the globe continue to
struggle to reach the as-yet-unrealized ideal of an Internet usable by
all people.

As with other forms of "otherness," it has been claimed that the
disembodied, anonymous nature of the Web has been a boon to people with disabilities. As some differently abled people have testified,
this can be true. But there is also a danger of once again pushing folks
with disabilities to the margins, making them invisible. Visibility

or invisibility, openly noting or not calling attention to conditions labeled disabilities, should be the choice of people with disabilities online, not something foisted on them by putatively able-bodied folks who'd rather not know.

While there are technical issues that cause difficulties in achieving universal access for persons with disabilities, the ultimate issues are social and political not technical. The issues begin with the very terms used and the hidden biases they conceal. Let's start with that phrase itself, "people with disabilities." That's the preferred term and is set against the commonly used phrase "disabled people." What's the difference? There is a world of difference. To say someone is a *person with a disability* is to stress the personhood first and the disability second. By contrast, to say *disabled person* makes the disability the defining feature of the person. That difference neatly sums up the attitudinal problem that people with disabilities face from the able-bodied population—their full personhood is lost in a focus on physical differences.

A person with a disability, or the differently-abled, exists on a continuum with everyone else. We all have certain abilities and disabilities, and to place people who have a particularly visible or more pronounced disability in a wholly other category of human beings from those of us whose abilities and disabilities are less visible is nothing but prejudice. Disability is a continuum, not a state of being. All of us at some point in our lives will be disabled, temporarily or with likely permanence, and most of us will be severely disabled if we live long enough. The most common form of prejudice is to speak of the "normal" body or the normal way of moving through the world. But which is the "normal" way to move over the course of a mile: by walking, by jogging, by riding a bicycle, by riding in a car, by train, by wheelchair? All but the last of these are considered "normal" ways to move by the world at large. Why not in a wheelchair? Disability is not a natural fact; it is a socially defined state. Over the course of history and across cultures today there are many different standards of normal bodily and mental functioning, and many different attitudes towards those currently characterized as physically or mentally disabled.

When asked what is the greatest difficult they face, the most common answer given by people with disabilities is "People's attitudes towards me" (Mullins 2010). According to disability activists, disabling responses to people with disabilities typically take one of these forms: *pity* (a useless emotion that makes the able-bodied person feel sensitive); *heroic appreciation* (how amazing that you can do

X despite being so messed up); *invisibility/avoidance* (find ways not to see or interact with the PWD); *annoyance/impatience* (find the presence of a PWD an eyesore or time drag when they must be accommodated). Each of these attitudes, though differing in moral weight, has the effect of reinforcing the non-normal nature of disability, of lessening the person with a disability's place in the world.

In light of these and other forms of medical and social prejudices, the Disability Rights and Independent Living movements argue that *social attitudes* and the *built environment* are major *disabling* features that are *falsely regarded as intrinsic to the disability*. Let me give you an example. Most of you can't read with your fingers. Is that a disability? It would be if the only books published were in Braille, just as the massive number of books not printed in Braille is a limitation for those who can only read with their fingers. Again, new technologies are helping, both in translation to Braille and in such other innovative approaches as text to audio readers. But the truly disabling factor is the assumption of those privileged with sight that limitations placed upon the unsighted are not their problem.

In a world in which the social construction of disability was recognized and dealt with fairly, so-called disabilities would be seen as *naturally occurring and accidental differences* in degrees of able-bodiedness that change over time. Various disabilities would be seen instead as socially imposed limitations on movement and access *created by cultural expectations and built into social spaces*. The larger disability in this perspective is *the failed ability of society to create accommodations* to varying kinds and degrees of able-bodiedness. And the term accommodations itself can misleadingly suggest special privileges, as if able-bodied persons are not accommodated everyday by sidewalks, elevators, escalators, and thousands of other things often built at the public expense to make their lives easier.

The most common justification for lack of access to the Web or other public media for people with disabilities is that accommodation costs too much. Disability activists respond by asking, what should we pay for basic human rights? What are the societal costs of not accommodating the many gifted people with disabilities? What would we not know about the origins of the universe if Stephen Hawkins' "disability" was not "accommodated"? What great music would we have missed if certain accommodations were not made for musicians without sight? Much of the expense of hardware and software accommodations is greatly minimized if an access expectation is built in initially as opposed to an afterthought. Again the disabling factor is more attitude than economics. Activists argue that when differing dis/abilities are normalized, when so-called able-bodiedness is no longer the definition of normal, all spaces, including cyberspaces, will be enriched by extending access to folks currently excluded by socially constructed limitations.

At the same time that people struggle to change the attitudes which inhibit wider access to digital cultures for persons with disabilities, others have been using digital technology to create a host of new assistive devices and virtual therapeutic environments that enable many kinds of physical and cognitive limitations to be lessened or virtually eliminated. However, each of the two main technical elements enabling digital culture impacts the access of people with disabilities: 1) hardware that is difficult or impossible to use; 2) software and applications with limited functionality vis-à-vis certain physical and cognitive conditions. And so long as hardware and software makers do not fully take people with disabilities into consideration at the earliest stages of design, each new iteration of technology only compounds the problem by requiring new accommodations to new devices and software. Given the generally lower income of people with disabilities, these recurring costs can be, well, crippling.

Not taking into consideration the needs of people with disabilities can also show up in the arena of innovations. While most people welcomed, and the industry greatly hyped, the move to a more visual Web, progress to visual interfaces proved to be a regression for unsighted users who had been able to read text with screen readers that were not prepared to convert visual information. In sum, access for people with disabilities is a continuing, economic, social, technical and frequently changing issue that must be dealt with as an issue of rights and equality.

There are, however, many creative ways in which people with disabilities have used cyberspaces. The organization Able Gamers (*Able Gamers* n.d.), for example, is tackling the issue of e-game access for people with disabilities (*Videogamerability* n.d.). There is an entire realm in the virtual reality space Second Life where people with disabilities interact in a variety of ways, from playing to having sex to strategizing about how to improve access to and experience of online worlds for people with disabilities. Technoculture theorist Sherry Turkle relates the story of a graduate student who had lost a leg, and then created a one-legged avatar who had a romance online that helped her come to terms with her real life changed body (Turkle 1995 262–263). Stories of this kind abound, incidentally reminding us that not all avatar creation has to take the form of muscle-bound men and cyberbabes.

Another positive side of the ledger regarding digital technology is the multifaceted and fascinating area of technologies used to offer people with disabilities new abilities. Every day new devices are being invented to give people with disabilities not only better access to the World Wide Web, but to the world at large. The variety of new assistive devices with digital components range from the use of virtual environments to retrain human movement to direct brain–computer interfaces that allow the brain to control prosthetic arms and legs to video games used in psychological and physical therapies to more sophisticated wheelchairs that can climb stairs. The possibilities are staggering (though so too, often, is the cost) (*Usable Web* n.d.).

Much discussion in cyberculture studies focuses on the issue of bodies and embodiment, in large part because so many people experience cyberspace as disembodied. Most of the time users do not even see each other's bodies when communicating online, and as they become immersed in online environments they tend to become less aware of their own bodies. Questions of embodiment obviously have special meaning for people whose bodies have been defined as not normal, including people with physical disabilities. The idea that in cyberspaces no one knows who you really are as an embodied being can seem attractive to people whose physical differences have been stigmatized as somehow less than fully human. In the many cyberspaces that do not include visual cues, we meet the person before we meet the body, if we meet that body at all. This can short circuit many prejudicial attitudes attendant upon viewing the non-normative body, just as is true to some degree around the illusory invisibility of race and gender in online worlds. But as in these other examples, social invisibility is not the solution; it can be temporarily useful in side-stepping prejudices, but too often these return when the invisibility stops. The real target is not the visible markers, but the social attitudes and structures that unequally treat the life prospects of people based solely upon those physical markers.

This returns us to the issue of access but from a new angle. While these new technologies are exciting, for a variety of reasons, not all persons with disabilities choose to avail themselves of these "fixes," not all want to be "fixed." A famous example of this is the long-standing resistance in some deaf communities to cochlear implants, devices that can enhance hearing but that are seen by some deaf people as a betrayal of fellow members of their community. Thus, respecting various disability cultures may include in some cases acknowledging the rights of people to *refuse to use technologies* that might otherwise allow them to approximate behaviors and abilities defined as normal by dominant, non-disabled communities. Just as folks have suggested that people have a perfect right to opt out of digital culture entirely, so too people have a right to refuse particular technologies as not necessarily enabling from their perspective. But the societal task is to make accessibility to digital realities as rich and complete as possible for people with a range of dis/abilities, so that they have the freedom to choose the kinds or degrees of dis/engagement they value.

5

Digitizing Desire?

Sexploration and/or Sexploitation

The impact of the Net on sexual attitudes, practices and knowledge can provide a vivid case study in how online cultural knowledge relates to the offline world. Granted, sex is a particularly charged subject that may not prove "typical" of other kinds of impacts. Nevertheless, the very intensity and ubiquity of the subject matter has made it one of the most studied and thus most amenable to exploration. Some suggest that there is no aspect of contemporary life that has been impacted more deeply by the Internet than sexuality. The exact amount of sexual content on the Web is very

- → Real Virtual Sex Education
- → Digital Diddling: Varieties of Cybersex
- → The "Mainstreaming" of Porn
- → Digitized Sex Trafficking
- → How Queer are Cyberspaces? Alternative Sexualities in Cyberspaces

difficult to measure, and has at times been wildly overestimated (reports of a third of websites being pornographic, for example, proved to be wildly exaggerated; it is closer to 4 or 5 percent (Ogas and Gaddam 2011; Ruvolo 2011)). But by most any standard, the amount of online sex material is staggering. Then again, most Internet statistics are staggering, and the stats on sex should perhaps not be so surprising. Everyone after all at some point learns the "facts of life" entailed by sexuality. Even the small number of people who choose not to engage in it physically during their whole lives would not be here without sex. Sexuality of all kinds is available in virtually all places where the Net has "penetrated" (as digital marketing researchers call "access"). But in this chapter I am going to make the perhaps seemingly perverse suggestion that the problem with the Web is not that there is too much sex on it, but that there is not enough.

⊡ REAL VIRTUAL SEX EDUCATION

To look carefully at what sexuality in digital cultures is all about, it is initially helpful to temporarily put aside questions about the morality or immorality of pornography and other forms of sexual activity. Because sexual mores will vary immensely among the readers of this book, I want to make it clear that my work here will be more descriptive than prescriptive. That is, I am not primarily interested in judging these practices but instead in describing them and characterizing some of the various positions and debates that cybersexualities have generated, though, as in the rest of this book, I will not try to hide my own views or prejudices when relevant. And in one regard I have already done so as I suggested above one abiding principle that shapes my discussion. My seemingly perverse claim that there is not enough sex on the Web is a claim that there is not enough sexual variety online, or perhaps, more accurately, that pornography crowds out other varieties of sexuality that is and could be more available in digital spaces. The Net has undoubtedly become the most pervasive medium of sex education on the planet. But I concur with the view of psychotherapist Marty Klein that pornography is about as useful for serious sexual education as a car chase scene from a movie is useful for a driver's education (Klein 2012).

Previously difficult or impossible-to-come-by information about sexuality, from medical facts to dating, mating or hook-up facilitation to academic sex research to more hands-on ways of getting off online, has been made more available by the Net. Some of this information has been literally life-saving. Some of it has been life-endangering. What is clear is that the online realm provides a panoramic view of the world's sexual possibilities, and makes this information available discreetly. Because of this it allows people to safely explore sexual alternatives.

Sexual positions, or rather, positions on sexuality, in regard to pornography and cybersex more broadly run the gamut (what is a gamut, anyway, and why does no one ever walk it?). Politically, morally and culturally the Net offers and critiques every imaginable form of sex, from the most libertarian to the most rigidly moralistic. But even the most rigid of positions do not fall neatly along ideological lines. Any serious analysis of sexuality on the Web must look at but get beyond the question of pornography to look at a range of topics, including sexual hook-up sites, Internet-assisted sexual trafficking, sex worker rights campaigns on the Web, sexual chat, sexting, online sex games, teledildonics and related digital diddling, and a wide variety of formal and informal digitized sex education by therapists, teachers and sex workers.

⇒ DIGITAL DIDDLING: VARIETIES OF CYBERSEX

The term cybersex has both a narrow and a broader meaning. In the narrow definition it refers to *sexual acts performed through the medium of digital technology*. In the broader definition, it refers to *all the ways in which sexuality is represented* in digital spaces, including but not restricted to sexual acts mediated by digital means. Obviously, these two definitions overlap to some degree; watching cyberporn, for example, may or may not lead to those physical manifestations defined as sex acts, but a strong argument can be made that viewing pornography is itself a sex act. But for now, let's try to use the distinction to help sort out the ways in which the sexuality and cyberculture shape each other.

Beginning with cybersex in the narrow sense of one, two (or more) people seeking sexual gratification with the aid of digital communication, the first thing that might be said is that it is in one sense among the safest of safe sex practices. There is no chance of the exchange of bodily fluids if the medium of sexual interaction is confined to pixel sharing, or verbal intercourse. In this sense, cybersex has as a precursor phone sex, another safe medium. Cybersex includes SkyperSex, sex chat rooms, cellphone sex (phone sex made easier and more mobile), sexting, teledildonics (sex toys mutually controlled via online connection), sex-centered digital games and sex in virtual worlds (Second Life, for example, has been a very active sexual play field, with at least one in ten users engaging in virtual sex there). These and various other modes of digital diddling in and of themselves are safe sex, in terms of physical health (issues of psychological health, or moral health, are of course far more complicated; and computer viruses from sex sites are another kind of "health" issue altogether). In this context, then, cybersex has been seen by some as a very positive thing in the era of HIV-AIDS and other STDs when sex can literally be a matter of life or death.

Online spaces are, of course, also being used to facilitate offline sex in a variety of ways, from dating sites to transnational "e-mail order bride" sites to explicit sexual hook-up sites like Grindr where locative media are used to find nearby willing sex partners. In addition, some online activity can lead to offline sexual harassment, cyberstalking and other unwanted forms of sexual attention (as discussed in Chapter 4). There are also larger issues as to how things like easy access to pornography shape offline sex habits. This may especially be a problem regarding young people and others with limited sexual experience. Klein's remark about porn being a terrible way to learn about real sexuality is echoed by former porn actress and now porn director Nina Hartley who remarks: "Pornography is a paid, professional performance by actors. It is a fantasy, it is not meant to be a rulebook and guidebook or a how to as a general rule. And it goes to show how poor our sex education is in this country that people are reduced to looking at an entertainment medium for information about the body." This point is reinforced humorously as well in the viral video "Porn Sex vs. Real Sex" (n.d.), in which the difference is illustrated using vegetables.

Anecdotal evidence suggests that cybersex has both destroyed and enhanced relationships. On the enhancement end, SkyperSex and related forms have been helpful for couples separated by long distances. While reliable statistics are hard to come by, it appears that a large percentage of cybersex is between two partners already in a sexual relationship offline (and remember, as always, that the online/offline split is largely illusory), and online sexual information accessed free of potential embarrassment has apparently enhanced many relationships. Nevertheless, there appears to be a considerable amount of cyber-cheating, online mediated sex with someone other than the partner with whom one is in a putatively monogamous relationship. As with virtually all aspects of cybersex, some argue that this can provide a healthier outlet for extra-marital or extra-commitment impulses (the "safety valve" theory), while others argue that cheating is cheating, and almost invariably harms a relationship. Incidents of both outcomes are not hard to find, and are clearly dependent on particular individuals in particular relationships. The preponderance of evidence, however, seems to be on the downside. Porn, for example, leads to unrealistic physical and behavioral expectations in the real world, and has been the cause of much disappointment and sexual dysfunction offline (Lambert et al. 2012). The issue has hit the mainstream media in a fairly nuanced way in Joseph Gordon-Levitt's "Don Jon," a film that argues, moral issues aside, that the problem with porn is that it leads to bad sexual experiences in the real world, that the best sex in the real world is very unlike the mechanical kind found in porn.

▣ THE "MAINSTREAMING" OF PORN

The aspect of cybersexuality that has received the most attention, from both scholars and the wider public, is the role of the Web in the *mainstreaming of pornography*, the movement of porn from the hidden edges of society to near the center. It is now routine for talk shows, sit-coms, reality shows and various other forms of mainstream entertainment to make allusion to consumption of pornography, and in recent years porn stars have been seen mingling with other kinds of celebrities in ways that clearly suggest increasing acceptance. One critic suggests an alliterative threesome is largely responsible for this mainstreaming: accessibility, affordability and anonymity (Cooper cited in Nayar 2008 2). What this means in terms of sexual practices beyond watching is difficult to measure. The largest sex survey ever undertaken, as summarized in the often interpretively misguided, but statistically rich book, *A Billion Wicked Thoughts,* suggests that the vast majority of pornographic searches fall within a fairly small range of rather tame, traditional sex practices (Ogas and Gaddam 2011). However, the fact that millions of people who had never accessed pornography have now done so on the Net is no doubt having a variety of novel impacts. Much of this access is legal, some is illegal, or legally ambiguous. As we have noted before, censoring the Net is a difficult thing to do, and pornography purveyors have been expert at getting around attempts to limit access. In the US, the standard for legal pornography remains "local mores," a concept that has been rendered virtually meaningless by the ways in which Web content travels nationally and transnationally. Internationally, attempts to censor online pornography have had little success, especially since censors in less-than-open societies tend to focus more on political than cultural censorship when monitoring resources are limited. And even countries with the strictest anti-pornography laws that do try to contain it have found it impossible to keep their citizens from accessing porn, given the many workarounds possible in the digital world.

By way of context, it is important to remember that pornography is as old as human representation, and that all major historic cultures have included graphic representations of sexuality that could be considered pornographic. In modern times, pornographic films were born almost simultaneously with film itself. And each new medium (TV, video, etc.) has extended the amount and availability of pornography. But in terms of scale of access, the Web has brought an exponential growth in the amount and kinds of porn available, and thereby in the porn industry. This includes the problematic fact that young people ill-prepared to put the kind of sex portrayed online in a social context are accessing it at younger and younger ages (Papadoupoulus n.d.). Some online sites have sought to address this fact with more socially responsible sexual education for youth (e.g., *Scarleteen: Sex Ed for the Real World* n.d.). It is not clear what greater access to porn has meant to what is probably the most impacted group, teens and young adults just discovering their sexual identities. Research on the topic reveals a complicated mix of impact on sexual attitudes, body image, self-concept and social development, with certainly enough evidence to suggest that there are matters of concern for parents, teachers, health professionals and youth counselors to be aware of (Owens et al. 2012). The issue of "porn addiction" at all age levels has also garnered increasing attention, and has been documented as a serious social problem (Wilson n.d.).

Pornography was a major source of social controversy before the Net, and it has become ever more so since mainstreaming has occurred. The major protagonists have included some strange bedfellows. On one side, you have conservative groups attacking porn on religious and moral grounds, along with, in a decidedly shaky alliance, some feminist groups who see porn as inherently degrading to women and, in one analysis, a violation of women's civil rights. On the other side, you have various social libertarians, including "pro-sex" feminists interested in promoting the liberation of female and queer sexualities, and in protecting the rights of the primarily female cohort of "sex workers" (the non-pejorative name for prostitutes, phone sex operators, strippers and so on) (Li 2000; Nayar 2008; Rajagopal and Bojin 2004).

It is important to realize that the many who reject efforts to restrict pornography can nevertheless be quite critical of various forms. They recognize that there is much truly repugnant sexual material, especially violent, non-consensual material, online. But they advocate education rather than censorship as the best means of eliminating socially offensive or degrading forms of graphic sex depiction. Certain forms of porn, especially child pornography, are both virtually universally condemned and illegal. It is also important to realize that porn is a highly racialized commodity. On many porn sites, "Asian" is not a geographic or cultural location, but a category indicating supposedly submissive Oriental dolls, cute slutty school girls and Dragon Lady dominatrixes. "Interracial" is another category of porn that plays off historical fantasies of oversexed men of color. And where ethno-racial categories like "Indian," "Latina" and "Ebony" (Black isn't exotic enough) have their own niches, the default norm of white women is not treated as a race, but rather the category is sub-divided by things like hair color, breast size or sexual proclivities. The interesting category "female-friendly" on some porn sites (by which they usually seem to mean mildly more romantic in focus) ironically points up the fact that much of the rest of the material on these sites is decidedly "female-*un*friendly." Moreover, there is some general evidence linking porn use to sexism among hetero-sexual males (Hald, Malamuth and Lange 2013).

There is little doubt that the Internet has not only moved por-nography out of the shadows and into homes, it has also seemingly reshaped attitudes about sexuality in a relatively short time, bringing not only consumption, but also production of porn into the house-hold. As Chuck Klosterman acerbically but tellingly puts it,

> Everyone knows that the Internet is changing our lives, mostly because someone in the media has uttered that exact phrase every single day since 1993. However, it certainly appears that the main thing the Internet has accomplished is the normaliza-tion of amateur pornography. There is no justification for the amount of naked people on the World Wide Web, many of whom are clearly (clearly!) doing so for non-monetary reasons. Where were these people 15 years ago? Were there really mil-lions of women in 1986 turning to their husbands and saying, "You know, I would love to have total strangers masturbate to images of me deep-throating a titanium dildo, but there's simply no medium for that kind of entertainment. I guess we'll just have to sit here and watch 'Falcon Crest' again."
>
> (Klosterman 2004 109–110)

While presented ironically, Klosterman is asking a serious question: Did the medium create the message? Did the technical feasibility to upload amateur porn excite a response that would not otherwise have happened? He cleverly suggests that it did, and that claim is one that of course has implications for all kinds of DIY production across the Web on sites like YouTube and Vimeo.

Some anti-pornography forces look upon the mainstreaming of porn as one of many signs of steeply declining moral values in what-ever particular national culture they are located (often articulated from one or other form of religious fundamentalism), while others see it as a deepening of the objectification, degradation and exploita-tion of women (as argued from one branch of feminism). So-called anti-porn feminists point to what they see as a high level of overt violence against women in pornography, and argue that those who engage in the industry do so either due to coercion or to low self-esteem (often arising from earlier sexual abuse). Having fought for years to limit or eliminate pornography, the vast expansion of porn online and the concomitant lessening of social taboos on porn is seen as tragic by these folks.

On the other hand, libertarians, including many cyberlibertarians, argue against restricting porn at all on general freedom-of-speech grounds, while so-called pro-sex feminists often argue for legalization and minimal regulation of pornography on the basis that making sex work illegal places sex workers (the vast majority of whom are female) in greater danger of exploitation than would legalization. They argue in relation to online porn that it is about the safest kind of sex work that can be engaged in, since no exchange of bodily fluids and no chance for physically violent encounters exists in virtual spaces (though this does not address the issue of coerced performance). They also point to the increasing numbers of women in executive positions in the pornography industry, and claim that the vast majority of women working in porn do so willingly and with a significant degree of autonomy.

Evidence-based studies suggest some truth on each side of this debate. Violent pornography is a horrifying phenomenon that has no justification, and there is some evidence that exposure to porn can increase sexual aggressiveness (Owens et al. 2012). Statistics suggest that violence is not as prevalent as some claim, and has been declining as a percentage of overall porn production, partly because more women have assumed positions of power in the porn industry, and more women are watching porn. But non-consensual violence in porn remains a very significant concern, and some anti-porn activists see all pornography as a form of violent objectification of women, and/or a violation of women's civil rights (MacKinnon and Dworkin 1988). At the same time, there is a great deal of testimony from sex workers themselves supporting claims to voluntary involvement in the industry, greater female power in the industry and safer conditions due to the virtualization of much sex work, including much self-production by women. As we will see in the next section, however, the darkest impact of the enormous growth of the pornography industry has to do with the most unprotected group of sex workers, those forced into sexual servitude.

▣ DIGITIZED SEX TRAFFICKING

All sides of the online sex debates agree that one absolutely indefensible form of violence as implicated in pornography is the trafficking and forcing of women, girls and boys to engage in sex acts online (and offline). Without doubt this is the ugliest, most exploitative dimension of technology: its deployment to assist in sexual trafficking and other forms of violence against women, girls and boys. Trafficking of women, girls and boys long precedes the rise of new communications technologies. But many suggest the new media have played a role in expanding trafficking in recent decades, and there can be little doubt that ICTs have changed the nature of trafficking. Trafficking has long been a transnational phenomenon, usually from poorer countries to richer ones, and increasing global economic inequality due to the forces of globalization has intensified trafficking. The current phase of globalization itself is of course deeply dependent on new media technologies (Kee 2005).

Mobile phones, GPS devices and e-mail have facilitated communication among traffickers and allowed them to better track their victims. Legal "e-mail order brides" websites promise pliant, marriage-ready women and girls; on the surface they represent "soft" forms of trafficking, but they often serve as a front for hardcore trafficking. Underground illegal websites have digitized the promotion of trafficked women, girls and boys. Once again, the anonymity that comes with using the Net plays a crucial role, allowing traffickers and their customers to conduct business online with little risk of being identified. Peer-to-peer trafficking networks, where individuals arrange the transfer of trafficked women, girls or boys, has arisen alongside older organized trafficking networks. The vast increase in the amount of pornography represented by the mainstreaming of porn has significantly increased the demand for sex workers, and a considerable portion of the new recruits to the porn industry are trafficked individuals. Some argue that the "trafficking in images" is a less dangerous, less overtly violent form of trafficking, but far too often the publication of images is accompanied by or enabled by other physically exploitative activities.

Neither the general expansion of trafficking nor its various digital manifestations has gone unchallenged. And many of the same digital communication technologies that have been used by traffickers have been used against traffickers and trafficking. Anti-trafficking organizations can use ICTs to track traffickers, and help locate trafficked people. Online information for victims and potential victims of trafficking has proven vital, especially in the typically isolated conditions that trafficked individuals often find themselves. Online-capable cellphones have been particularly useful in these situations.

The Web has also been used by governments at all levels, from the United Nations to neighborhood watch groups, to provide useful information on trafficking. But the most important work on the issues has been done by non-governmental organizations and social movement groups. NGOs have found the Web to be a major resource for spreading the word about general trafficking dangers, for organizing anti-trafficking campaigns and pushing for political policy changes, for exposing specific traffic zones and traffickers, and for educating about available help for trafficked women, girls and boys. Even one of the strongest groups fighting against online trafficking, Take Back the Tech, concludes that there is no definitive evidence that digital technologies *have worsened* the terrain of trafficking, but the expansion of the porn industry into online spaces has intensified demand which in turn translates into greater amounts of trafficking. Trafficking remains an international tragedy of epic proportions that must be fought with all the resources, online and off, that can be mustered.

⊡ HOW QUEER ARE CYBERSPACES? ALTERNATIVE SEXUALITIES IN CYBERSPACES

As is the case with virtually every kind of cultural minority, the story of sexual minorities in digital culture is a decidedly mixed bag. LGBTQ folks and other practitioners of marginalized sexualities have often found that important new spaces for discreet connections and community formation have been opened online, while at the same time the anonymity and disinhibition allowed by online discourse have unleashed a great flood of rhetoric that is viciously homophobic and heteronormative (attitudes and practices that presume only opposite-sex relations are acceptable).

The Web has provided safe spaces with a degree of anonymity that have allowed some people whose sexual orientation is unwelcome or treated with active hostility in their home communities to find each other, share knowledge and offer support. Particularly in cultures with deep strictures against same-sex desire, information available online—sometimes just the information that "others like me" exist—has proved deeply reassuring. Many members of sexual minority groups have attested that online communities literally have saved their lives. At the level of organized pro-queer advocacy, again, the Web has many benefits in creating safe spaces for strategizing and communicating. LGBTQ social movement groups have found the Web to be a vital tool, especially in working transnationally, but also within given countries (King 2012; Phillips and O'Riordan 2007; Pullen and Cooper 2010).

On the other hand, the same anonymity and disinhibition that have provided openings for LGBTQ connections, have provided safe cover for the unleashing of a variety of forms of gay bashing and heteronormative hate speech. Accusing someone of being a "faggot" has been one of the most common forms of cyberbullying, and has caused great pain for many young people; in all likelihood it has contributed to the high rate of gay juvenile suicide. (Eighty percent of young people interviewed say they are more likely to bully online than face to face.) Many online communities, perhaps most notably gaming communities, are also riddled with homophobic slurs. The term "gay," adopted as a positive term for same-sex loving individuals, has become a widely used slur in English language youth communities. Many users of the term claim that phrases like "that's so gay" do not actually reference gay people, but even when this claim is sincere it does nothing to mitigate the fact that for most users the equation of gay (people) and disliked ideas, attitudes and/or practices, is implicit in this ubiquitous usage. Campaigns against the use/abuse of this term, including online campaigns, are under way (*Think B4 You Speak* n.d.).

As with representation of other marginalized populations, media watchdog groups have been a bit slow to catch up with the regression to stereotyping and abusive representation of sexual minorities in new media. The best known LGBTQ media justice group, GLAAD (Gay Lesbian Alliance Against Discrimination), for example, held its first (very informative) conference on anti-gay harassment in digital cultures only in 2009. GLAAD admitted as it did so that it should have been on the case sooner. (Still, GLAAD's otherwise comprehensive website has no category for digital media, though it does have a director of that subject area.) That conference offers a model for a multifaceted strategy for dealing with these issues. The invited representatives from digital game companies addressed the existence of homophobia in games, the possibilities of and obstacles to creating more gay characters in games, and their efforts to monitor and address anti-queer hate speech in online gamer communities. Many gay ITC professionals are talking about attitudes in the industry, and ways to intervene to bring more gay people into new media production and more gay people already in the business out of the closet and into discussions about improving the climate for LGBTQ professionals and users of new media as well. Finally, many of the panelists addressed the responsibility of new media users to call out and/or report gay abusive participants in digital cultures. Clearly, there is much more work to be done to make cyberspaces LGBTQ-friendly ones, but no one can now claim that either the problem or viable solutions have not been set forth. Perhaps a sign of things to come is the recent addition of a cross-dresser to the panoply of Pokemon characters in the popular Japanese game!

While one should always be careful not to extrapolate too much from one example, as a case study sexuality provides some very suggestive intimations as to how digital knowledge works. Even advocates for one of the strongest groups fighting violence against women in general and online techno-violence in particular see a complicated picture in which digital culture is both an enemy and an aid:

> Whether new forms of ICTs replicate, amplify or destabilize power relations will depend largely on how closely we monitor their development and discourse. This requires we first understand what digital technology means, then interrogate its impact on society in light of multiple and shifting strands of political discourse. The process has already begun: feminists and women's rights advocates are consciously and deliberately "taking back the tech" and indelibly changing what technology is and means.
>
> (Kee 2005)

This strikes me as precisely the right way to approach not only issues of sexploration and sexploitation online, but all social issues impacted by the Web. It is imperative to understand technologies as tools that can be wielded in many different ways, to resist both pro- and anti-tech discourses that see their impact as automatic or techno-determined, and instead find ways to use technologies and new media to fight for the values you believe will better the world.

6

Does the Internet Have a Political Bias?

E-Democracy, Networked Authoritarianism and Online Activism

The impact of new media on political culture has many aspects, from digital voting and the possibility of instant polling on controversial issues, to availability of governmental and extra-governmental political information, to digitized campaigning to use of the Web for legal and illegal forms of organizing to incite revolution or other major forms of social change. Questions like these arise: Are digitally linked citizens better informed and smarter voters? Is the increased amount of political information available leading to greater understanding across political differences and a deeper degree of democratic participation? Has

→ Citizen Cyborgs? E-Voting, Online Politicking and Partici- patory Democracy

→ Can Social Media Over- throw Governments?

→ Netroots Activism or Just Slacktivism?

→ Hacking, Wiki-Leaking and Cyberterrorism

→ Digitizing the Arts of Protest

this meant a more active, engaged and broad-minded citizenry? Or are others right to claim that the Web creates a political silo effect in which users echo, amplify and make more rigid their existing political biases? Is it true as some assert that the Internet is bound to bring down authoritarian regimes and spread democracy? Are social movement organizers expanding the possibilities of dissent, or lapsing into complacent slacktivism where clicking on an e-petition takes the place of real political work? How has the availability of digital culture changed organizing for social change? What are the legitimate limits of new digital forms of civil disobedience ("hacktivism" to supporters, "cyberterrorism" to detractors)?

⇨ CITIZEN CYBORGS? E-VOTING, ONLINE POLITICKING AND PARTICIPATORY DEMOCRACY

Many scholars and activists have expressed great faith that the Internet is a force for expanding democracy, both in existing democracies and in countries with currently non-democratic governments. At the same time, other observers have questioned just how deep or important the kinds of democratic interaction, or cyber-citizenship, currently available are. Many have also challenged the assumption that given new media the future inevitably entails greater and greater democratization.

Electronic voting, or e-voting, is already under way in a number of places. Electronic voting machines have been used for many years, and the more direct form of online voting is increasing in viability. Its benefits include speed of counting, and perhaps most importantly ease of access for people who are homebound due to illness, infirmity or some other limitation. On the other hand, the existing digital divides would effectively disenfranchise people with no or difficult access to a digital device. The potential is great, but at present the drawbacks largely outweigh advantages. The biggest problem, as with much in the digitized world, is security. Possibilities for fraud in electronic voting are quite serious. In countries like the US and UK where voter fraud is extremely low, turning to electronic voting at this historical moment could well lead to increasing amounts of falsification of voting records. The temptation is great; the modes of digital fraud are numerous.

Digitized campaigning has also drawn a lot of attention in recent years. Some people, for example, credit Barack Obama's two presidential election victories to superior use of digital resources. There is little doubt that the Obama staff did wield a variety of digital technologies. These included sophisticated computer models of voter profiles, extensive involvement with social networking sites, a mobile app that allowed on-the-ground canvassers to download and upload data without ever entering a campaign office, and a Web app called Dashboard that turned volunteer activity into a game by ranking the most active supporters. Much of this organizational framework did in fact prove superior to the use of technology by Obama's opponents. Looked at in context, however, the role of digital technologies is revealed as a factor, not *the* factor, and a factor subject to historical reversal. Obama had a built-in advantage with younger voters who are both more likely to vote liberal and more likely to be deeply connected to digital cultures. That affinity will not necessarily continue over time.

Another key area of political contestation concerns the degree to which the vast amounts of political information available online have impacted political attitudes and practices. Have digitized information sources led to greater political wisdom, or to greater political understanding across ideological differences? One keen observer, former political consultant Cass Sunstein, thinks not. The "Sunstein Thesis," elaborated in his book *Republic.com* (2000), argues that most people using the Web to follow politics do not seek out a variety of perspectives, but instead seek out informational and opinion sources that match their existing ideological biases. Moreover, spending time on reaffirming silos produces what he dubs "cybercascades" that drive individuals to ever more rigid and extreme positions to outdo each other in political intensity. This tendency can be reinforced by algorithms on sites like Google and Facebook, where searches lead to personalization (aka, profiling) that reinforces the searcher's politics, and "likes" become locks, zeroing in only on what a user already believes. Sunstein is most familiar with US politics, in which he has been deeply involved as a consultant, and his views seem to have been confirmed by the greater polarization of American ideologies since the emergence of digital cultures. But whether this is causality or mere correlation is difficult to measure, and comparative studies with other countries would be needed to prove the case. Others, like cultural studies scholars Henry Jenkins and Tim Wu, have challenged the Sunstein thesis, taking a somewhat more optimistic view, but likewise with too little evidence to be ultimately persuasive (Jenkins 2008; Wu 2011).

Can we at least say that the vast amount of political information available online is making citizens better informed? Statistics are not encouraging. A Pew Internet study of the US populace, for example, "Public Knowledge of Current Affairs Little Changed by News and Information-revolutions," shows US citizens, among the most digitally privileged in the world, were not better informed in 2007 than in 1989, pre-Internet ("Public Knowledge" 2007). On the other hand, at least one other statistical study, by Matthew Gentzkow and Jesse M. Shapiro, seems to contradict the Sunstein thesis:

We find that ideological segregation of online news consumption is low in absolute terms, higher than the segregation of most offline news consumption, and significantly lower than the segregation of face-to-face interactions with neighbors, co-workers, or family members. We find no evidence that the Internet is becoming more segregated over time.

(2010 1799)

So, as with most things digital, the jury is still out. But certainly Sunstein is right to argue that it is a dangerous disservice to democracy to fail to use the opportunities provided by the Web to expand the range of political ideas we expose ourselves to.

A different kind of politics, civic engagement and community building has benefited more unambiguously from the use of digital tools. Local community planning has become much more interactive in the digital age. One of the best examples of this is a project in Boston known as Participatory Chinatown. The project is a joint one between city officials, community organizers, and residents. The website introducing the project describes it as follows:

Participatory Chinatown is a 3-D immersive game designed to be part of the master planning process for Boston's Chinatown. You assume the role of one of 15 virtual residents and you work to complete their assigned quest—finding a job, housing or place to socialize. But look out! Sometimes language skills, income level, or other circumstances can make your task more challenging. Whatever your experience, you'll then be tasked with considering the future of the neighborhood by walking through and commenting on proposed development sites. Every one of your comments and decisions will be shared with real life decision-makers.

(*Participatory Chinatown* n.d.)

Recognizing that this approach toward re-thinking the neighborhood could be biased toward youth and others more likely to be tech savvy, the project included a techno-literacy component that not only allowed anyone to learn to play the game, but taught other valuable computer skills to those previously lacking them.

A key feature of the game is that in order to do well players need to assume several different identities among the 15 characters who represent diverse ages, income levels, genders, ethnicities, and immigrant/long-term resident statuses. As they move about in a virtual representation of the Chinatown's various neighborhoods, they face particular situations matched to their ascribed characteristics. Quite literally (and virtually), the game encourages residents to walk in the shoes of others in their community, facing the daily possibilities and limits those others face, and seeking out solutions that balance the needs of diverse groups. This imaginative variation on a theme of the town hall meeting proved wildly popular, and suggests the potential to use digital means to revitalize community meetings, circumventing hardened battle lines and opening up new channels of dialogue. A somewhat more pointedly playful version of this approach can be found in the GPS-enabled game, Gentrification (*Gentrification: The Game* n.d.).

To summarize, while no one disputes that digital media have made more political information available more easily to more people than ever before, they differ as to the impact of that fact. Bottom line, information is not knowledge and knowledge is not wisdom. Political wisdom can only arise from substantive discussions that, while potentially more widely available through digital technologies, do not arise automatically from those technologies. Ease of voting, and ease of registering public opinion, is only as good as the political intelligence behind the votes and opinions. To think otherwise is to fall into technological determinism. The political impact of new media technologies will depend on how the informational and communicational powers of the technologies are put to use. If information gathering is simply used to further already existing political beliefs, then our political lives will be no richer, and may in fact become more polarized and dangerous. If information gathering leads to expanded knowledge and more substantive exchanges of ideas, then greater political wisdom may emerge. But the technology is only the means; the ends, once again, will be decided by who uses the technology most imaginatively and effectively.

⬚ CAN SOCIAL MEDIA OVERTHROW GOVERNMENTS?

On the broader scale of international politics and revolutionary change, many have argued that the Internet is an inherently democratizing, liberating technology. Events like the Arab Spring Revolutions, in which social networking and other elements of digital culture played a prominent role, give credence to the idea that digital technologies can bring down authoritarian regimes. Some even argue that the spread of these technologies will inevitably bring down such regimes. However, the evidence is mixed at best. Other closed regimes, including Iran and Saudi Arabia in this same region, have used the Web to spy on, track down, harass, arrest and in some cases torture and murder dissenters (as have other authoritarian and quasi-democratic governments around the world) (Fuchs 2008; Mozorov 2011). To what extent does the Net have a bias toward freedom and democracy? Is it only a matter of time before digital technology opens up even the most closeted regimes, like North Korea, or have we overestimated this particular kind of technological determinism?

Particularly after the Arab Spring Revolutions of 2011–2012 in the Middle East, and versions of the Occupy movement in the US and elsewhere, strong claims were made for the Internet and digital media as an irresistible force for democratization across the globe. How valid are those claims? Let's begin with naming; some in the press came to call these events the Twitter or Facebook Revolutions. But activists actually involved in these movements by and large rejected such characterizations. And it is not hard to see why. No one calls the American Revolution the Pamphlet Revolution, yet pamphlets and broadsides played a crucial role in awakening dissent. No one calls the French Revolution the Salon/Saloon Revolution, yet salons for the bourgeois revolutionists and saloons (taverns) were crucial communication centers for working-class revolutionaries. The point is that communication devices are communication devices, not revolutionary in themselves. The revolutions in the Middle East did indeed make very positive use of new media, especially cellphones, including ones with video capabilities, and the Twitterverse and Facebook were important for communication, especially to the world outside. But the revolutions emerged from years of deprivation and years of organizing. Worker unions, student groups, women's groups, legal and clandestine NGOs, these and smart tactics, not smartphones, made the revolution. Further evidence that it was more than new media can be seen by contrasting Egypt, Tunisia and the other more or less successful revolts with the failed revolt in Iran two years earlier (it was that revolution, by the way, that was first dubbed the Twitter Revolution). All the new media deployed in Iran could not overcome the fact that the regime there was more stable than dissenters inside and outside the country believed. Without better organization, communication was not enough.

The other, darker side of this story is the use of digital technology by authoritarian regimes to squelch protest and punish dissenters. Iran, China, parts of Eastern Europe and numerous other undemocratic regimes have used the trail left by online communication to track down activists, often leading authorities to harass, threaten, jail and sometimes to outright murder dissidents (Fuchs 2008; Gladwell 2010; Mozorov 2011). In Iran, it remains unclear who will ultimately win the online political wars, but suffice it to say that the regime still stands, and activists are further underground and more cautious online than before the failed Green/Twitter Revolution. Even in states where the Arab Spring revolts were more successful, as in Egypt, the aftermath has included members of the new regime using digital tracking to locate and punish revolutionaries who are now viewed as enemies of the new regimes.

These caveats, however, do not detract from the basic fact that, as I detail in the next section, the Net and related technologies have much to offer in terms of social protest and social movement organizing. It simply means that we need to be more level headed and realistic about the use of technologies by forces opposing the expansion of democracy in the world as well as those seeking to expand it.

⊡ NETROOTS ACTIVISM OR JUST SLACKTIVISM?

Social movements arise when traditional political forms—elected or autocratic leaders, parties, lobbying, etc.—fail to address pressing economic, social or cultural concerns. Protest movements have long been a driving force of modern history. The American and French Revolutions ushered in the modern form of democracy. Labor movements ended child labor, brought worker safety rules, set reasonable wages and hours, and ushered in a host of social benefits enjoyed by all. Women's movements around the globe got women the vote and continue to push for full gender equality. Anti-colonial movements in Africa, Asia and Latin American utterly changed the map of the modern world. Movements for ethnic rights and global human rights have deeply challenged racisms and ethnocentrisms around the world. Environmental social movements have profoundly reshaped attitudes and practices towards nature. Indeed, it is hard to find another form of human activity (including technological innovation) that has been more influential in shaping and reshaping societies than organized political protest through social movements. It is not surprising, therefore, to find social movement activism very much present in digital spaces, with many new kinds of electronic activism added to the standard repertoire of protest forms.

Long before the Internet, social movement scholars studied the crucial importance of social networks to the growth of protest. Social networks, including transnational ones, existed long before the rise of new electronic media, but the Net has added virtual communication networks and digital cultures that have reshaped, for better and worse, the pursuit of social change. Dissenters with romanticized names like hactivists, camcorder commandoes, data dancers, code warriors and culture jammers engaging in cyber sit-ins, electronic civil disobedience and meme warfare have created a rich new media culture of resistance that has become a vital part of many social movements. Not only the Arab Spring uprisings, but also the anti-globalization/global justice movement, the Occupy movement, the *indignados* in Spain, and numerous other twenty-first-century protests have imaginatively used digital media. And, appropriately enough, digital protests have been key in protecting Internet freedom, as in the massive online protests in 2011 against the SOPA legislation in the US that would have given greater corporate control of the Web (*SOPA Strike* n.d.).

Wiki-leaking, live streaming of demonstrations and electronic communication during events, inexpensive alternative media, and a wide variety of other digitally based activist forms have arisen. Some of these developments have been controversial, and some, often labeled cyberterrorism, have been condemned. What is certain is that, apart from a few hardcore neo-Luddites (advocates of destroying technologies), digital technologies are acknowledged as important new forms of social movement activism that have enhanced, but not replaced, more traditional forms (Boler et al. 2010; Gerbaudo 2012; Hands 2011; Joyce 2010; Juris 2008; Raley 2009).

The term netroots activism is a common descriptor for online protesters meant to echo the term grassroots activism, the traditional form of organizing protest. Those who do not believe serious social movement activism can take place online invented the pejorative slacktivism (i.e., slackers posing as activists) to disparage digital politics. Some charges of slacktivism raise legitimate issues regarding overreliance upon or complacent technological determinism among some activists. But other charges seem merely to reflect anti-technological bias or resistance to new forms. Some are also misinformed about activism, as is the case of a well-known *New Yorker* article by Malcolm Gladwell (2010). Gladwell attacks the anti-hierarchical, network approach common in digital organizing, contrasting it with what he misrepresents as the hierarchical organizing in the US Civil Rights Movement. In fact, the most successful movement group in the CRM was the radically network-oriented, anti-hierarchical Student Non-violent Coordinating Committee (SNCC). Moreover, the networking model of organizing, in the wake of SNCC, has been the dominant form in US and transnational left-liberal movements for several decades now. In this regard, the analogous relationship between networks as a major metaphor for the organization of the Web, and networks as the major form of contemporary movement organizing, has created a natural affinity between the Net and progressive social movements.

In order to make the general case that slacktivism best characterizes protest organized in online environments one would need to show that offline forms of activism like marches, street protests, sit-ins and other forms of civil disobedience have declined overall in the Internet era, and then show precisely how the Net has contributed to that decline. In fact, since the former is not true, there is little point trying to prove the latter. On February 15, 2003, for example, with the US clearly approaching war on Iraq, the largest protest event in human history took place in over 600 cities on every of continent on the globe. The event was so huge that while no one doubts it was the largest event of its kind ever, no full count has been possible (estimates range from a mere(!) ten million to as high as 15 million protesters). Regardless of which figure is more accurate, that stout source of humanity's statistics, the *Guinness World Records*, certified it as the largest anti-war protest in history. Not only did this event show that getting millions of people into the streets in protest could happen in the Internet era, the organizing and coordinating of the events largely took place online and would most likely have been impossible to achieve before the Net arrived. Interestingly, it was also a pre-war, anti-war protest. Typically significant resistance to wars happen only after they have been going for a while. And it was not an isolated event; between January 3 and April 12, 2003, 36 million people across the globe took part in almost 3,000 anti-war protests ("February 15, 2003 Anti-War Protest" n.d.). A digitally enabled timeline created by John Bieler that graphically maps "every protest on the planet since 1979" illustrates greater and greater amounts of dissent in the twenty-first century (Bieler n.d.; Stuster 2013). Social conditions under neo-liberal globalization account for this more than digital media, but it seems clear that online activism has helped accelerate it, contrary to charges of slacktivism.

Digital social movement activity includes both new ways to accomplish older forms of organizing, and truly new forms only possible in the Internet era. Even the most traditional of political activist work (i.e., writing letters to officials) has been enhanced greatly by the low-cost, high-speed and extensive geographic reach of the Internet. But critics argue that the very ease of digitally signing an e-mail or online petition has cheapened the experience, rendered it less impactful on politicians than personal letters snail mailed the old-fashioned way. Are social networks and microblogs just updated versions of group meetings, or do they fundamentally transform interactive experience? That seems to depend primarily upon age. For digital natives who grew up web-connected, these forms feel natural and legitimate, while older activists express reservations that the experience feels less substantial, artificial and limited. Whether or not this is elder wisdom or mere generational prejudice remains to be seen. The great Civil Rights activist Ella Baker, a woman as important to the movement as Martin Luther King though far less appreciated, made a distinction between mobilizing people and organizing them (Payne 2001 [1995]; Reed 2005). Mobilizing refers to the process by which inspirational leaders or other persuaders can get large numbers of people to join a movement or engage in a particular movement action. Organizing entails a more sustained process as people come to deeply understand a movement's goals and their own power to change themselves and the world. Mobilizing creates followers; organizing creates leaders. (Note how Twitter speaks of "followers.") Baker makes clear that we need both mobilizing and organizing. And thus far, while the Net has proven to be a highly effective tool for mobilizing, the jury is still out as to how effective it can be at organizing, at deeply empowering people who become self-activating leaders themselves.

We are now at a point where it is pointless to deny that digital activism has a role to play because the medium is so pervasive, and people are finding a variety of creative ways to use the massive potential of so many intercommunicating people. One example that might be called remediating activism is a group built on the massive literary and cinematic phenomenon that is the Harry Potter franchise. Recognizing that the immense popularity of the Potter books and films had potential to be used for social change, a group of Dumbledore devotees got together and formed the Harry Potter Alliance to tackle a range of social issues. As their Mission Statement puts it:

> The Harry Potter Alliance (HPA) is a 501c3 nonprofit that takes an outside-of-the-box approach to civic engagement by using parallels from the Harry Potter books to educate and mobilize young people across the world toward issues of literacy, equality, and human rights. Our mission is to empower our members to act like the heroes that they love by acting for a better world.
>
> (*Harry Potter Alliance* n.d.)

With more than 100,000 members, the group has had real social impact on issues ranging from poverty in Haiti to marriage equality.

Rather than adding to the lament that youth are not as politically engaged today as in past generations, these organizers sought out and found new points of motivation by linking Rowling's virtual world to the virtual world of the Net in order to bring real change. One of the secrets to successful social movements is mobilizing existing social networks and turning them on to activism. The Web provides exponentially more publicly visible social networks than ever before, and offers the communication media to make them more available for organizing than has ever been even remotely possible in the past. The HPA offers one clever example of how to imaginatively tap into this potential.

Excitement about the possibilities for digital activism should also be tempered by the fact that such possibilities are open to all political persuasions, including extremely reactionary ones. White supremacist, anti-immigrant, Islamo-phobic, sexist and homophobic groups, not to mention terrorist ones, have also been given a boost by digital media. The anonymity of the Web in particular has proven attractive and useful to groups whose ideas are anathema to most, or that otherwise need to be carried out in a clandestine way. These groups have availed themselves of the range of other available features of the Web (Daniels 2009; Klein 2010; Rajagopal and Bojin 2004). Stormfront, for example, a white supremacist hub, has put up fake websites, like one promising to inform about the life and works of Martin Luther King that on closer inspection proves to be riddled with lies, half-truths, and racist propaganda. The amount of blatantly racist, sexist and homophobic imagery on the Web promoted by these groups is deeply disturbing, and certainly gives lie to the idea that we are living in a post-racial, post-sexist, gay-positive world.

Nevertheless, the imaginative variety of digital activism by progressive movements is especially impressive. Digitization has clearly changed the nature of and added to the repertoire of protest. Digital protest takes many new forms. From digital civil disobedience to digitized protest art to strange-sounding innovations like maptivism, culture jamming and meme warfare (plus, in the next section, wiki-leaking, political hacking and electronic civil disobedience). Networked cameras, smartphones and a variety of other digital devices have, for example, changed the nature of face-to-face protest events. Importantly, the presence of video recording devices has proven effective for activists seeking to get their version of events out past a mainstream media often suffering from "protest fatigue" (the drama of protest inevitably becomes less dramatic when routinized, while the media rely on drama to raise circulation or viewership). The presence of many videophones and mini-camcorders during the "battle of Seattle" protests against the World Trade Organization in 1999 proved crucial to the legal process after the events were over. What were often characterized by the police and the mainstream media as anti-globalization riots were reclassified as a "police riot" once video showed many incidents of unprovoked police attacks on protesters. Virtually all charges were dropped against the activists, and many received monetary compensation for the abuse suffered at the hands of the authorities. This process of vindication of protesters and condemnation of police overreaction has been repeated a number of times through the use of digital video (Reed 2005).

Similarly, the OccupyWallStreet movement received a large infusion of sympathy and support when an activist video of police surrounding and harassing a group of peaceful female protesters went viral on the Web, and was picked up by mainstream media in the US and abroad. More generally, the ability of movement groups to live stream coverage of their events can be crucial in several respects. Perhaps most importantly, younger people, many of whom have grown quite distrustful of mainstream politics and mainstream media, partly due in the English-speaking world to the influence of brilliant satirical news shows like "The Daily Show" and "The Colbert Report," are more likely to view and trust direct streaming from the movement than filtered coverage. While various forms of independent media, like the presence around the globe of numerous Independent Media Centers, (Indy Media), still work at a great disadvantage compared with news coverage backed by huge multinational media conglomerates like Time Warner, Viacom, Vivendi, News Corp, or Bertelsman AG, they are making significant inroads, again, particularly among younger people.

Another interesting form of activism made possible by a different set of technologies, including Global Positioning Systems (GPSs), has been given the portmanteau designation *maptivism*—the using of mapping techniques to visualize, represent and organize around a given social issue. A particularly rich example is HarassMap, a project centered on Egypt and aimed at reducing and hopefully ending sexual harassment in that country. Like most successful e-activist projects, the digital elements are never seen as sufficient but rather as a starting point or augmentation to face-to-face organizing.

HarassMap is just what it sounds like. It is an online tool that maps the places around Egypt where acts of sexual harassment have occurred. The site is "crowdsourced" in the sense that anyone who has experienced sexual harassment or sexual assault, whether on the street, in a store, in school, at a doctor's office—anywhere—can submit their story to the site and have that story appear both as a narrative and as a point on the HarassMap. The organizers of HarassMap see the map itself as a taking-off point, a tool for deeper work. They also protect their work from government interference by hosting the site outside of Egypt itself. The map provides concrete visible data and a variety of moving stories that they in turn leverage into information used in neighborhood-by-neighborhood, door-to-door organizing that can cite facts, figures and specific cases to overcome denial (not here, not in significant numbers, not to "good girls," etc.) and bolster their argument that the problem exists, is serious and is prevalent in a particular neighborhood they are targeting at that time. All of the volunteers must be from the particular village or part of the city they intervene into, assuring utmost local credibility and sensitivity to specific class, religious and cultural contexts.

The organizers are also aware that there was once a stronger cultural intolerance for harassment (in earlier decades harassers were routinely run down, and had their heads shaved as a form of public shaming), so the publicizing made possible by the Web is part of a strategy to shame Egyptians into resisting a growing problem, and an attempt to recall a time when this problem was dealt with by collective community action. HarassMap has been amazingly successful, and has spawned similar projects on harassment or on other issues around the globe. Would they have been able to do their work without digital technology? They readily admit that they could, indeed they had been doing anti-harassment work for several years prior to their creation of HarassMap, but the technology set off a firestorm of information and recruitment that would have taken years to organize without the technology. The main technology they use, the Ushahidi platform, was originally used to monitor election fraud and, like other mapping software, has been used for a variety of activist ends in what has been nicknamed Global Positioning Subversion.

The HarassMap model grew from earlier forms of maptivism (Kreutz 2009), and has been adopted by activist groups in other countries around the world, from Yemen to Canada, with each group shaping the materials to meet particular local cultural values and specific needs. One such group, Hollaback, tracks and protests street-level sexual harassment by collecting and sharing via the Web information on places and individuals harassing female passersby, a process that nicely illustrates how real world and virtual world can interact very directly and effectively. A related but slightly different example of maptivism has been carried out by groups seeking to give greater historical depth to protests in particular locations. The "Re: Activism" project has worked in a number of cities in the US to set up (analog) games that trace and interact with the history of activism in a given community by using locative media to take players to various sites where important protests occurred in the past ("Re: Activism" n.d.). Such games would seem capable of deepening understanding of the protest tradition, and inspiring continued commitment. They are also an excellent example of working simultaneously in so-called real-world and virtual spaces. Some tech-savvy activists in London took this a step further through the invention of a suite of apps called Sukey to help dissenters avoid being caught in police "kettles" (often brutal formations in which dozens of riot-gear-attired police suffocatingly surround or fiercely funnel a group of protesters: see Figure 6.1). The apps use a Google maps mashup, GPS and encryption to instantly and securely monitor police movements to allow maximum activist effectiveness in protest blockades. Seemingly thinking of every contingency, Sukey includes a Twitter link called sukeydating that can help jailed protesters to find "activist love"; a sample tweet: "Do you know why they're called kettles? Because they are hot and steamy . . ." (*Sukey Apps* n.d.; Geere 2011).

Adaptation to local conditions along with traditional face-to-face organizing are what has turned these many digital activist projects from interesting technical tools to truly effective agents of social change. The same can be said for digital protests generally; it is close connection to "real-world" away-from-keyboard sites that makes online netroots activism most effective.

FIGURE 6.1 *Police kettle in London protest, 2011. (Courtesy: 1000 Words/ Shutterstock.com.)*

⊡ HACKING, WIKI-LEAKING AND CYBERTERRORISM

Three of the most controversial forms of digitized protest activity are, unfortunately, often misleadingly lumped together. Politically motivated disruption or alternation of websites or databases (hactivism), leaking corporate and government documents (wiki-leaking), and using the Net to promote or engage in terrorism (cyberterrorism) need to be carefully distinguished from one another. Hacking is a multifaceted phenomenon. Working from imagery from old Westerns, some practitioners distinguish between white-hat hackers who break security for non-malicious reasons, either to test a security system, sometimes with authorization, sometime just to prove a point, or for positive political goals (including hactivists) and black-hat hackers, sometimes also called crackers, who use hacking for personal gain or purely malicious intent such as cyber-vandalism, identity theft or electronic bank robbing. Tacitly acknowledging that sometimes this distinction is not entirely clear cut, a third term, gray-hat hacking, has been invoked at times to denote ambiguous hacking practices.

One of the main strands of hactivism includes electronic or digital civil disobedience. The long tradition of civil disobedience dating back at least to Thoreau in the US and as practiced famously by Gandhi and Martin Luther King has several, sometimes debated, major strands. The putatively purist principled form is the direct breaking of a law or social custom deemed to be unjust, and accepting the consequences of that law breaking in the interest of drawing attention to the injustice. A classic example of this form is the breaking of racial apartheid laws in the legally segregated American South during the Civil Rights Movement. Thousands of US citizens went to jail to protest these unjust laws. A second strand breaks a law less directly connected to the injustice, and takes the consequences. A well-known example here is Henry David Thoreau going to jail for refusing to pay taxes because a portion of those taxes were paying for a war on Mexico Thoreau thought unjust (there is a long tradition of civil disobedience in the US in opposition to unjust wars). Thoreau, upon being asked by his friend and mentor Ralph Waldo Emerson, 'What are you doing in jail?' famously replied, 'What are you doing out of jail?' (in other words, why are you not protesting a war you too believe to be unjustifiable). A third strand believes in breaking laws either directly or indirectly linked to injustice, but with the aim of evading capture and consequences. To use a final US example, those famous Boston revolutionists, disguising themselves (not very convincingly, it would seem) as "Indians" threw large quantities of tea into Boston harbor in protest of British taxation, but then slunk away undetected and unarrested to fight another day.

For the most part, current-day practitioners of electronic civil disobedience prefer this third mode, creating mayhem through legally fuzzy or outright illegal activities while escaping punishment by covering their digital tracks. The only harm done by hacktivists is to the pride and reputation of corporations and governments they aim to embarrass by exposing either their undemocratic practices or vulnerable security. When economic damage is done to a corporation through hacking, the hactivists typically justify it by suggesting it is a small sum compared with the money these companies beg, borrow and steal from the populace and from government.

The form of hacktivism that has received the most attention in recent years is that practiced by the groups like WikiLeaks and Anonymous. WikiLeaks refers to itself as a form of investigative journalism that relies on whistleblowers within corporations, governments and militaries, to expose practices they deem illegal or harmful to the public's right to know. The organization has been phenomenally successful in obtaining and e-publishing such data. It has therefore come under fire and legal prosecution by those who wish to keep their secrets. The most serious charge against WikiLeaks is that they have endangered military and civilian intelligence officers through some of their leaks. In response they claim to have sought to redact all such names from the documents they have made available online. The leaking of secret documents is hardly a new phenomenon (one of the most famous such cases was the Pentagon Papers scandal of 1971 in which a former defense department employee copied and had published a secret history of the US war on Vietnam). Wiki-leaking is becoming a verb far larger than a single organization (the hacker group Anonymous is increasingly using this mode of operation as well, for example) and it has spawned a rich expansion of the debate about the public's right to know, private property rights and legitimate forms of national security. There is no doubt that every government has a right to keep certain things private. But it is equally the case that every government, however ostensibly democratic, abuses this right to privacy to protect not their citizens, but to keep their citizens from knowing of the misdeeds, especially the most horrendous ones, of the government. There is no a priori formula for sorting out legitimate from illegitimate forms of leaking (which of course is also done by analog means, not just digital ones). But wiki-leakers have done the world a favor by bringing this issue more forcefully into the arena of public debate.

Another significant category of digital political action is cyberterrorism. Like the term hacker, cyberterrorist is a highly ambiguous designation. The major problem with this concept is that it is almost infinitely expandable. As Sandor Vegh was among the first to argue, governments can expand the term to fit any opponent they wish to discredit, harass or imprison (Vegh 2002). To help assure that this does not happen, critics argue that the term should properly be used in two main contexts, to describe offline terrorists who use digital spaces to communicate about their plans to terrorize, or to designate individuals, groups or governmental entities who use hacking and other techniques to purposely cause death and destruction. Broader definitions are almost invariably misused to suppress legitimate forms of protest.

The issue of cyberterrorism ties into the larger question of cybercensorship. While it is easy to decry censorship of the Net in authoritarian regimes like China and Iran, putatively democratic ones are also making strong efforts to limit, control and surveil the Web. US government attacks on Chelsea Manning, Julian Assange and Edward Snowden, for example, have all been pursued at a level out of proportion to their alleged actions. And revelations in 2013 of the extent of illegal digital spying on American citizens were deeply disturbing (Gellman 2013). Often using cyberterrorism and national security as excuses to vastly overreach reasonable protection of the populace, from the so-called Patriot Act onward the US government has tried again and again to legitimate extensive invasion of digital spaces to spy on and gather information about citizens who pose no threat. As part of the battle to decide whether the Net remains a truly open public space, or becomes one dominated by corporate and governmental control, keeping a close watch on legislation aimed at limiting Web freedoms or allowing online and cellphone surveillance should be a task for citizens of all countries.

DIGITIZING THE ARTS OF PROTEST

Virtually every art form has been transformed by the rise of digital technologies, and new forms of art—variously called new media art, digital art, computer-mediated art and so forth—have also emerged. One way to survey this massive terrain is to look at a few examples of political protest art as representative of larger trends in the digitization of the arts overall.

The range of art media, styles and forms used as digital protest is extremely broad. To begin with one of the most ubiquitous forms of protest art, the poster, has had renewed life in the digital world. The anti-AIDs activist group ACT-UP pioneered the digitizing of graphic protest art, using every form from small stickers to placards to huge posters, and they did so mostly in the pre-Internet era (Reed 2005). While spreading posters and other graphic images online is immensely powerful and can instantaneously reach thousands of people, the best protest poster producers realize that it is equally important to reproduce and disseminate their works out into the offline world. Like the best social movement organizers in general, poster makers realize that it important to reach those people, the majority of the world's population, who do not have the privilege of access to digital culture.

Another aesthetic form that has long had a major role in protest, the mural, has also been transformed in the new media era. While murals painted on walls the traditional way are still very much alive, they have also been augmented by digital murals that can be made and remade in a more timely fashion. Self-described queer Chicana art-activist Alma Lopez, for example, executes her striking protest murals in both traditional and digital form. Two distinct advantages of digital murals over painted ones are that they are almost infinitely reproducible—rather than being confined to one wall in one neighborhood, they can be appear in many neighborhoods, and they are scalable—they can be projected on the side of a building in grand scale, but they can also be reproduced in every size from gallery-sized painting to postcard to poster (at which point they indeed become posters). Of course, the special power of murals largely stems from their size and their permanence; they are literally larger than life and they become fixtures in neighborhoods offering their powerful imagery to all who pass by. But that need not be lost, since digital murals can have that scale and can be rendered permanent. Already existing murals can also be photographed and then be reproduced in near-to-original quality via digital techniques, allowing classic murals to migrate to new locations, and be preserved for longer periods. Of course, as with all things digital, there are purists or traditionalists who argue that some essential human quality is lacking in digital murals, an argument that in many ways parallels the preference for vinyl records over digitized music. Fortunately, no one is forced to choose, since traditional style murals continue to be created as well. For example, one of the most important digital creation and preservation institutions in the world, SPARC (Social and Public Art Resource Center) near Los Angeles, uses digital means to document classic traditional murals and remains committed to both older and new forms of political mural making.

Traditional satiric and parodic protest art has also been reshaped for and by digital cultures. One striking example is the site "Cybracero" (*Cybracero* n.d.). The parody site began as a student project by Alex Rivera while an undergraduate at Swarthmore College, and has been elaborated through several iterations. Cybracero works with an utterly straight face, much in the spirit of Jonathan Swift's famous suggestion in "A Modest Proposal" that the solution to the famine in Ireland was to eat babies. It purports to be the website for Cybracero Systems, a corporation that is solving the messy problem of Latino immigration to the US by using robots controlled from Mexico to pick fruit and do other agricultural labor without Mexican bodies actually crossing the border. Elites in the US can have all the benefits of Mexican immigrant labor without having those laborers actually near them. (The made-up word cybracero combines cybernetics with bracero, the name for workers who in previous decades were bussed or flown into the States to do backbreaking agricultural field work, and then were shipped out again as soon as that work was done.) The shiny bright site brilliantly mimics the callous rhetoric of corporations for whom workers are work units not people; indeed, it does so with such perfect pitch that many of my students when exposed to it without explanation have taken it for a real corporation (a few, alas, even thought it a good idea). Similar sites (for example, "Rent-a-Negro") use parodic website imitation to address other issues from gender and ethnic justice, to environmentalism. The theatrical parody group The Yes Men, while focused primarily on live performance, has also used the Web to spread news of their outrageous impersonations of transnational corporate executives and high-ranking government officials.

The emphasis on participation, interaction and collaboration in much digital culture has also played a role in re-shaping the protest arts. These are qualities particularly apt for adaptation to the collective process of political protest. In many of these works the artist is a co-producer along with those previously known as the audience. This is not a wholly new development in the arts, but, again, it is one that is enhanced and extended via the possibilities provided by digitizing cultures. Some of this work seeks to challenge both previous highly individualized art processes and previously commercialized artworks in much the same way as others see the Net as providing more participatory and less commercial forms of social interaction generally.

Two interesting examples of highly participatory art also address the issue of borders using digital technology. The "Border Haunt" project is a one-time event that subsequently has life as a website. Using GPS it carried out a unique protest (*Border Haunt* n.d.). Each year many people die in vain efforts to cross the Mexico/US border without proper authorization. The project seeks to honor those who have died, while also demonstrating how surveillance technologies can be turned against themselves. Ian Alan Paul, the creator or facilitator of the action, invited anyone sympathetic to the plight of immigrants to participate in the intentional misleading of border patrol officers tasked with tracking down border crossers. Close to 700 participants from 28 countries around the world called the border patrol to falsely report the whereabouts of suspected illegal migrants, using the names of the departed, of those who had drowned, died of dehydration, been shot or otherwise perished in previous failed attempts to make the perilous crossing. These actions at once threw the patrol officers off course, aided folks trying to cross, and most importantly drew attention to and paid homage to the hundreds who had lost their lives in previous crossings.

The second example is from another part of the world and uses a different kind of digital geography tool, Google Maps. "The Wall-The World," conceived and executed by Paula Levine and Christopher Zimmerman, presents you with a map of the 439-mile-long wall Israelis are building between Israel and the West Bank to effectively ghettoize Palestinians. You are then asked to take part in the project by typing in the name of the town or city in which you now live. Quickly, the Palestine wall is superimposed on your town, emblematizing what it would be like to have that kind of apartheid forced upon your neighborhood. With minimal commentary, a simple but powerful image is offered to quite literally bring the Israeli-Palestinian conflict "home."

Looking closely at the digitization of politics shows a complexly mixed terrain. At every level of politics today the question of whether digitization deepens or cheapens politics will depend on which groups of people get most involved in putting digital technology at the service of civic engagement, and how thoughtfully and imaginatively they do so.

7

Are Digital Games Making Us Violent and Sex Crazed, or Will They Save the World?

Virtual Play, Real Impact

Digital games have become a pervasive part of the lives of millions of people. This chapter will examine the nature and role of games from several angles. After looking briefly at some theories of how to think about games and gaming, we take up the issue of games as forms of education. We know games teach, and not just so-called educational games, but how and what do they teach? Much concern has been raised that games teach violence and other forms of anti-social behavior. How valid are those concerns? Do games promote aggression? Are games particularly sexist? Beyond the general critique of violent games, one particular phe-

→ What's in a Game? Playing Theories

→ What Do Games Teach?

→ Do Video Games Make Players Violent?

→ Digitized "Militainment"?

→ Gender Games, Race Games

→ Can Video Games Save the World?

nomenon known as militainment (war-related entertainment) has received special scrutiny. While there has been much criticism of games, there have also been eloquent defenders of the form. Some proponents claim that the most often disparaged form of new media can actually make us smarter and improve the world. They claim that the intellectual skills developed by game playing can and desperately need to be turned into socially useful real-world actions. Can both perspectives be true?

⊡ WHAT'S IN A GAME? PLAYING THEORIES

Play seems to be an inherent part of human life, and much animal life as well. I've disparaged kitten videos in this book a couple of times, but one thing we can learn from things like kittens at "play" is that play is educational. While kittens learn primarily how to catch and eviscerate prey, what humans learn from game play is rather more complicated, but we learn many kinds of skills and values in the midst of play. Studies of digital games often draw upon a wider category of human play studies (Bateson 1976; Huizinga 1971) that have long sought to understand the role of gaming in social and personal life. In terms of digital gaming, early researchers tended to fall into one of two broad categories, those who emphasized narrative or storyline in games (narratology), and those who concentrated more on interactions and rules shaping game play (ludology). The extent and importance of story to games varies greatly, from a minor backstory to a highly elaborated narrative. Likewise, the interactive variable elements and rules of games run from the simple to the highly complex. Clearly, both sides of the narrative/playful dyad of analysis have things to teach, and more recent game research has gotten beyond this binary into more supple and subtle analysis that draws on both traditions as well as utilizing other contemporary cultural concepts like *assemblage* (Deleuze and Guattari 2007; Haraway 2003 [1984]; King 2012), the idea that so-called individual identities are less like coherent things than an assembly of parts that can be reassembled. Assemblage theory is important in that it reminds us, on the one hand, that game characters are pixels, not people, and on the other hand, that as we play games we are revealed as pixelated ourselves in the sense that our identification with characters may reshape our own identities. Assemblage theory reminds us that game characters are both pixels and bits of us, not people in little virtual worlds separated from us, but human creations that recreate us as we become in some sense absorbed, cyborg-like, into game worlds. The plasticity and variability this entails make games a particularly rich place for experimenting with and analyzing human (and posthuman?) identities.

Games have long been a key component of digital cultures. In fact, game cultures can be considered the earliest of all digital cultures. Today many untold millions of people play digital games all over the world, and the most popular games have millions of individual players. While the stereotype of the gamer remains the adolescent boy, in fact the average age of video gamers by the second decade of the twenty-first century was 32, and as of 2013 there were more adult women players than teenage boys. This changing demographic also represents some changes in the nature of games, but in many ways the game industry still lags behind its user base, just as the stereotype of the teen boy gamer misleadingly still dominates the popular imagination.

Digital gaming comes in several flavors these days—computer games (played on laptops, desktops, smartphones, etc.), console video games (Xbox, Playstation, Wii), as well as various handheld devices, with many variations (from the literally one-shot Angry Birds to vast online games that never end like World of Warcraft). Within the supergenres of sports, strategy, arcade, adventure, role playing, action, shooter, racing and so on, there are dozens of genres and subgenres of games, each with vastly differing versions. Each type of game has its own rules, its own environments (game worlds), and its own communities of players (Aarseth, Smedstad and Sunnan; Wardrip-Fruin and Harrigan 2004, 2007, 2009; Wolf and Perron 2003). And beyond these main modes, the category of playable media is sometimes used to push past somewhat narrow definitions of what constitutes a game. Therefore, generalizing about games and game culture is impossible, and thus the intent of this chapter is only to highlight certain aspects of some games. Certain overall patterns can, however, be noted, beginning with the fact that while still very much a "boys' club," especially at the top, game design and game play both are no longer exclusively a male-only or youth-only endeavor. With the average gamer now in their mid-30s and equal numbers of female and male players (though console games remain male dominant in terms of numbers of players) a new world of gaming is clearly emerging ("Essential Facts about the Computer and Video Game Industry" 2013).

⊡ WHAT DO GAMES TEACH?

Play has always been a form of education, and video games too are teaching devices. The amount of time that many, many people spend with them means looking into *what* they teach is a very important social task. Before looking at some of the specific claims about the kinds of education taking place through games, one general point seems worth emphasizing: digital games teach you how to learn. Every game you pick up, no matter how simple, requires you to navigate an unfamiliar interface and uncover the causality behind that game world. This may be one of the most significant things games have done, especially for digital natives, and it's a large part of what enables them to tackle new technologies and systems more easily than digital immigrants. As we will explore below, questions about how well they prepare gamers for other dimensions of social life are more complicated. Games teach about race, class and gender, about what is appropriate and inappropriate behavior across the cultural realm.

There is clear evidence that a great deal of mental and physical activity is going on during gaming, but what that activity means is as yet less clear. Certain kinds of visual acuity have clearly increased. Hand–eye coordination is improved. And while games were once tainted as sites of physical inactivity, more kinetic games are changing that story. A variety of other positive impacts of video games have been traced by neuroscientists, though seldom without skeptical reception by other researchers (Connolly et al. 2012; Holt 2012). Some researchers have even found that violent games, the most vilified, were the *most* educational in several respects (Bavelier 2012). The category of educational games (see Chapter 8) makes sense as a name for games with particular explicit teaching goals, but it is important to keep in mind that all games teach things, all games are educational, for better and for worse.

▣ DO VIDEO GAMES MAKE PLAYERS VIOLENT?

Concern about the impact various modes and genres of media may have on "real-world" behavior has long been a fraught territory of claims and counter-claims, much of it surrounding the controversial social science field of "effects studies." The strongly immersive nature of many digital games has intensified this debate. Video games have come in for more than their share of grief, particularly for allegedly promoting social violence.

In the UK, Canada and Australia, they call them "moral panics." In the United States, there is no name for them, but they occur in abundance. They usually take the form of "phenomenon X is destroying the moral fiber of the nation," or "corrupting our youth," or "bringing about the downfall of civilization." In the past these youth-corrupting influences have been spotted most often in popular music. Elvis Presley's wild hips and "Negroid inflections" were morally damaging, then it was "acid rock," then "punk," then "heavy metal," then "rap" and so on that signaled the end of civilization.

Now digital cultures in general, and game culture in particular, have become a major target of moral panic. But having survived all these previous end-of-civilization scenarios, it is unlikely that any aspect of digital culture represents the end of the world. As we have seen, the Internet in general has been portrayed by some as the end of civilization, and various phenomena associated with the Web like social networking, texting, or, worse, sexting have also. But it is clearly video games that have generated the largest and most sustained panic attacks in the twenty-first century.

The most enduring of these attacks have revolved around the issue of violence in digital games. The most common form of criticism is to point out that a certain mass murderer (usually in the US) spent a lot of time playing violent video games. This is an example of what social theorists call mistaking a correlation for a causality. Millions and millions of young men all over the world play violent video games, and do not commit acts of murder. That a handful of serial killers also played violent video games is not a causal link (97 percent of Americans have played video games; 15 percent of that market represents mature games likely to include violence; "first-person shooter" is the most played genre at 21 percent). Those serial killers also no doubt had dozens of equally meaningless correlations based on simple statistics. To call something a moral panic is not to dismiss all the issues behind the panic. In fact, almost all moral panics have some substantive issue behind them. This is certainly true of the issue of violence in video games, but violence is a presence in the world above and beyond video games. The amount of carnage seen on nightly news telecasts is enough to make anyone believe violence is the preferred solution to all problems. It is also the case that attacks on games tend to backfire; Rockstar Games, maker of the frequently critiqued game Grand Theft Auto, for example, reportedly encouraged and perhaps even paid reviewers to boost game sales by fueling a moral panic through playing up the amount of sex and violence. In any event, we have to get past the panic in order to get something like a clear analysis of the various kinds, degrees and meanings of violence in a range of video games, both online and on consoles.

The question of violence is often also debated in terms of "real world" versus "game world." Nothing riles gamers more than the suggestion that people are too dumb to know the difference between games and reality. In fact, however, critics of games almost always acknowledge this fact, and it is not the basis of most criticism. In the academic study of media the question of cultural "effects" is an extremely complicated and difficult one. Media scholars recognize that there is almost never a direct link between what happens in media and what happens in the world. No one, for example, simply plays a first-person shooter game, gets confused, and goes out and shoots someone in real life. Nor do people watch pornography and then run out to commit rape. Though in both of these examples there is some (contested) empirical evidence that inhibitors to violence, general and sexual, can be lowered by repeated exposure to violent games and violent porn, respectively. But there is also evidence that violence in games has positive impacts, including a cathartic effect by providing a safe outlet for aggressive emotions. One neuroscience researcher even found that violent games were in some respects the most educational (Bavelier 2012). Several scholars have noted that youth violence in the US and elsewhere has declined in the era of video games, suggesting at the very least that other countervailing factors have kept games from making young people more violent (Ferguson 2010). In any event, to the degree that there turn out to be measurable impacts of games on phenomena like violence, they will not take the simplistic forms certain moralistic critics put forth.

Lack of direct measurable correlation does not mean that what goes on in games has no real-world impact. Those impacts while contested are no doubt very extensive given the pervasiveness of gaming. The point is not to show a direct correlation between what goes on in games and the wider world, but rather to look at the way in which games and game cultures unintentionally and indirectly create positive or negative cultural echoes, climates and impacts. Violence is undoubtedly the most studied element of gaming, and as computational analyst Joshua Lewis, who studied effects on 2,000 computer game players, has noted, "There has been a lot of attention wasted in figuring out whether these things turn us into killing machines. Not enough attention has been paid to the unique and interesting features that videogames have outside of the violence" (quoted in Holt 2012). In fact, while issues of violence have dominated the field, there has been a good deal of evidence gathered on other possible impacts too, by a range of neuroscientists, psychologists and other social scientists, as well as humanities scholars, but with few absolute conclusions. A review of more than 7,000 articles on video games and education, for example, came to the conclusion that far more careful and comprehensive research, combining qualitative and quantitative methods, is needed before any definitive claims can be made about the positive or negative impacts of gaming on the brain (Connolly et al. 2012).

⊡ DIGITIZED "MILITAINMENT"?

There is another, more specific issue of gaming and violence that is equally complicated but rather different in nature. Computers and war have been increasingly interrelated since the middle of the twentieth century (Edwards 1996; Gray 2004; Halter 2006), but computer games have added a new twist to this interaction. This is the increasing involvement of games and the game industry in the phenomenon known as militainment. Militainment can be defined as the depiction and usually the glorification of the military and warfare in the popular entertainment industry; in recent years this also entails increasing interconnection and cooperation between the military itself and entertainment corporations. This phenomenon precedes the rise of military video games, and is at least as old as wooden toy soldiers (Halter 2006). But the nature and extent of the phenomenon have grown exponentially with the rise of first old media like television, and now new media, especially video games. Combat-based digital games, particularly as they have become increasingly real-seeming and immersive, are carrying militainment to new levels, while at the same time video games are being used by the military for both recruitment purposes and actual combat training. The fact that the US and Australian militaries, among others, have actually created commercial video games (America's Army and Arma, respectively), with help from the game industry, and that in turn military personnel have become more and more deeply involved as consultants in the making of combat video games, represents a further blurring of the line between entertainment and warfare. In addition, the game industry has become increasingly involved in creating training games and combat simulators for the military (Arma actually started as a simulator, and was then turned into a commercially available game). Clearly, digital cultures, especially in the form of video games, have become a significant component in the intensification of the military–industrial–entertainment complex and the transformation of war into a game.

To understand and place the importance of digital militainment socially, it is necessary to do a bit of historicizing. Dwight Eisenhower, president of the United States in the 1950s, gave a famous farewell address upon leaving office. Eisenhower had been the Supreme Allied Commander, and a five-star general during World War II. But he had grown increasingly concerned that the United States was becoming dependent upon its military industries. In his famous address, Eisenhower warned of a growing "military–industrial complex." By this he meant that corporations that were profiting from the arms trade and by building new airplanes, ships and armaments, were putting pressure on the military and the government to buy weapons that were not really needed. Despite Eisenhower's great credibility as a former general, his warning went largely unheeded by those with the power to change things. But over the years the phrase military–industrial complex came to have more and more resonance in the US and around the globe. Indeed some came to talk about the US as having a "permanent war economy." By this they meant that military spending had become so integral to the US economy that subtle and not-so-subtle pressures for a militaristic posture, if not open warfare, were ever present in the society. Evidence for this is overwhelming, given that even during times of peace, a fairly rare occurrence for the last 50 years of US history, pressure to build more and more weapons has remained. Driven initially by the Cold War with Russia, the military–industrial complex continues unabated despite the US being the one lone remaining Superpower. At present, the US has more weapons than all the other countries on the planet combined, and is a major purveyor of weapons to most of those other countries.

In more recent years an additional term has been added to the phrase military–industrial complex. People now speak of a military–industrial–entertainment complex (sometimes the word "academic" is added to the label since much military research is done at universities). The recent period has brought old media and new media into militainment alliance. The increasing militarization of the television news, for example, is entangled with the great popularity of combat video games. Many noted that in coverage of the US wars in the Middle East, "embedded" reporters in effect put the viewer in the position of being a soldier, much like playing a video game does. Many of the images conveyed through these media, such as video shot by a bomb with a camera in its nosecone, look eerily similar to video war game imagery. Or is it the other way around? This should perhaps not be surprising given that the military and the digital game industry have been for several decades increasingly involved with one another in a variety of ways. But many argue that this similarity presents the danger of lessening the reality of war, rendering it playful. Even anti-war activists report feeling a certain thrill in being positioned as soldiers during the invasion, a reaction difficult to imagine apart from the messy merging of the real and the simulated via militainment.

This increasingly deep intermixture of popular entertainment and the military has raised a number of critical questions, both within the military and among civilian scholars. Perhaps the biggest question is whether militainment is increasing militaristic feelings among non-military players, and whether that has spilled over into support for military action over other kinds of international engagement. As noted above, virtually all game players insist they know the difference between virtual violence and the real kind. But the absoluteness of this claim has been challenged, and the instance of the soldier/game player may be an especially confusing case. Some in the military have worried that pre-enlistment game playing is poor and even dangerously misleading training for real warfare. Some combatants on the ground have complained that new recruits with a video game mentality can endanger themselves and their fellow soldiers.

Virtual reality and video war games are now being used to treat US veterans and still-enlisted soldiers suffering from war-inflicted PTSD (post-traumatic stress disorder) (*Coming Home* n.d.; Drummond 2012; Khaled 2011; Moore 2010). This fact has a myriad of interesting implications. First, it will be a wonderful thing if game war proves useful for lessening the impact of the horrors witnessed in real war, wonderful if it can help some of the thousands of casualties of war. (A more general elaboration of this work, a set of "health games" called Coming Home, extends this idea to a variety of approaches to virtual readjustment to civilian life.) In the US alone, according to an Army study, at least 250,000 men and women who have served in the Middle East have PTSD. There are nowhere near enough resources to treat these ex-soldiers, and at present there are no plans to use the technology to help the millions of Iraqi, Afghani and other civilians traumatized by US wars. The theory behind the use of games in treating PTSD includes the notion that if vets can re-experience war in the safety of a game situation, they can gain control over the terrifying emotions set off by flashbacks to real war situations. That this therapy can apparently be successful to some degree suggests just how close game war and real war are these days, and perhaps belies the assumption of those who claim they can tell absolutely the difference between game war and real war. As real war becomes more game-like, and game war becomes more "realistic," this confusion is likely to deepen in unpredictable ways.

A different but related set of technocultural issues emerges around the increasing gap between front-line and online warriors. Unmanned drones wage war on people thousands of miles away from the "combatants" who control them. These issues are not wholly unprecedented. Concerns have been raised historically that pilots flying bombers that never see their bombs land on human targets may be shielded from the realities of warfare, and that they may suffer retroactively when that reality hits them. But now we are talking about a whole other level of magnitude and perhaps moral confusion. Some of these combatants are actually on the "home front." Being at the front and at home at the same time presents a whole new set of concerns. Soldiers can spend all day raining death on people half a world away, and then go home to dinner with their families at the end of the day. This kind of blurring of military and civilian life can be deeply, dangerously confusing (Gray 2004; Singer 2009). War games have long been a part of military preparedness, and digital war games are among the most popular genres on video consoles and computers. But war is no game. Some observers have asked how the justifications for war are transformed if one side of the conflict fights far away from the dangers of the front. Anti-war movements have long been fueled by the dead bodies coming home from the front. Dead bodies of the "enemy" have generally made less of an impact. Will one-sided warfare, more commonly known as slaughter, become more acceptable?

More generally, is militainment making it more difficult for the general citizenry to sort out justifications for war and blurring the line between civilian and military roles? Just as civilian control of the military has been a key, defining element of modern democracies, so too has the clear line between military and civilian life been important to maintain. So the larger, more difficult to measure questions concern how militainment, and especially digitally driven immersive militainment, may be blurring the socially important line between the military and civilian sectors of society overall. Has all this increased militaristic feelings among non-military players, and has that spilled out into the wider society? Is militainment making questions of war and peace more difficult for the general citizenry to sort out?

These questions are deepened by the fact that combat games are among the most popular of genres; more and more people are having the experience of playing digital war games. How is that changing the perception of war, the willingness to support military interventions? Even when they portray realistic blood (as they increasingly do given ever advancing digital resolution quality), they are profoundly sanitized. However realistic they seem, they lessen the reality of war. Whatever else you can say about digitized combat games, real people seldom die while engaging in them. They are also unrealistic in that the good guys are almost invariably American and almost invariably win; the powers of the US military seem unlimited. In fact, as Chris Hables Gray and others have argued, US military capacity has been greatly overestimated, as prolonged, still unresolved wars in the Iraq and Afghanistan make clear (Gray 2004). Few if any of the mainstream games question justifications for US wars, let alone hint that motives might include securing economic domination over other nations rather than "spreading freedom and democracy."

The literature on militainment has grown to be fairly substantial, but there is much more that could be done. A cross-cultural comparison of the impact of military games in Japan and the United States, for example, might be especially revealing. These, the two countries most responsible for the video game market, have very different recent histories in regard to war. The United States is a highly militaristic culture that has been at war somewhere in the world for all but a handful of years out of the last 50, while Japan, forced to demilitarize at the end of World War II, continues to have an official state policy of pacifism. How have each of these quite distinct cultural contexts shaped responses to digitized militainment?

▣ GENDER GAMES, RACE GAMES

Years of experience suggest to me that a significant segment of hardcore gamers respond very harshly (not to say hatefully) to anyone who is in any way critical of any social aspect of games or gamer culture. From the cry of "It's just a game" to "Screw this political correctness!" Gamer Guy seems strangely defensive, but methinks he doth protest too much. It should go without saying that there are hundreds of wonderful games and millions of great gamers. But this is not a book dedicated to celebrating digital cultures; it is dedicated to improving them. And, strangely enough, in order to improve things you have to point out things that need improvement. So, unless you can make an argument that racism, sexism, xenophobia and homophobia, for example, are intrinsically necessary to games, then I invite you to think about how you might make the games you love better by supporting efforts to open up gaming to people who are currently unable to enjoy their pleasures because they often feel more like targets than players. Pointing out that some games engage in problematic stereotyping, or exhibit extreme violence, is not a charge that any particular gamer is racist, sexist or violent. But taking some action (even as small as one post on a game site objecting to a slur or a blatantly sexist depiction) will make you a part of solutions that will make game play better for all gamers.

As with other issues we've looked at, much of the problematic content in video games and other digital games reflects the problems in the larger society. That doesn't get them off the hook, but it does remind us that these games did not invent things like violence or racism or sexism or homophobia. But what concerns many critics is that while other older media—television, film, and music, for example—have made some strides to limit these social blights, some parts of digital gaming seem to have moved backwards in time, making these problematic representations more prevalent. In other words, video games seem to have brought back to prominence some of the worst features of old media.

Why might this be the case? Two partial causes are economics and technological limits/capabilities. In establishing a new type of commercial media, companies frequently rely on old formulas because they seem the most economically safe. That is why so many Hollywood films or TV sitcoms seem like clones of so many others. But in a new medium like digital games, the pressures are even more intense to rely on the familiar and previously successful images, and storylines. As everyone knows, or at least thinks they know, sex sells. It's not surprising then that so many digital games, especially those marketed to teenage boys, are full of adolescent male sexual fantasies (i.e., beautiful, titillating, scantily clad and apparently sexually available girls and young women). For this reason, the example of female images and characters in games provides a particularly rich example to explore social representations.

The line between sexiness, and sexism, isn't always easy to draw. But years of critical work in media studies give us some clues as to what to look for. Two key things that can help move a representation toward or away from being sexist are *agency* and *complexity*. Agency in this context means the ability to impact the world (or, in this case, the game world). To have agency is to have the ability to make things happen, rather than just have things happen to you. Representations of girls and women as simply eye candy, as characters who do nothing active in a game and apparently have no ideas, interests, or goals other than to please men sexually are not only unrealistic but potentially dangerous to real-life females. Conversely, images of female avatars showing real skill, intelligence, strength and impact can be empowering.

Related to the issue of agency is the question of personality complexity. When you portray people without complex thoughts, feelings and motivations, you in effect dehumanize them, turn them into objects to be manipulated by others (a particularly tempting thing when quite literally the control mechanism is in one's hands). There is nothing wrong with sexiness, and all human beings objectify potential sexual mates. The problem lies in the imbalance of gender power in and around such depictions. Physically exaggerated male bodies are almost as common in video games as exaggerated female ones. But the contrast is illustrative. While women (some women warriors notwithstanding) often have their sexual allure attuned to near naked helplessness, male fantasy figures most often take on the form of exaggerated musculature and aggressiveness. While women bear the major burden from these exaggerated bodies, some studies suggest that this pixilated perfection has contributed to the rise of eating disorders and steroid abuse among boys and men, and moved many from healthy to obsessive work out regimens.

Some statistics can illustrate the core of the gender imbalance. According to one British government-funded study on the sexualization of teens, 83 percent of male characters in digital games were portrayed as aggressive, while 60 percent of female characters were highly sexualized in a generally subordinate way, including 39 percent who were scantily clad in ways that made little game sense (the equivalent figures for male characters were 1 percent sexualized, 8 percent provocatively clad) (Papadoupoulus n.d.). This means that both females and males are being victimized by game-world representations, though hardly in equal ways. In addition to providing impossible to reach and therefore frustrating masculinity models for boys, game play sets up expectations for how girls and women will react to male aggressiveness that are likely to meet with rejection in the offline world, rejection that may trigger stronger aggression in some cases.

While as noted in Chapter 5, amateur digital representations provide the most extreme and egregious forms of sexism online, professional forms also exhibit a great deal. Gender stereotyping in digital game characters has been particularly well documented. One comprehensive study of over 250 games found that over two out of three contained objectifying, hypersexualized and/or derogatory images of women (Yao, Mahood and Linz 2009). Compounding the problem is the fact that only about 15–20 percent of games contain significant female protagonists at all. Where strong female leads do exist, like Lara Croft, their representation often mixes that strength with sexual objectification (Norris 2004). Women and (fewer) men are fighting back against this reality, and because game producers are a recognizable community, they have had some success in improving content. Anita Sarkeesian, a prominent feminist pop culture critic, uses her blog Feminist Frequency to take on all aspects of media sexism, but in recent years she apparently has decided that some digital cultures are most in need of reform. She traces not only dominant sexist tropes in game worlds, but also how those images seem to play into harassment of female gamers (Sarkeesian n.d.). She has identified a variety of forms of stereotyping that dominate far too much of game characterization. Among those she names are the damsel in distress, the smurfette, the evil demon seductress, the manic pixie and the straw feminist. Each of her analyses (available in video form in the "Tropes vs. Women" series) is eminently reasonable and backed by extensive examples from a range of game genres and platforms. Yet in response she has received every imaginable kind of abuse, including threats of rape and murder. Ironically enough, the viciousness of the misogynistic attacks on Sarkeesian for daring to criticize games reinforces her point as well or better than her analyses themselves.

The most famous female figure in the history of digital gaming, Lara Croft (she even has her own star on the Hollywood "walk of fame," and is on a stamp in France), can illustrate some of the complexities involved in evaluating game characters. When I teach about video games and gender in my courses, I have students debate the following question: is Lara Croft more of a cyberbimbo, or an empowering image for women? The class is almost always equally split in their answers, and each side is usually equally represented by males and females. One obvious thing to see in this is that as in all media culture, audience experience of the same phenomenon varies, sometimes immensely, that the true impact is partly in the eye (or more broadly, the mind) of the beholder. But the degree of variation in interpretation is not random. Some images, and Croft is a great example, are more ambiguous than others (by contrast no one in any of my classes has ever defended the hookers in Grand Theft Auto as empowered sex workers). Croft's ambiguity was built in from the design stage onward, a fact that also usefully illustrates the complexities of game creation. In one sense, Lara is a female impersonator. In the mind of Tomb Raider's lead graphic designer, Toby Gard, the character that became Lara was a male hero with a whip and floppy hat that made it too obviously an imitation of the then immensely popular Indiana Jones (note that routinely old and new media exchange characters, as when later Lara becomes a movie hero). Recognizing they could be accused of unoriginality, if not plagiarism, they floated the idea of making the main character a female. There was initial resistance from the head of the team, but he relented when convinced novelty might make up for the awkwardness of getting a then primarily male game community to play as females (the second level of female impersonation in the game?). So Gard proceeded to create a female protagonist, reporting that he wanted to invent a richer character, not one of the bimbos or dominatrixes he felt then dominated the game scene. His first female version was Latin American, and dubbed Laura Cruz. But pressure from the default subject position dictated that she be Anglicized, so Laura Cruz was reborn as Lara Croft. What happens next reminds us both that accidental things happen in game design, but also that cultural patterns generally win out over chance or creative risk taking. As Gard was playing with the polygons that made up Lara, he one day made a mistake that increased her bust size by 150 percent. Before Gard could fix the problem, the rest of the (all-male) design team weighed in arguing that they loved the new, exaggerated proportions (Goldman 2007; Jenkins 1998; Marie 2010; McGlaughlin 2008).

Would this have happened if even one female was on the team? We'll never know, but we do know that the highly improbable, if not impossible, body of Lara Croft was launched in 1996 to highly positive reception, as well as strong criticism as an eye-candy sexist depiction. The claim was seemingly supported by the quick proliferation of nude, and later, explicitly pornographic, images of Lara on the Web, though, alas, almost all female and some male digital characters undergo pornification at some point (known among the digerati as Rule 34). Other critics have complicated the issue by asking what it might have meant genderwise for those who played as the Tomb Raider avatar. What did adolescent boys make of having to play as a "girl"? Did it unconsciously bring them to identify with a female, maybe even make them more sensitive to women? Or did they simply take pleasure in watching Lara's posterior as they manipulated her at their will? Or both? And were young female players able to identify with a strong heroine, or were they daunted by her eye-candy physique? Or both (Kennedy 2002)?

Over the years, through several game iterations and films with Angelina Jolie as a no-nonsense Lara, and in response to feminist criticism, changing markets and technological breakthroughs, subsequent Laras have become more realistically proportioned, stronger in character, and in general less bimboesque. A visual comparison of the figure of Lara Croft between her arrival in 1996 and her 2013 version illustrates this small but not insignificant degree of progress, which might be characterized as moving from Bimbo to Rambo (see Figure 7.1; Hall-Stigerts 2013). At the same time, in another twist, this move has somewhat downplayed the intellectual dimension (Lara's ostensibly an archaeologist) in favor of more kick-ass action elements.

To broaden the picture, video games regularly limit agency and complexity, in both male and female characters, though far more fully for the latter. This is not a good thing for either gender, but

FIGURE 7.1 *Evolution of Lara Croft, 1996–2013.*

it's especially an issue for girls and women in cultures that still deny them equal rights, equal pay and equal respect. The situation seems to be improving somewhat. As a result of more sophisticated technology backed up by large amounts of social criticism, both the physical and subjective characteristics of female avatars are generally becoming more realistic. Yet, it is a reflection of political timidity that we have game ratings for violence and harsh language, but no ratings for racism, sexism or homophobia—far more socially dangerous components of many games and too much game culture. Again, the point here is not to single out gaming as uniquely featuring these socially regressive qualities; all media, new and old, have contributed to this problem. The point rather is that as new media in general, and video games in particular, have become the most pervasive forms of entertainment they have brought with them, and arguably deepened, highly problematic representations and attitudes that contribute to the epidemic of violence against women, rampant homophobia and ongoing racism. Some of this can be attributed to technical issues, to the tendency in early games to rely on stereotypes in part because richer representation was not technically feasible, but such technological determinist claims take us only so far. Improvements in the variety and depth of representations in games have come about not just through greater technical capacities, but more because game makers have responded to criticism and to the changing demographic nature of their market, especially the displacement of white adolescent males as the core user base.

Women of color often face double jeopardy online in general and in games in particular, as racism is as prevalent in gaming as sexism. This phenomenon has been studied convincingly as well in the creation of characters and avatars in digital games (Chan 2005). Often new "races" created in games (elves, dwarves, aliens, etc.) are poorly disguised stereotypes of actual ethnic groups. Unlike the best science fiction and fantasy works that imaginatively attempt to get beyond real-world racialization in order to better reflect on it, many digital game representations are deeply mired in existing stereotypes. In the fantastically popular MMORPG World of Warcraft and its spinoffs, for example, pixelated racisms include dark-skinned Worgens controlled by white wizards, Asian cybertyped pandas, thinly disguised nature-loving primitive Natives, and so on (Corneliussen and Rettburg 2008; Nakamura 2009; "Racism in WoW" n.d.). This doesn't make all WoW players racists, but it may mean that racial misrepresentation may subtly shape the experiences of all players, even those of strong advocates of racial justice.

In war games, especially in the wake of the 9/11 bombings, anti-Arab, anti-Muslim stereotyping has been rampant (Sisler n.d.). In addition, a host of games seem to reanimate colonialism and subconsciously support contemporary transnational corporate empires in a variety of disturbing ways (Dyer-Witheford and de Peuter 2009). African American cybertyping has been particularly egregious in sport games and urban street games (Chan 2005; Leonard 2004, 2006). As in pop culture generally, indigenous peoples ("Indians" as some native people prefer, to remind us of how geographically confused Christopher Columbus was) in digital culture remain largely confined to the past, where they are either war-painted fierce warriors, long-haired buckskin-clad princesses, or nature-loving ultimate ecologists (Sturgeon 2009). What arguably makes game play more disturbing is the fact that as players, rather than simply viewing an offensive stereotype, people may be more actively engaging the stereotypes, may, for example, be killing racially coded aliens or fantasy creatures, or shooting "redskins."

In fact in the real world of the twenty-first century, indigenous peoples, despite being among the groups with the least digital access, have used the Net extremely well, including setting up very important global networks of Natives facing similar forms of cultural domination on several continents (Christensen 2003; Landzelius 2006). Native peoples of the Arctic region are also using the Web to warn that the impacts of global climate change are already here (Banerjee 2012).

Game play has also exposed a good deal of anti-Asian racism from North America and Europe. Waves of anti-Chinese racism, for example, were unleashed when large numbers of Chinese players began earning a living playing games like Lineage 2 by winning virtual weapons in the fantasy role-playing game and then selling their online loot to people in the United States who did not have time to play as many hours to arm their characters. Many of the Chinese players chose to play as a female dwarf, a class in the game that can more easily win treasure on solo missions. In response, US players began killing all dwarves in the game, often adding anti-Chinese slurs in the chat section of the game as they did so. Similar forms of anti-Japanese, anti-Korean and anti-Chinese sentiments have been chronicled in other game chat spaces. With China now widely portrayed as the "enemy" in a new struggle of world economic supremacy, this cybertyping plays into some very dangerous racist discourses in US and European society.

Continuing elements of sexism, racism, homophobia and other socially destructive elements of contemporary games will not go away automatically, any more than they will go away automatically in the wider social world. In the specific case of games, critics argue that it will take pressure on game companies, revolts by gamers and the diversification of the game industry workforce to do that. Hope that this may occur is offered by surveys that suggest despite immersion in the regressive side of digital culture, young people are generally somewhat less sexist, homophobic and racist than their parents.

Rockstar's Grand Theft Auto series provides a case study in the possibilities and complexities of making progress in game worlds. Grand Theft Auto is the single most lucrative media product of all time (the fifth installment in the series, GTA V registered $800 million dollars in sales on the day of its release alone). It is also one of the game franchises that has been most severely criticized over the years. The pressure not to mess much with the formula of a multi-billion dollar enterprise is immense. Large changes, like adding a strong female protagonist to the mix for example, seem unlikely. Advertised improvements in the 2013 version focused mostly on technical improvements in "realism," and a more developed storyline. Widely criticized for racism, sexism and homophobia in earlier versions of the game, part of Rockstar's defense often was to claim it was satirizing, not endorsing, the violent, gangster-based regressive social attitudes portrayed. In subsequent versions, and most overtly in GTA V, the satirical element has been brought more to the foreground (touches like a white thug character with "privilege" tattooed on his neck), without significantly changing their goldmine of a game (having their virtual cake and eating it too?). That approach raises interesting questions about audience. No doubt a large portion of GTA players get the jokes, while others may endorse the racism, sexism and homophobia. And there remains the question of whether, since much of the social educational impact of games goes on unconsciously, deeply disturbing social values are being exorcised or reinforced through over-the-top satirical representation.

Nevertheless, Rockstar can be given some credit for responding to critics. And, particularly under the influence of indies (small independent game companies) more pressure is being applied to make games less stereotyped, more socially complex and more aesthetically rich. For example, a game like Beyond Two Souls (2013), produced by the French company Quantic Dreams and featuring actor Ellen Page, may open space for more female action heroes in games. And at another extreme, the game Journey (2012), from the indie company ironically named Thatgamecompany, offers a contemplative, voiceless sojourn through the desert as a different kind of "adventure" game. Such progress is encouraging to continuing efforts to make this particular branch of digital culture a more livable place for people currently more victimized than welcomed into game play. But it clearly has not ended criticism (Martens 2013), nor do many think it should. Progress in terms of gradual improvements in the social consciences and imaginations of game designers suggests that change can come without loss of revenue. Critics would argue that this (limited) progress should lead to greater pressure, not to complacency, but they do recognize that some positive things are in motion.

Gaming is still a very young genre that has not come close to reaching its potential, particularly as an art form. Gaming has produced amazing things already, but it probably has not yet found its Shakespeare, its Rembrandt, its Kurasawa. But it is bound to. The aesthetic potential of playable media is too rich to be left only to (often highly creative but genre-bound) commercial designers. Four decades of game art and much interesting indie game design have stretched the medium in exciting directions (*Digital Meets Culture* n.d.). The form will increasingly attract more and more great narrative artists, visual artists and musicians, who will fully utilize the full range of the medium's immersive and ever expandable verbal, visual, aural and playable dimensions. A focus on the far better known commercial game industry products makes sense in mapping the larger social impact of digital cultures, but a growing body of non-commercial game art reminds us that there is another dimension altogether that is likely to have greater and greater cultural impact in the future.

CAN VIDEO GAMES SAVE THE WORLD?

At quite the opposite pole and partly in response to folks who see video games as signs of a cultural apocalypse, or deepening militarization, are people who wish to use the great potential of games for positive social transformation. Most prominently Jane McGonigal, in her widely read book, *Reality Is Broken: Why Games Make us Better and How They Can Change the World,* has sought to demonstrate how games are not only useful, but potentially vital to solving many of the world's most pressing problems (McGonigal 2011; McGonigal, *You Found Me,* n.d.). She starts by asking two important, related questions. Why do so many people play e-games so passionately, with often great investments in time and energy, but without monetary reward? And why do many of those same people say they can't find that passion in the work they do in the "real world" despite being compensated monetarily? In a stimulating set of answers to these questions, McGonigal makes a case, much of it based upon empirical social psychological research, that the real world is "broken" in that most people do not experience the sense of excitement, accomplishment, or involvement in their everyday lives that they experience in games. From this premise, she argues that in order to unbreak the world, to make it a better place, we need to learn from digital games how to transfer the elements of excitement, accomplishment and involvement found in games to solving real-world problems. In other words, she argues, we need to make the real world more like the virtual world of games, and that actually using games to tackle collective problem solving may provide the energy needed to find real solutions.

What are the qualities in games that McGonigal would like to see harnessed toward dealing with real-world problems? McGonigal names four qualities: Urgent Optimism, Social Fabric (trust), Blissful Productivity, and Epic Meaning. These aspects include a sense of engagement that is personally challenging, but also connected to a wider community (gamers love to compare experiences). This entails connection to something bigger than oneself, but with the specific contribution of the individual clearly evident. Many games, especially MMORPGs, require teamwork in which each player's participation is vital and visible. In addition, accomplishment is palpable, with tasks in games broken down into levels that clearly demarcate progress towards the goal. Finally, games by definition entail playfulness, a positive emotion that we tend to think of as the opposite of work. Taking pleasure in work is too often a rare thing these days, notes McGonigal. McGonigal's ideas are bolstered by a psychological theory of what in games gives pleasure, and by her years of work as a game designer and game player. More than just talking, she has put her ideas to the test by building real-world, game-based projects. Whenever I ask my students to think up an anti-war game that is as exciting as a war game, they draw a blank and claim it is not possible. Are they right, or can the making of peace and justice become as exciting as blowing up enemy tanks (Castronova 2008; Whitson and Dormann 2011)?

McGonigal's work is part of a larger movement seeking to build alternative games that offer more positive forms of social and political engagement. Her own games like EVOKE, World Without Oil, and Superstruct tackle real-world problems that require collective solutions. Others, like Edward Castronova in *Exodus to the Virtual World* (2008), for example, argue that games may come to be important shapers of public policy. In addition, game companies are adapting their games to the classroom without lapsing into the dull traps of many "educational" games; the education edition of the highly popular game Minecraft is one excellent example (*Minecraft Educational* n.d.). There are also several groups of game developers working together on a socially progressive vision. Prominent among these is the organization Games for Change, a coalition of game designers who work singly and collaboratively, and meet once a year at a "festival" to compare, discuss and celebrate attempts to create world-improving, if not world-saving, digital games (gamesforchange.org; gameful.org). While no social activist game has broken through into the commercial market where profit remains the bottom line (and doing what has already worked always seems safer than trying something new), more and more games that are both socially conscious and engaging are emerging. Some of these games are quite rich and impressive. The excellent puzzle game Papers, Please, for example, does a fine job of capturing the terrifying experience of immigration (in this case into an Eastern Bloc country) and the life-and-death decisions a border patroler must sometimes make amidst a highly entertaining game. Half the Sky, about global gender equity, has a million players worldwide. Climate Defense involves players in finding solutions to global climate change. Peacemaker requires players to negotiate the Israeli–Palestinian dispute. The amount of talent and energy currently being focused on using games to deal with real-world problems is impressive, and is a phenomenon surely worth supporting, whatever one's ideas are about what solutions are needed, since game worlds are currently among the most pervasive and active cultural spaces on the planet.

8

Are Kids Getting Dumber as Their Phones Get Smarter?

E-Learning, "Edutainment" and the Future of Knowledge Sharing

Few areas of contemporary cultural life have been as deeply impacted by digital technologies as the realm of education. From pre-school to graduate school and on into all areas of professional scientific, social scientific and humanities scholarship, the field of education has been profoundly reshaped by computers and related technologies. The exceedingly rapid digitalization of all forms of education has led to great expectations and more than a little anxiety and consternation. Parents

→ "Is Our Children Learning" Digitally?

→ What is Technology Doing in the Classroom?

→ Is Knowledge a Commodity or a Human Right? MOOCs, Information Feudalism and Scholarly Publishing

wonder if our kids are becoming dumber as their phones become smarter. Teachers wonder if new technologies will render them obsolete. Scholars wonder if it is still possible to get a research grant without a digital component to their research projects, or conversely if their colleagues will not take their online publishing seriously. Is the D-generation (those immersed from birth in new media) a generation of spoiled know-nothing, mental D-generates who must be edutained? Or are they a generation of informed, active learners with different, but, perhaps, better, ways of gaining and making knowledge?

Digital technologies have no doubt put more information at Net users' fingertips than has ever been available in human history. All of the tragically lost ancient library of Alexandria (the greatest knowledge source of its time) could now be contained on a microchip the size of the tip of a single finger. But what are we making of all this information? Information, after all, is not knowledge (knowledge is information organized intelligently), and knowledge is not wisdom (wisdom is knowledge put to good use). Is all the information available via the Web and other digital sources mostly making us smarter, or just more superficial, confused and overwhelmed? Should "too much information" (TMI in web talk) be our battle cry? If a future anthropologist were to look back to the birth of the Internet would she be stunned that a network that put all the world's accumulated knowledge at their fingertips seems mostly to have inspired human beings to share pictures of cats playing the piano and dancing dogs?

⊡ "IS OUR CHILDREN LEARNING" DIGITALLY?

The short answer to this variation on an ungrammatical question posed by former US president George W. Bush, is Yes. Whether we like it or not, our children is/are learning digitally. While this chapter will focus primarily on the role of digital media in formal education (pre-school through graduate school and beyond), it is important to remember that digitizing education is a wider phenomenon than computers in the classroom. The Web is an educational device in a myriad of ways, and as shown in Chapter 7, video games play a major role in the education of youth in terms of the information and values they imbibe. One of the most important studies of the impact of the Internet on the learning of youth was part of the Pew Internet and American Life Project. Published in 2008, its findings have been replicated with few variations ever since, and the basic conclusions are summarized thusly: "Contrary to adult perceptions, while hanging out online, youth are picking up basic social and technical skills they need to participate fully in contemporary life" (Ito et al. 2008 2). Studies also suggest, contrary to parental fears and moral panics, that over 90 percent of the time students spend online is with the same people they spend time with offline, not with potentially dangerous strangers. Also, perhaps on the positive side, unless you have stock in Facebook, a 2012 Pew survey found that youth increasingly resent social media as a burden; many are fed up with the inanity and lack of privacy (only 14 percent have their accounts set for open access), though, paradoxically, they are sharing more personal information. Only 5 percent deny access to their parents, though complaints about trolling parents is another reason some are now less thrilled with Facebook. In general, there is a pattern that suggests the novelty of social media wears off for even the most enthusiastic of young users; many consciously limit their time online, and evidence suggests as they become aware of privacy issues, they shape their activity more carefully: "Teens take steps to shape their reputation, manage their networks, and mask information they don't want others to know; 74% of teen social media users have deleted people from their network" (Madden 2013 2).

Some of the answers to questions about the impact of digital technology on learning come from the emergent scientific disciplines that are themselves significantly impacted by advances in digitized research tools. Study of the brain has made remarkable strides in the last couple of decades. New interdisciplinary fields like neuroscience and consciousness studies have emerged to try to pull together a rapidly proliferating body of knowledge about what the brain is and how it functions. Startlingly new insights about the brain and its relation to that mysterious thing called consciousness seem to appear in the media almost daily. Much of this information is being incorporated into more effective teaching. Unfortunately the press, not to mention scientists seeking recognition or larger research grants, has frequently hyped these "discoveries" far beyond what the science actually suggests. Among those most susceptible to this type of hype have been writers about computers and the brain. From the misleading metaphor that the brain *is* a computer, or the slightly less misleading claim that it in *some* ways functions like one, to a host of arguments about what computers and computer culture are *doing to* our brains, news sources and bookstores are now littered with titles along the line of "How computers are destroying our minds" or "How computers will make us all geniuses," with far too few offering more subtle analyses avoiding these extreme claims. As noted throughout this book, a certain degree of exaggeration, both utopian and dystopian, was a part of early cyberculture that has never completely gone away. This same spirit has inflected and infected much of the popularization of neuroscience generally, and neuroscience looking at the human computer interaction specifically. So the best advice when reading about the latest study showing what your brain looks like when googling, is *caveat emptor*—buyer beware. Instead of the hype, let's look at the facts, particularly as represented by the use and misuse of digital technology in education.

⊡ WHAT IS TECHNOLOGY DOING IN THE CLASSROOM?

Computers and digital technology are now pervasive in classrooms throughout much of the overdeveloped Global North, and increasingly present among elites in the less developed Global South. Whether one likes it or not, digital education is here to stay. It is certainly here to stay outside of the classroom, as I suggested above, because the amount of time young people spend online is clearly significant (in the US children aged eight to 18 spend an average of seven hours and 38 minutes per day online or 53 hours per week, 94 percent of children 12 to 17 go online, 75 percent own cellphones, 73 percent use a social networking site; stats are slightly lower for less tech-accessible countries, obviously, but often startlingly high nonetheless). For better and for worse, children around the globe are learning many things about society through digital media.

Unofficial online learning is clearly rampant, and not likely to go away, and it is also here to stay in formal, classroom-centered education. This should be seen as neither a cause for alarm nor elation, because computers are neither the problem nor the solution to issues in education in the twenty-first century. Both those who assume computers in the classroom are inherently negative and those who see in them utopian possibilities, often also assume that they are somehow replacing teachers. Such is not and should not be the case.

It is important to remember that computers are tools, and tools are only as good as those people who wield them. There are no doubt some teachers who use computers in the classroom to escape from rather than enhance their jobs as teachers. But these are a small minority. Good teachers recognize that digital technologies create opportunities, but opportunities that only careful, thoughtful pedagogy can take advantage of. One thing that computers are especially good at is creatively teaching routine things that both teachers and students tend to dislike in rote form. When utilized to carry out the necessary but historically boring baseline work required in education, computers can actually free up teachers to do the more important face-to-face interactive and creative learning. But computers can also do great personalizing and creative things face to face (or interface to face, if you want to be more technically accurate).

One typical set of dystopian images of computers imagines students being cloned into exact replicas of each other. Here again, the imagery is far off the mark. In fact, the great virtue of computers in education is their capacity to individualize the learning process.

Increasingly computers are more sophisticated and can be excellent devices for giving students the opportunity to learn at their own individual pace (sometimes using what are known as *personalized learning channels*). There are many kinds of learners. Some learn best visually, some aurally, some through written words, some with hands-on tactile involvement. And each form can reinforce the others. The multimedia capacity of computers and online learning widens the spectrum of useful pedagogical possibilities open to teachers and students. Studies make clear that students can learn as much from each other as they can from their teachers. Computers can be used creatively for group projects, ones that again can free up teachers to spend time with students who need extra care.

The Web also opens the classroom out onto the wider world in ways that students find deeply engaging. Lack of obvious connection to the real world can be a major block for students, while using the Web to connect to an engineer or architect who explains how they use math, or to a writer who can discuss the joys of crafting a sentence no one has imagined before, can vividly awaken students. Hearing business owners talk about the tangible benefits of having people from a variety of backgrounds in their workforce can remove resistance from those inculcated with the silly notion that promoting diversity is some form of liberal, politically correct conspiracy. While in many communities there are too few such potential contacts to bring into the classroom, the digital classroom knows no such boundaries, and can draw literally on a world of experience.

Digital education allows many, many kinds of geographic and cultural boundaries to be crossed. I have participated in classrooms where students from the US and Japan engaged in animated conversations about how the popular cultures of their respective countries were received and understood in the other country—hip-hop in Japan, manga in the US, video games from each, and so forth. Hundreds of conversations like this take place every day at every level of education, conversations only made possible by new technologies that have immense potential to deepen cross-cultural understanding for mutual benefit. But again, this only happens when good teachers make smart use of the technologies now available, and it only happens in well-funded classrooms.

On the creating side of the ledger, knowledge that things they produce can be shared with more than one person (the teacher) can also inspire far more thoughtful, careful work in students. Putting students to work on real-world problems can deepen engagement immensely. Classroom blogs, wikis and other digital formats can put already popular genres students use outside of school into the classroom in ways that feel familiar and less like drudge work. There are templates based on popular gameshows available in PowerPoint form that can be adapted to virtually any subject matter for turning the generally less-than-exciting form of question and answer into a more engaging activity (while, if you must, still teaching to standardized tests that require baseline cultural knowledge).

Some critics of digitizing education use the dismissive term edutainment, with emphasis clearly on the *tainment,* rather than the *edu,* to disparage this kind of learning. The assumption here seems to be that real learning is being replaced by mindless play. Ironically, these doubters are often the same people who scare folks about the impact of video games because of their deeply immersive nature. Much recent empirical study, not to mention the application of common sense, suggests that students might in fact learn more if they were enjoying their education rather than being bored out of their minds. And the skillful use of multimedia digital pedagogy can do just that. Play is a fundamental form of learning throughout the animal kingdom; just watch two kittens for five minutes and correlate their play with the challenges they will face in the real cat world. In the world of human animals, play can be used quite thoughtfully to engage students with varying learning styles. Some people learn best through the written word, others through visual stimulation, still others through sound, and almost everyone learns better through multiple modes of stimulation acting simultaneously. These various modes are made far more accessible via digital technology. Playful digitally delivered multimedia learning forms provide flexible options that help reach more students, engage them personally and give them more control over their own education. The best digitized learning tools designed by the best teachers can improve all teachers' effectiveness to a degree. They are almost infinitely adaptable to the needs of each student and teacher. Indeed, the irony of images of computers cloning students is that, when used well, they are doing just the opposite; they are personalizing situations where one-size-fits-all education is foisted upon a classroom of 20 or 30 or 40 students, each of whom has a different learning style, pace and set of needs.

While there are many great teachers in the world, there are never enough of them. Digital technologies make it possible for the best teachers to be available to wider and wider audiences of students. Teachers have different gifts, and wise teachers can use digital means to make up for their own limitations and free themselves to do what they do best. For example, few teachers are great lecturers. But the handful of truly great lecturers in the world are now being used via things like podcasts to great advantage in capturing the interest of students. Subsequently, classroom teachers build on the enthusiasm generated by great lectures to get into the next level of questions best worked on with individuals or small groups working interactively.

Figure 8.1 offers a useful chart summarizing the dos and don'ts of using educational digital technology. Note the key distinction being offered being *using* technology in the classroom and *integrating* technology into the classroom. The former is based on narrow technological determinism (we use computers because we should), the latter on smart technocultural planning (how best can we use digital media to improve learning).

Using Technology	Technology Integration
Technology usage is random, arbitrary & often an afterthought	Technology usage is planned & purposeful
Technology is rare or sporadically used in the classroom	Technology is a routine part of the classroom environment
Technology is used purely for the sake of using technology	Technology is used to support curricular goals & learning objectives
Technology is used to instruct students on content	Technology is used to engage students with content
Technology is mostly being used by the instructor(s)	Technology is mostly being used by the student(s)
Focus on simply using technologies	Focus on using technologies to create and develop new thinking processes
More instructional time is spent learning how to use the technology	More instructional time is spent using the technology to learn
Technology is used to complete lower-order thinking tasks	Technology is used to encourage higher-order thinking skills
Technology is used solely by individuals working alone	Technology is used to facilitate collaboration in & out of the classroom
Technology is used to facilitate activities that are feasible or easier without technology	Technology is used to facilitate activities that would otherwise be difficult or impossible
Technology is used to deliver information	Technology is used to construct & build knowledge
Technology is peripheral to the learning activity	Technology is essential to the learning activity

FIGURE 8.1 *Best practices of teaching with technology.* © *Aditi Rao, Teachbytes.*

Where computers are seemingly least adequate as pedagogues is the affective dimension, the emotional context and emotional contact crucial to education. That is one of the many places where human teachers can play a crucial role in even the most tech-heavy classrooms. This includes a range of factors from recognizing and addressing degrees of emotional comfort with the technology itself to all kinds of mood variations that can impact the success of students. Great teachers connect with students, investing in a relationship full of nuances no computer can read or replicate.

There is nothing magical about computers in the classroom. Like all forms of technological determinism, the assumption that computers can automatically augment education is mistaken. If you want to answer the grammatically correct variation of the question asked above, "Is your child learning digitally?," you need to know not how many tablet computers or digital projectors your son's or daughter's classroom has (though that is good to know), but rather what are teachers doing with the technologies they have. Are they using them creatively or dully, are they using them to escape their role as teachers or deepen that role?

Another key set of issues that especially impacts education while having wider social implications, concerns what certain kinds of digital experiences are doing to our minds. Most frequently cited among these is a possible decline in certain intellectual functions due to the nature of much online experience. Some claim online spaces may be undermining our ability to think linearly, to pay attention to long narrative storylines, and to grasp complex sustained logical arguments. The best known popular book on the dangers of the Net for human intelligence is Nicholas Carr's *The Shallows: What the Internet is Doing to Our Brains* (2010). To my mind, what I have left of it after years working online, the book would have been better if the subtitle had been in the form of a question, What is the Internet doing to our brains? Which is to say, that Carr makes a strong but one-sided case that humans are losing the ability to have deep thoughts, to delve substantially into topics, because clicking on so many hyperlinked web pages has rendered us "shallow," flitting about from bit of knowledge to next bit of knowledge, in a kind of distracted dance of the mind. Much of Carr's evidence is anecdotal (he and many of his friends say that after being on the Web for years they find it difficult to read whole books), but not implausible (though to toss back an anecdote, my digital generation son has devoured hundreds of fiction and non-fiction books over the years while also spending uncountable hours on the Web). But I hear this claim often enough from teachers at all levels of education to take it seriously. At present, however, we do not have enough consistent data from neuroscience studies to thoughtfully answer the question, are we becoming less thoughtful? The bottom line suggested in Carr's book, however, that we spend a good deal of quality time in non-digital environments, quiet our minds at times with meditation and/or contemplation, and stretch our minds at times by reading long narratives strikes me as extremely sensible (though, full confession, as a sometime professor of literature, I do have a vested interest in people continuing to read novels). Perhaps tellingly, many executives at Google, Apple, eBay and other hi-tech firms apparently enroll their children in Waldorf schools partly because the "schools discourage the use of electronic gadgets in early childhood" (Utne 2013).

Less thoughtful

Another less ambiguous downside to computers in the classroom is the fact that in the US, the UK, and other countries where strong movements to standardize and narrowly quantify educational progress have been put in place, often as part of drastic cuts in school budgets, computers are being used to do not very useful, if not downright useless, things. They are used to prepare for largely meaningless tests that teach memorization, not thinking. Every major study of education around the world makes clear that the best students, including the ones who do best on so-called standardized tests, are students who work in very interactive, open-ended, problem-solving environments. Real education is interactive in every sense of the word. Standardization is taking place not because of computers, but computers facilitate or provide a rationale for this kind of unimaginative pedagogy (standardizing is something digital tools can do quite well and easily). However, the countries consistently producing the highest-achieving students (South Korea, Finland, Japan, and Canada, for example) are places where students are challenged to problem solve, not regurgitate. They also happen to be places where the role of teachers is respected, valued and compensated at the level of other professionals (doctors, lawyers). In contrast, the US, where teachers are overworked, underpaid and often under attack, ranks 30th in the world in math education, 21st in science, 15th in reading, and unspeakably low in writing skills. Rankings for the UK are comparably abysmal.

Instead of focusing on the alleged dehumanizing effects of computers in the classroom, or fetishizing the technology itself as the sole solution, it is far more useful to focus on the real issue with hi-tech (and not so hi-tech) education. Real concerns about digitizing education take us back to issues of social fairness, equality and digital inclusion, as linked to creative teaching. Vast inequalities in the funding of schools between richer and poorer communities is mirrored and multiplied by inequalities in the amount and sophistication of digital tools available in particular school districts. Damaging inequalities also exist between households in the same districts, since studies show that school success in computer use is greatly enhanced for students who have access at home in addition to in the classroom, a situation that obviously varies with family income. These disparities are in turn often translated into different educational *tracks* where degrees of computer literacy become a basis for pointing students to future roles in a workforce divided between more tech-literate white-collar managers and the less tech-literate blue- or pink-collar work forces (Monroe 2004).

⧉ IS KNOWLEDGE A COMMODITY OR A HUMAN RIGHT? MOOCs, INFORMATION FEUDALISM AND SCHOLARLY PUBLISHING

The digitizing of college- and university-level education includes the general issues discussed above with regard to K–12 education, as well as some additional unique concerns and unique opportunities. Many professors are deeply trained in their fields but very thinly trained as teachers. In my experience, the transition to online teaching has brought many college professors to think more carefully about pedagogy. Much literature on teaching shows, to the chagrin of some of the more arrogant among the professoriate, that peer-to-peer learning is often superior to prof-to-peer learning. Online courses, when they include a strong element of student-to-student discussion made possible by the technology, tend to generate a good deal more student interaction. The physical absence of a professor often stimulates a good form of disinhibition, especially among shyer students who would have difficulty speaking in a room full of people (students tend to forget, or put to the back of their minds, the fact that in most cases the instructor is there as a sort of "lurkerprof," to coin a phrase). Bottom line, bad teaching can happen online or offline, and so can great teaching.

Just as some forms of community could only be virtual, so too virtual education is the only option for some. Fortunately, as suggested above, it is an increasingly rich option. Online education is the only option for placebound people, people who for reasons of work or other commitments cannot travel to a college or university site. This is also true for people who may be within a reasonable distance of a higher educational institution, but whose work schedules would preclude enrolling were it not for the timeframe flexibility of asynchronous (not time-bound) online courses. In addition to geographic isolation, many people with physical or psychological conditions that limit mobility have had new educational vistas opened up by distance education via new media. Moreover, increasing numbers of students who have none of these reasons driving them to the online option are taking these courses simply because they prefer it as a mode of learning.

At the same time, in the US, the UK and much of the developed world, support for public higher education has eroded at the governmental level, with public funds increasingly replaced by higher tuition and fees. This is effectively privatizing education, and making it more and more difficult for even middle-class, let alone working-class, students to afford a university education. But just as short-sighted government policies are raising the costs of education, new technologies and new digitized sources are making more and more knowledge accessible and affordable for more and more people. This contradiction cannot stand for long. Already students in many countries are rebelling against these policies, and increasingly the professoriate is coming to support more and more open-access forms of education.

Part of this stems from the fact that increasingly college and university administrators, boards of regents and the politicians who fund public education speak of higher education as a business. This is largely nonsense for a number of reasons. Most importantly, treating students like clients or products (both terms have been applied by CEO-like administrators) misrepresents and degrades the complicated interactions that make up an education. Educational institutions should be run efficiently and effectively, but the measures of efficiency and effectiveness in academe do not match the measures used in the business world.

As for the "business" of professing, few professors go into education thinking of it as a business, including, or maybe especially, business professors. Whatever field of knowledge they pursue could have been pursued in more financially remunerative ways outside of academe. Moreover, the vast majority of the knowledge professors produce does not lead to financial reward. Professors seldom make significant amounts of money from the academic books they publish, and even more rarely from the research papers they publish. Most profits go to publishing houses which serve as cost-increasing middle persons, often with little direct connection to the knowledge. This contradiction cannot stand in the age of digital production and distributions systems like the Web that make it quite possible to eliminate these middle persons and greatly decrease the cost of knowledge dissemination.

Many authors would rather have their work made available to more people at lower cost than fewer people at a higher cost. And this is even more true for professors, since very few count on getting rich by selling their work, both because they have another job, teaching, and because they care more about spreading knowledge than profit. What professor (indeed, what author of any kind) would not rather have 1,000 people pay $1 for their book, than 50 people pay $20. So what stands in the way? In technological terms, nothing. In practical terms, a mechanism of review that ultimately has little or nothing to do with the actual publication venue. The value of academic work is measured in significant degree by the place where it is published, the "best" university presses, and the "top" scholarly journals. The prestige of these sites is based on two things, historical reputation (they have published highly regarded stuff in the past), and peer review (the quality of the people associated with the publishing site who deem the book or article to be worthy of publication in their reputable publication). But these review processes have nothing whatsoever to do with how the knowledge is then made available—at high cost, low cost, or no cost, through expensive books and journals, or online for little or no cost. While, contrary to the slogan, not *all* "knowledge wants to be free," much of it does and most of it should be free in both senses of the word, now that we have the technology to make it so. Granted, there are complex issues involved in transitioning from the current system to a new, better one, including issues of copyright (where law is decades behind digital innovations), and ease of transition for employees in the current publishing system. But these issues can we worked out, to the benefit of all.

Critics like Peter Drahos, John Brathewaite and David Parry refer to the large publishing conglomerates that control much academic publishing as among the "knowledge cartels" that are engaging in "information feudalism" (Drahos and Brathewaite 2002). Parry (2012) has laid out an action plan for displacing the higher-education branch of the cartel in order to open up academic knowledge to wider and wider publics. His recommendations include using Creative Commons licensing instead of publisher or university copyright for academic books, publishing articles only in online open-access journals, pressuring universities and academic field organizations to embrace open access, and boycotting jobs with academic cartels. Parry and other advocates realize that this is best done on a large scale because few individual academics and individual institutions will have the courage to opt out of the current system. But a few breakthrough efforts like some highly ranked journals going open access, or a couple of major universities embracing these principles, could quickly start a landslide toward a more equitable and accessible knowledge system. These issues matter not only in the US, but widely because the US controls so much of the world's knowledge.

A second controversial area where higher education and digital technology meet is the arena of MOOCs (Massive Open Online Courses). These are courses offered online for free (open) to up to thousands of people at a time (massive). The courses differ from ones offered in universities and colleges in that they can lead to at most a certificate of completion, rather than adding up to an undergraduate degree. From one angle, free online courses that differ little from ones available for (ever more expensive) tuition seem to threaten the very foundation of higher educational institutions. From another angle, they promise to actually fulfill the mission for which higher education exists at all. In any event, given the MOOC mania starting in 2012, the future is looking very MOOC-y. The positive side of making more and more college and university courses available to more and more people is simply too strong to be resisted for long. But, as with changes in the educational publishing industry, change will not come without a fair amount of chaotic dislocation and much social struggle. More important, the form that MOOCs will take is very much up for grabs. MOOC precursors arose in the UK and Canada, but it was MOOC-offering technology organizations in the US who hit upon a popular formula. In the states, three major operations, edX (started by Harvard and the Massachusetts Institute of Technology), Coursera (started at Stanford University) and Udacity (also with roots at Stanford) monopolized the early market. The phenomenon is spreading world-wide, with major efforts under way in Brazil, Japan and the EU, among others. At present, one constraining issue is that elite institutions (like MIT, Princeton and Stanford in the US) have the financial resources to overcome the initial costs of MOOC creation in ways that give them a distinct advantage over state-funded and other less well funded schools.

This could be referred to as the MOOC digital divide. It is also not clear whether these free courses will remain free under pressure from those who continue to think of higher education as a business, rather than a collective social good. Two of the three major MOOC offerers in the states, Coursera and Udacity, are for-profit enterprises that may not continue to provide free classes forever. Business-minded administrators simply can't imagine having thousands of students learning without profit accruing to their institutions. Advocates of openness argue that the difference between uncredited MOOC courses and those offered as part of a regular, tuition-funded and accredited curriculum leading to a degree will be a sufficient distinction to retain the current role of universities and colleges. But once the good publicity gained by apparently altruistic offerings of free courses runs out, there will be great pressure from administrators to "monetize" these courses, to limit the open part of Multiple Open Online Courses.

MOOCs also can be quite retrograde pedagogically. Many are based upon talking-head lecture formats that have proven to be among the least effective forms of teaching. While many offer "interactive" elements, it is not clear how many of these are actually used and how interactive they really are. Truly interactive forms of teaching, including much student-to-student activity, are far more useful than most kinds of lectures, and technologies have been used thoughtfully by many to create more student-centered, as opposed to professor-centered, courses. If MOOCs continue to develop based upon a kind of star system of elite lecturers, they will still prove useful to some students, but they will set back more than they advance higher education pedagogy overall. They may also greatly deepen an already growing divide between tenure-line faculty, and adjuncts hired at far lower pay, with higher teaching loads and far less job security. Some forms of MOOC-ing could shrink the number of full-time faculty, and expand the group of exploited adjuncts who would manage the massive numbers of students through machine-graded tests and other far from creative forms of learning.

Alternatives to these kinds of MOOCs are emerging. FemTech-Net's Distributed Open Collaborative Course (DOCC) model, for example, challenges both the pedagogical style and the hierarchical structure of MOOCs. These alternatives will be up against the greater economic resources of the corporate academic types, but with imagination and effective networking they will have an impact. It will take demand from students for courses embodying more of the interactivity they have come to expect of education in the digital age to turn the dominant forms of MOOCs into something better.

There is also a great deal of rich, digitally enabled scholarship now available through the Web, from the sciences, social sciences, arts and humanities. Given this book's focus on culture, the rise of extraordinary "digital humanities" projects is particularly relevant as detailed in sites like HASTAC, Digital Humanities Now and the Center for History and New Media. Digital humanities work ranges from rich online data bases and resource sites on particular artists and writers to vast projects like MediaNOLA that seek to map something approaching the whole history of cultural production in a city over the generations and across a range of fields (MediaNOLA n.d.). Hundreds of free cultural resource sites now available worldwide represent an inestimable gift enabled by digital technologies. Protecting and expanding these kinds of resources in the face of increasing commercialization, however, will require continued vigilance and creative action. Scholar Robert Darnton, for example, leads a project that represents a public alternative to Google's stated goal of digitizing virtually all the books in the world (the Digital Public Library of America http://dp.la/). Ironically, at a time when universities are moving ever more toward reductively vocational approaches to education that stress business, engineering and natural science over the social and human sciences, three out of four employers say they want schools to "place more emphasis on the skills that the humanities and social sciences teach: critical thinking and complex problem solving" (American Academy of Arts and Sciences 2013). Digital humanities are well placed to help bridge this division, and help restore art, literature, philosophy and related fields to the center of higher education.

Innovations in the digitization of educational resources raise the larger question of whether knowledge is something that should be hoarded and made financially inaccessible to all but the few (the business model), or a human right that should be available to anyone with the intellectual skills to benefit from it, regardless of ability to pay. There are complex issues of copyright and intellectual property rights that need to be untangled in this context. Laws on these issues around the globe are decades behind digital technology. But surely at a time when humanity faces extraordinarily daunting problems—wars, famines, poverty, ecological crises and more—we should be doing far more to use digital and other means to increase the flow of knowledge and the number of educated people in the world, rather than creating roadblocks. Yet that is precisely what we do when we think of formal education and knowledge more generally as a commodity. Markets can do some things extremely well. But the idea of a knowledge market makes no sense. Do we really want to increase profits for a few institutions by creating a shortage of supply? Is that really a good strategy for creating the smartest possible world?

At a time when exciting new educational vistas are opening up, many countries, under the dubious slogan of austerity, are gutting education. In both the UK and the US, for example, massive government funding cuts and other ill-conceived policies have led to the privatization of much that was once public in education, especially at the college and university level. Higher education is more and more expensive, less and less available to all but the wealthiest students

(Couldry and McRobbie 2010). Moreover, in the US there has been a three-fold increase in the amount of state funds going to students without financial need in recent years (based on a notion of merit that does not factor in the impact of family income), and that means far less for students from low-income families (Rampell 2013). No amount of digitization is going to help much if these trends are not reversed, because intelligence is never found in only one economic or social class, especially the kind of intelligence needed to see the world in all its diverse complexity, and tackle mounting economic, social and ecological problems plaguing the planet. The Internet and related digital communication technologies open up vast possibilities for expanding the amount of information, knowledge and wisdom in the world. All that stands in the way is lack of accurate information about what tech can (and cannot) do in education, lack of imagination in using the technologies, and lack of the political will to support these innovations.

9

Who in the World is Online?

Digital Inclusions and Exclusions

Throughout this book we have been examining those who are part of digital cultures, but what about those who are not? Who in the world is *not* online and why aren't they? While I have discussed aspects of digital inequality throughout this book, before concluding, we need to look more closely at the so-called digital "have-nots." It is no accident that the opportunity and ability to take part in the benefits of digitized life vary immensely, both between countries and within countries around the globe. And those differences are sometimes matters of life or death.

⧉ THE WORLD WIDE WEB ISN'T

One thing to always remember about the World Wide Web is that it isn't. Isn't worldwide, that is. As its name makes clear, the World Wide Web seeks to be a universal phenomenon, and it *is* a very widespread phenomenon, but the Web and other aspects of digital culture are far from worldwide. Statistics make clear that the spread of the Internet around the globe has been deeply uneven, with vast differences across continents, between countries, and along class, gender and ethnic lines within regions and nations.

Who in the world is online, and who is not or cannot take part in the digital realm? The quick answer is that only a small percentage of the world's population has significant access to the wonders of the digital realm, and even the more than two billion people who have some kind of (often quite limited) access make up less than a third of the global populace (currently approaching seven billion). In other words, 70 percent of the world's population (five billion people) have no engagement with digital culture at all. Three broad lacks shape this fact: lack of economic resources, lack of computer literacy skills and lack of information relevant to many cultural groups, combined with a lack of information on the benefits of the Net for those groups. The last of these three is a function of the relative lack of linguistic and cultural diversity in the material available on the Web.

The highest access rates are in North America and Europe, the lowest access rate is on the African continent, with Asia and Latin America in the middle range. Within countries rates of access also vary greatly, depending primarily on economic wealth or lack thereof, and majority or minority ethnicity status, with age, gender and educational level also shaping amount and quality of access. To begin with, access is distributed extremely unevenly across continents: 79 percent of North Americans have access, 63 percent of Europeans, 49 percent of Middle Easterners, 42 percent of Latin Americans, 27 percent of Asians, and only 16 percent of Africans (*World Internet Stats* n.d.). These statistics are telling, but also incomplete in that deep disparities also exist between countries on a given continent and even more drastically by income within countries. And since virtually every country on earth currently shows increasing economic inequality, these are key statistics.

Some key aspects of digital culture this book has explored can be called issues of "digital diversity." Digital diversity is at once a fact and an unrealized promise. The Internet is a vast web of words, images and sounds created by millions of people all around the globe, and thus certainly reflects a very diverse range of cultures and ideas. On the other hand, data show that there are not only vast inequalities of access to these new media, both within and between countries, but also deep disparities in amount and quality of information online depending upon language and relative cultural power. Put bluntly, the English language and Anglo-European cultures are vastly overrepresented on the Web (relative to population), rendering other languages and cultures severely underrepresented. This is turn means there are even greater disparities in terms of who *produces* most of the content in digital culture. That is, even much of the information about non-Anglo-European cultures on the Web has been produced and uploaded by Anglo-Europeans. This does not inherently invalidate the information, but insiders to a culture are generally far more sensitive to the nuance and specificity of their culture. These various inequalities involve both questions of *access* (who is online) and *representation* (what is online and how truly it reflects the diverse peoples and cultures of the world). There are in fact several different divides reflecting various aspects of a multifaceted set of deficits. These statistics are startling, but how much do they matter? Why should we care? How much do these disparities really matter? Are digital divides really that important?

⊞ WHO NEEDS THE INTERNET?

The gap between those who do and those who do not enjoy the benefits of digital communications technologies matters because every aspect of current social life—business, education, government, family life, social change movements—has been reshaped along digital lines. With more and more economic, political, social and cultural information available exclusively via the Net, the fact that billions do not have solid access to these resources is a major societal concern. This gap is most commonly referred to as the digital divide. But it is important to realize that the digital divide is not one thing, but many things. To begin with, there is not so much a divide as many divides, and within each divide there is a continuum from extremely high-level access to no access at all, with many gradations in between. Access itself is a very complicated phenomenon that goes far beyond hardware and software to the "wetware" (human culturally variable brains) that alone makes the system work.

Why does using new media to address economic social inequality matter so much? Recall these statistics from the introduction: 80 percent of people live in countries where the income gap is widening; the richest 20 percent of the population controls 75 percent of world wealth; 25,000 children die each day from poverty; only seven in 100 people have a college education; a billion people in the world are illiterate; one in five people on earth have no clean drinking water; four to five billion have no Internet access (*Statistic Brain* n.d.; *UNESCO Institute for Statistics* n.d.). Moreover, an analysis of long-term trends shows the distance between the richest and poorest countries has been growing almost exponentially. The wealth gap between richest and poorest countries was about 3 to 1 in 1820, 11 to 1 in 1913, 35 to 1 in 1950, 44 to 1 in 1973, 72 to 1 in 1992, and 107 to 1 in 2010. This trend is not socially sustainable. It can only lead to greater and greater strife.

At the turn of the twenty-first century, New York City had the highest concentration of fiber optic wired buildings on the planet, yet only one of these was in predominantly African American Harlem. Similarly, in high-tech Los Angeles, the Latino barrio of East LA had no wired buildings at all (Sassen 1999). Inequality in relation to digital culture has many different dimensions, and varies in terms of quality and intensity, not just pure access. The city of Tokyo, to take one example, has a greater density of Internet use than the entire continent of Africa. But in the (over)developed First World vast disparities exist among populations, based primarily on income and ethnicity. The most recent research in the US has identified inherited wealth, not income, as a more direct determinant of upward mobility, and gaps between whites and people of color are particularly stark in that category. Generational poverty due to systemic racism or ethnocentrism ensures that certain groups never accumulate enough wealth to pass on to the next generation. This means the problem of poverty will not go away without serious action to create more egalitarian conditions.

Ethno-racial disparities are compounded by another key dimension of the digital divide, the languages prevalent on the Net. The Internet was born in English, and the English language continues to have disproportionate overrepresentation in digital cultures worldwide. Japanese likewise, despite far fewer speakers, is overrepresented, while Chinese language content on the Web is nowhere near its percentage of native speakers worldwide. Ditto for Arabic speakers, Spanish speakers, and speakers of virtually all smaller linguistic communities.

Many of these disparities arise from governmental policies as shaped by corporate domination of decision makers. And here the issue isn't entirely based on overall national wealth. Susan Crawford, in her book *Captive Audience: The Telecom Industry and Monopoly in the New Gilded Age* (2013), notes that in the most prosperous country on earth, the US, consumers have fewer choices for broadband service, at higher prices and lower speeds, than in dozens of other countries, including most of Europe and parts of Asia. As one reviewer of Crawford's book noted,

> Reasonable people can and do disagree about policy solutions, but the facts are not in dispute. Americans have fewer choices for broadband Internet service than millions of other people in developed countries, yet we pay more for that inferior service. The reason for that, according to Crawford, is that US policy

makers have allowed a small number of highly profitable corporate giants to dominate the market, reducing competition and the incentives for these companies to improve service and lower prices.

(Gustin 2013)

This matters a good deal because in the twenty-first century those lacking broadband access face yet another digital divide as increasing amounts of Web content are available only to those with broadband. In the US, this has meant that certain previously declining numbers in terms of gaps between whites and ethnic/racial minorities have begun to rise again because of the greater cost of broadband access. This too is a reminder that technology changes can impact the nature of digital inequalities, sometimes improving things, sometimes setting trends moving backwards.

These and related facts about growing digital disparities led scholar Andrew Carver to argue that "The digital divide is *the* [human] rights issue of the 21st century." Why? Because the Internet is (potentially) the greatest educational invention since the printing press. Here are just some of the many areas where the Net can be immensely important: health education to areas without medical professionals; economic education to areas lacking economic knowledge and opportunity; political information to areas suffering severe ideological control and censorship; multimedia (visual and aural) information even to those lacking written literacy; multiple formats to match multiple learning styles and vast cultural variability, including broadly oral cultures, written cultures and visually oriented cultures. As a scholar deeply involved in studying digital divides, Mark Warschauer summarizes,

Whether in developed or developing countries, urban areas or rural, for economic purposes or sociopolitical ones, access to ICT is a necessary and key condition for overcoming social exclusion in the information society. It is certainly not the only condition that matters; good schools, decent government, and adequate health care are other critical factors for social inclusion. But ICT, if deployed well, can contribute toward improved education, government, and health care, too, and thus can be a multiplying factor for social inclusion.

(Warschauer 2003 30)

If not dealt with, lack of meaningful digital access will increase all forms of poverty (economic, social and informational) and deepen all forms of inequality. Despite the problems with and limitations of digital cultures discussed in previous chapters, by and large for most people, having significant access to online worlds is preferable to not having that access. So how do they get it?

⇨ FROM DIGITAL DIVIDES TO TECHNOLOGIES FOR SOCIAL INCLUSION

The concept of "the digital divide" came to prominence in the mid-1990s in the United States. The term has been widely criticized, and does have some misleading connotations, but it remains the most commonly used shorthand for the gaps between those who have access to digital technologies and those who do not. The term digital divide was first used by journalists, and then enthusiastically adopted by members of President Bill Clinton's administration. Under the leadership of then Vice-President Al Gore (no, he didn't really *invent* the Internet but he was an important force in increasing access to it), a series of initiatives and national report cards were put forth aimed at bridging the gap between those who did and those who did not have easy access to the Internet. The first of these report cards, "Falling through the Net: Defining the Digital Divide" (1999), largely set the parameters for use of the concept for a number of years. While immensely useful at first, the term rather quickly also became misleading in that it had defined the "divide" narrowly in terms of access to hardware, and suggested that there was but one such divide when there are in fact many kinds of divides.

While much of the work addressing the divide between the so-called digital "haves" and "have-nots" has focused on the important task of providing access to hardware, software and basic computer literacy, there is an additional issue—the cultural digital divide—that has received far too little attention. Research increasingly shows that one of the essential ways to attack digital inequalities is by addressing the fact that technologies are always created with in-built cultural biases that limit their use. This means that the divide will be lessened only when, in addition to providing basic access, we address seriously cultural differences and the differences in power that come with them. Significant lack of representation or misrepresentation of particular racial, ethnic and cultural groups in the media has long been shown to have profound negative psychological effects on the groups. In turn, this misrepresentation has strongly adverse implications for social justice and equitable social policy because of the broad consumption of these media by the general public and policy makers.

Progress in closing various digital divides needs to include improving the quality and quantity of diverse *cultural content* in new media like the web and video games. In turn, this will make those vital new media resources more effective in dealing with issues of economic, social and political inequalities. Most attempts to solve the problem of the digital divide have also used a shallow interpretation of technical literacy as simply learning computer programs, unaware that technological forms are culturally shaped and need to be reshaped to fit a wider variety of cultural styles and forms.

Mark Warschauer coined the term "technology for social inclusion" to describe this more proactive approach to new media than bemoaning digital divides, and he suggests that this changed perspective has three main aspects:

> The shift from a focus on a digital divide to social inclusion rests on three main premises: (1) that a new information economy and network society have emerged; (2) that ICT plays a critical role in all aspects of this new economy and society; and (3) better access to ICT, broadly defined, can help determine the difference between marginalization and inclusion in this new socioeconomic era.
>
> (Warschauer 2003)

A technology for inclusion perspective recognizes that multiple social variables create differing degrees of social power in relation to all things, including high technologies. Social inclusion refers to the extent that individuals, families and communities are able to fully participate in society and control their own destinies, with the goal of furthering equal access to economic resources, employment, health, education, housing, recreation, culture and civic engagement.

Below is a chart (Figure 9.1) mapping the various components that need to be considered in any technology for social inclusion analysis or project. Note that the arrows are meant to suggest that these various elements are not independent but rather interact with each other.

The process Warschauer's chart seeks to illustrate must address four levels or components that are key in the success or failure of a digital inclusion project: *physical resources* (the hardware needed to access the web), *digital resources* (culturally relevant content of interest to the full range of potential users), *human resources* (in terms of people competent to assist in helping users achieve techno-literacies of various kinds), and *social resources* (in the form of a supportive, culturally competent cohort of fellow users).

FIGURE 9.1 *Technology for social inclusion.* © *Mark Warschauer, reprinted with permission.*

Physical resources, the almost exclusive focus of many early digital divide projects, focus on getting the required hardware (desktops, laptops, smartphones, etc.) and software (operating systems, web browsers, word and image processing programs etc.). It goes without saying that not much can be done without these, but even deciding which kind of hardware and software is needed is not a culturally neutral issue. What particular kinds of hardware and software match the lifestyles of the users you hope to serve? Is mobility (as with smartphones and tablets) a high concern, or are more place-bound devices likely to be more useful. It might be a huge mistake to locate hardware in homes in a town that had a particularly lively community center where seeing one's neighbors using the Web could potentially create a snowballing effect of interesting other community members.

Digital resources form an area frequently overlooked in inclusion projects, often because the proponents are already so engaged with online life, so aware of its riches, that they forget others must be introduced to and convinced of the value of being online. While showing of some of the generic features of the Web like Wikipedia can be useful, what is really necessary is showing content of specific interest to the users for whom the project is being created, content directly addressing the age, ethnicity, gender, religion or other cultural features and values found among users. Obviously, this is even more important when dealing with a community where two or more different languages are spoken. Sometimes what will be needed is highly practical information about jobs or health care. At other times it may be something addressing particular cultural values like a religious site, and still other situations may call for something more recreational as the entry point to spur interest. But, again, this is not something easily determined by people with no deep knowledge of the community.

Human resources consist of people who can provide proper training in the techno-literacies needed to successfully access and explore online worlds. One of the best ways to do this is to encourage and provide technical training for people who have lived experience as members of underserved groups (in the US and globally). These culturally competent, technically savvy individuals can then work as facilitators for marginalized communities to empower them to represent themselves in digital media on their own cultural ground via their own cultural forms. When it is possible to find people from the community being served to do this work, this is the ideal. When that is not possible, then finding folks with the cultural competence to interact with the community in sensitive and effective ways is next best. Many projects have been ruined by "trainers," as opposed to "facilitators," who lacked the social skills, patience or flexibility to reach a range of community members.

Finally, *social resources* refers to model users and support networks to break through any reticence in the community. Communities "targeted" (already an ugly word) for digital inclusion projects are approached precisely because there seem to be too few members in the village, town or city that the project seeks to serve. But there are almost invariably some people in the community, or from similar communities, however few, who already have been convinced of the value of online access. These serve as ice-breakers demonstrating that "people like me" can use and gain value from access. In most cases, the more public this kind of work is the more quickly it will spiral out to many others. Again, this is why privatized projects in the home may sound good, but often lack this key level of social resources.

These four levels are obviously connected, and work at either reinforcing each other or at cross purposes. Only hard work on the ground can create the right mix of these various resources, but finding that mix is what will make the difference between a merely well-meaning and an actually successful project for digital social inclusion.

There are projects at work all over the world trying to bridge the many digital divides, but there are far too few of them, and even fewer of those address this full range of resources. If we wish to live in a more just, less conflict-ridden world, far greater efforts will have to be made to bring digital haves and have-nots closer to parity.

It is also important to realize that the nature of digital divides shifts significantly over time, and that the planned obsolescence of technologies requires a plan to not just start, but sustain access for communities and individuals. For example, at the same time that progress was being made in achieving basic access for many previously unconnected people in the 1990s and early twenty-first century, the Web was becoming more and more a broadcast medium like television. Increasing amounts of streaming video and other bandwidth-hogging content meant that large parts of the digital world could only be accessed with high-speed broadband. As a result, a new broadband divide developed in which, once again, the least affluent users became excluded from much Web content. On the more positive side, the largest impact in increasing access was certainly the invention of cellphones with Internet connections. This did not do much to narrow the broadband gap because, as anyone who compares access via cellphone with access by laptop or desktop will readily attest, even the best phones fall short in many ways, and access by phone does not match computer access in a variety of ways. Having cellphone access, while itself part of the broadband divide, has nevertheless been immensely important in increasing the economic, political and cultural information available to poor and low-income people around the globe (Horst and Miller 2006). But so far, the Web ledger is on the deficit side. To a large degree economic poverty has generated information poverty in those cut off from the Net, which has in turn deepened economic inequality (Monroe 2004; Mossberger 2003; Norris 2008; Zaremba 2006).

Of course, an even more basic question is where will the funding come to create these projects? One thing we know for certain about digital divides is that no single social entity will overcome them. A "free-market" approach alone, for example, will not work because the expansion of digital access is not always profitable initially to ITC corporations. Clearly the people who need the Internet the most— those seeking jobs, those in need of better health care, those seeking to overcome an inadequate education—are precisely those least likely to have the means, financial or informational, to access the required hardware, software and know-how to use the Net effectively. And because of their lack of wealth they are the least likely to be targeted by tech corporations. Sometimes ethnic stereotypes are used to excuse the digital gaps when it is suggested that racial minorities are somehow less interested in high tech than white folks. This assumption is demonstrably untrue. To take but one example, African Americans who have been amongst those stereotyped as lo tech or not tech savvy have been major innovators in music technology since the early hip-hop era, and were disproportionately early adopters of cellphones. Such prejudiced attempts to explain away digital divides are both ill informed and bad for business (Nelson, Tu and Headlam Hines 2001). And the business world does have a key role to play. Corporations with longer-range visions understand that diversity is a value in their workforce, and that the initial cost of bringing diverse folks currently out of the hi-tech universe in may pay off not just socially but financially down the line.

Governments too have a key role to play. Government support for inclusion projects has varied immensely across differing countries, and not always as a function of the relative wealth of the countries. It has more to do with understanding that digital inclusion can build community, can improve overall economic and physical health, and can lead to a more productive, less conflictive populace to the benefit of everyone. Unfortunately, most governments do not focus on the long range, and the benefits of social inclusion into digital worlds seldom have quick payoffs. But even governments can learn, and the best digital inclusion projects are showing these benefits.

The third level involves individual community members or community members collectively who have the resources and the vision to seek out inclusion for the rest of the members of their tribe, village, town or city neighborhood. In many ways, given their closeness, key locally based initiatives are the most likely to succeed. But they are also the least likely to have sufficient financial resources. So, as a general rule it will be partnerships involving local folks, government and/or relevant companies that will put together the best projects, often with the help of a rich force of local volunteer labor.

⊡ SHOULD EVERYONE AND EVERYTHING BE ONLINE?

Critics talk about not only digital "haves" and "have-nots," but also about digital "don't-wants". Clearly there can be very good reasons to avoid the online world, for a time, or altogether. Much of the work studying the "don't-wants" is based on the dubious assumption that everyone should want to be part of the digitizing world. I've suggested why that assumption makes sense given the vast amounts of vital information now available exclusively via the Web. But the digital world is a limited world. Not everything can be translated into 0s and 1s, or at least not everything should be. We can take as an example the form of analog music known as the vinyl record. Virtually everyone with a nuanced ear for music agrees that non-digital music such as found on records sounds different, different in ways that many people prefer. So too with all aspects of the analog world; there are things about it that are different in ways some will always prefer, and it is vital to keep those differences alive rather than lose them in a mad dash to digitize everything. That is the reason behind many "don't-wants," and that particular "don't-want" should be respected and nourished.

"We are in great haste to construct a magnetic telegraph from Maine to Texas," the poet/philosopher Thoreau (1982) observed 200 years ago, "but Maine and Texas, it may be, have nothing important to communicate. . . . We are eager to tunnel under the Atlantic . . . but perchance the first news that will leak through the broad, flapping American ear will be that the Princess Adelaide has the whooping cough." Substitute "Twitter" for the telegraph, and ask whether we really need to know where our favorite celebrity had dinner last night, and you'll see that Thoreau's question remains relevant. Let's face it, humans invented the greatest communication mechanism since language, including the greatest library of all human knowledge, and then filled it up with piano-playing cats, talking dogs, pornography, stupid human tricks, insane conspiracy theories, and every kind of trivia imaginable. If the Net is partly a mirror held up to humanity, what is reflected there is often appalling. Sometimes it seems, as Thoreau wondered, that we have in fact "nothing important to communicate" across the tubes.

A character (with the same name as the author) in *Galatea 2.2*, a novel by contemporary writer Richard Powers offers something approaching a technological update of Thoreau's concern:

> The web was a neighborhood more efficiently lonely than the one it replaced. Its solitude was bigger and faster. When relentless intelligence finally completed its program, when the terminal dropbox brought the last barefoot, abused child online and anyone could at last say anything instantly to everyone else in existence, it seemed to me we'd still have nothing to say to each other and more ways not to say it.

(2004 14)

So, one good reason to not be online might be to avoid the vast amounts of non-sense and digitized loneliness often found there. On the other hand, as another great writer, Theodore Sturgeon, observed about his preferred literary genre, "True, 90% of science fiction is crap, but then 90% of everything is crap." The exact proportion of crap to value on the Web is beyond anyone's calculation, but Sturgeon's law is about as good a guess as any. And his point is that finding the 10 percent of truly valuable stuff in life is the necessary task any serious person needs to undertake, whether online or off.

There are also deeper reasons than the high non-sense content for keeping some things offline. While the slogan "information wants to be free" is a catchy one that has served advocates of an open Web well, it doesn't fit every situation, or everyone's cultural values. The long history of cultural theft by dominant cultures has made many on the margins of such cultures wary of claims that all culture should be shared. While the powerful in the Global North, and dominant cultures in the Global South, seem to be taking in the rest of the world's cultures in giant gulps, these same forces often fight like mad to protect what they call *intellectual property rights*. Such rights have cultural bias built right into them, since not all cultures believe things like ideas and art can be owned by individuals. But beyond that, intellectual property rights have failed to protect such things as the medical knowledge of indigenous communities, or to protect other forms of collectively held traditional knowledge.

Against both exploitative corporations and well-meaning cyber-libertarians, some, particularly in Native or indigenous communities, seek a more nuanced understanding of and control over communally based knowledges. In many cases, this has meant keeping information away from the digital world. In some other instances, this includes using innovative digital forms themselves to protect rather than project cultural knowledge. One of the most interesting of these efforts is the Mukurtu Project (Christen and the Warumungu people n.d.). Mukurtu began as a collaboration between anthropologist Kimberly Christen and the Warumungu Aboriginal community of Central Australia. While Christen was doing ethnographic research on the community, they became interested in the technological devices she brought with her. Eventually, they asked her to find a way to digitally archive some of their cultural knowledge and cultural artifacts. Out of this came the idea of creating software for a digital archive that would allow communities to provide but limit access to cultural materials based on their specific traditional protocols. In other words, some knowledge would be available only to elders, some only to post-pubescent girls, and so forth. In this way cultural preservation could be done in a way that is consistent with long-held community values. Based upon this highly successful model, Christen and her associates created and have made freely available world-wide a Content Management System (CMS) with which any community can preserve and protect its cultural heritage. The goal, as they state it, is to "empower communities to manage, share and exchange their digital heritage in culturally relevant and ethically minded ways" (Christen and the Warumungu people n.d.). Key here is the understanding that not all information needs to be free to all people, that communities have a right to restrict as well as disseminate the knowledge specific to their history. This process also makes clear that not all members of the community necessarily want access to their particular knowledge in digital form, and that too is fine.

The Mukurtu Project is part of a wider movement in participatory design as well ("Participatory Design" n.d.). The central principle of participatory design in the technological world is that the people who will actually be using a given device, program, application or platform should have a say from the early stages in the design of technologies. What that means in practical terms is that designers need to either reflect personally, or develop deep cultural competencies in, the range of cultural groups who will use the devices, apps, etc. This seemingly simple principle has long been the exception rather than the rule in the development of new media. Instead, until fairly recently, the default subject position of the white middle-class male technician has been the sole angle of vision from which most technological innovation has emerged. The fantastic success of many of these products for a time disguised the fact that they also had major cultural limitations. Slowly that is changing.

Many in the electronics industry have realized that diversity is not just an ethical value, but a business necessity. There are currently more anthropologists and sociologists working for Microsoft and Google than in any university in the world. And many electronics firms are actively seeking out employees from the full range of ethnicities, genders and cultural locations. Whether this leads to more commodification of cultural difference or greater representation of marginalized groups and individuals remains to be seen. Unfortunately, the social conditions that gave birth to the limited cultural knowledge base in the industry have not disappeared, and are not easily erased by corporate affirmative actions. Deep-seated bias in economic, social and cultural structures means that the number of marginalized group members in a position to take advantage of certain opportunities to enrich the diversity of the world of techno-creators remains limited. Without both specific changes in digital access policies along with broader social change, the world of digital creators, as with digital users, is likely to continue to reflect and exacerbate existing social inequalities.

➔ WHY DIGITIZING MATTERS

Why does digital inclusion matter so much? Digital technologies and the nearly instantaneous transnational communication links they enable have been almost universally cited as a key factor in the economic, political and cultural processes that make up contemporary "globalization." Just as the effects of globalization in general have varied greatly, especially between the elites of the Global North who have benefitted immensely from economic globalization, and the peoples of the Global South who, apart from a few elites of their own, have suffered new forms of domination under the guise of globalization, so too has the spread of digital empowerment been deeply uneven. Those suffering under globalization, however, have hardly suffered in silence. Many have used the same tools of digitized communication to create a worldwide Global Justice Movement that has created unprecedented solidarity across national borders. Nevertheless, most information exchanged across the Web is exchanged only among those in the Global North, principally the US, Canada, Japan and Europe, a fact that suggests cultural imperialism, intended or not, is alive and well.

When misused, the concept of the digital divide can perpetuate a very limited image of Global North development versus Global South underdevelopment, of a provider group and a needy group. This insinuates the hegemonic idea of Western modernization as the only reasonable course, and does little to take into consideration the actual conditions and desires of those who currently are not part of the digitized world. A one-way model of giving access needs to be replaced by a much more interactive set of relations in order to truly understand needs, desires, power imbalances and cultural differences that underlie the data presented as a digital divide (Potter 2006). The immense potential benefits of new digital media will be realized fully only when those of us with greater privilege take some responsibility for the devastating economic, social and, consequently, digital divides. This is not about assigning blame to individuals born into particular privileged races, genders, countries or classes. It is about a need for widespread structural changes, particularly in the economic realm, that can only be brought about through collective, political action. How can new media technology be made more useful to the billions of people facing economic inequality, discrimination and cultural misrepresentation? We need to ask this question because the majority of the world's people due to historic injustices and the accidents of birth are on the deficit side of the economic and digital divide, and because, as Martin Luther King (1963) noted, "Injustice anywhere is a threat to justice everywhere."

Conclusion
Hype, Hope and Possible Digitized Futures

> Technology is not going to save the world. We are, and we can use technology to help us.
>
> (Aleph Molinari, "Bridging the Digital Divide with Learning and Innovation Networks," 2012)

If you expect this chapter to tell you about all the exciting technical devices of the future that are going to change our lives for the better, you have not been paying attention. Yes, I will mention a couple of emerging digitized technologies that present some exciting possibilities, but as I have been arguing throughout this book, which new technologies get developed, which become widely used, and *how* they get used (to better our lives or make them worse) will be up to us, not to the technologies.

One thing that is easy to predict is that our relationship to digital technologies will become increasingly pervasive (if not invasive), increasingly intimate. By intimate I mean especially to suggest that those with access will become increasingly cyborg-like in respect to digital devices and processes. Wearable computers are already widespread, with the commercial interest in Google Glass perhaps marking a newly popular awareness of this phenomenon. This development will continue, and more and more digital devices will move beyond domestication to embodiment, to feeling like they are part of us.

This sense of embodiment will deepen even further with the increasing use of implanted digital devices, and the infusion of nanotechnologies into our bodies for medical and monitoring purposes (*Nanotechnology in Medicine* n.d.). Nanotechnologies, devised at a scale visible only under a microscope, will be injected into our bodies to repair it, or to map it at a level of specificity that puts our current imagining technologies (MRIs, CT scans) to shame. This too will change cultural mores with regard to our digital technologies. Increasingly, we will experience them as life saving and life enhancing in as yet unimaginable ways. While for the most part immensely positive, these developments may also lull us into uncritically accepting more dubious digitally derived medical experimentation, and will certainly raise a vast new set of concerns represented by what might be called neo-eugenics—our increasing abilities to design and redesign human beings.

As renowned computer scientist Mark Weiser once noted, "The most profound technologies are those that disappear. They weave themselves into the everyday fabric of life until they are indistinguishable from it" (1993). Throughout history, once seemingly bizarre or awkwardly new technologies have come to feel natural, to feel like a part of us. Disappearing into the fabric of life is the next step beyond the domestication of technology, and we would be well served to keep our critical intellects honed and questioning as this taken-for-granted quality begins more and more to settle in. We need to continue to think carefully about which technologies we should (not just *can*) weave into the everyday fabrics of our lives, and which technologies we need to abandon, avoid or substantially alter.

Virtual reality devices will also become increasingly affordable and sophisticated. They will once again cause us to rethink the relation of computer-generated realities to the realities generated by our own sensorium confronting the world outside of digital devices. What kind of virtual realities will we create and what will they be used for? Will they be used, for example, to help us more profoundly inhabit the experiences of someone different from ourselves, or allow us to more realistically obliterate people whose difference from us is always portrayed as a threat? Can we create virtual spaces that can help us avoid the human misunderstandings that lead to traumatic violence, or only continue to use such devices to deal with post-traumatic stress disorders arising from such misunderstandings?

Another area where major breakthroughs will occur is the area of Artificial Intelligence. There has long been a desire to create *true* Artificial Intelligence, by which computer scientists mostly mean computers that think and act just like people. Why? Why make AIs that are just like people? We already have people, lots of them; arguably too many of them. Why not make AIs that are distinctly different from people in their cognitive functioning? That position, associated especially with Thomas S. Ray (n.d.), makes far more sense and would avoid much of the philosophical and moral morass

FIGURE 10.1 *Google Glass. (Courtesy: Koby Dagan/Shutterstock.com.)*

surrounding attempts to closely replicate human thought, emotion and self-reflection. For all the advances in neuroscience and consciousness studies, understanding of the human mind is still in its infancy. It is pure hubris to think we have fathomed the vast array of human intelligences, and thus great folly to think we can artificially replicate any yet alone all such forms of consciousness.

We will also need to think about the extent to which the corporate monopolization of technologies could profoundly shift the economic and environmental balance in ways that will deeply impact all aspects of culture. Recall that electric cars and solar energy devices that might well have staved off global climate change were delayed in development for decades by the stranglehold the oil industry had on governments around the globe. In the near future, technologies like open-source 3D printing devices, which could radically lessen the cost of creating thousands of necessary products and radically decentralize economies, with immensely positive consequences for millions of people, will be fought tooth and nail by corporations with a vested interest in the status quo. Decentralized energy production that will be made more viable by new technologies likewise threatens energy monopolies. New technologies can be used to create far more democratic societies, with far greater equity and independence, but they will do so only if the right kinds of political decisions are made.

Anyone who tells you they know for certain what the future of new media technologies will be is full of shtml. Not because they mean to mislead, but because the *future is in your hands* as surely as this book is at this moment. (If you are reading this as an e-book leaning on your desk or on a monitor in your lap, this is still just as true.) Technologies will remake us as we make and remake technologies, but we, by virtue of consciousness and self-consciousness, have the edge in those processes, and with that advantage comes great responsibility.

Hopefully, something in this book will have provoked you to play your part in making the next wave of decisions about existing and future technologies more wisely. The bigger question is, in what kind of world will these technologies exist? Here perhaps science fiction imagery is needed to complement the social science statistics on economic and social inequality cited in the previous chapters. We need to ask ourselves if we wish to live in a world like that portrayed in films like "Hunger Games," "Elysium," or "Cloud Atlas," a world where a tiny elite lives in luxury while the rest of humanity is locked in devastated urban wastelands. Or, if we wish to use our human intelligence and astounding technology to make the world a place where all beings, human and otherwise, can thrive.

Bibliography

A more comprehensive bibliography is available on the companion website at: culturalpolitics.net/digital_culture/bibliography

Able Gamers. Website. (n.d.). <ablegamers.com>.

"A Brief History of the Internet." *Internet Society.* (n.d.). <www.internetsociety. org/internet/what-internet/history-internet/brief-history-internet>.

American Academy of Arts and Sciences. "The Heart of the Matter." Vimeo (2013). <http://vimeo.com/68662447>.

Andrews, Lori. *I Know Who You Are and I Know What You Did: Social Networks and the Death of Privacy.* NY: The Free Press, 2012.

——. "Internet Privacy Rights Constitution." (n.d.). <www.kentlaw.iit. edu/faculty/full-time-faculty/lori-b-andrews>.

Aarseth, Espen, Solveig Marie Smedstad, and Lise Sunnan, "A Multidimensional Typology of Games." Paper published by the Digital Games Research Association (2003). <www.sts.rpi.edu/public_html/ ruiz/EGDFall07/readings/new%20topology%20of%20games%20 A.%20Arsneth.pdf>.

Anonymous. Website. (n.d.). <www.anonyops.com> [NB: There is no such thing as an official Anonymous website; this one does provide a good deal of information, however.]

"Anthem." MCI WorldCom. TV commercial, 1997. <www.youtube.com/ watch?v=ioVMoeCbrig>.

Ascharya, Kat. "A Slow Tech Revolution." *Mobiledia* (July 19, 2012). <www.mobiledia.com/news/156804.html>.

Au, Wagner James. *The Making of Second Life.* NY: Harpers Business, 2008.

Banerjee, Subhanker, ed. *Arctic Voices: Resistance at the Tipping Point.* NY: Seven Stories Press, 2012.

Barak, Azy. "Sexual Harassment on the Internet." *Social Science Computer Review* 23.1 (2005): 77–92.

Bateson, Gregory. "A Theory of Play and Fantasy," in Jerome Bruner, Alison Jolly and Kathy Sylva, eds., *Play: Its Role in Development and Evolution.* NY: Penguin Books, 1976 (pp. 119–129).

Bavelier, Daphne. "Your Brain on Video Games." *TED talks* (November 2012). <www.ted.com/talks/daphne_bavelier_your_brain_on_video_ games.html>.

Berners-Lee, Tim. *Weaving the Web.* Phoenix, AZ: Orion, 1999.

Bieler, John. "Mapping Protest Data." Web post. (n.d.) <http://johnbeieler. org/blog/2013/07/03/mapping-protest-data/>.

Blum, Andrew. *Tubes: A Journey to the Center of the Internet.* NY: Ecco Press, 2013.

Boler, Megan, with Andrea Schmidt, Natalie Magnan and Alessandra Renzi, eds. *Digital Media and Democracy: Tactics in Hard Times.* Cambridge, MA: MIT Press, 2010.

Border Haunt. Website. (n.d.). <www.ianalanpaul.com/borderhaunt-201/>.

Boyd, Dana. "White Flight in Networked Publics: How Race and Class Shaped Teen Engagement with MySpace and Facebook," in Lisa Nakamura and Peter A. Chow-White, eds., *Race after the Internet.* NY: Routledge, 2012 (pp. 203–222).

Boyd, Dana, and Eszter Harigittai. "Facebook Privacy Settings: Who Cares"? *First Monday* 15.8 (August 2, 2010). < http://firstmonday.org/article/view/3086/2589>.

Calleja, Gordon. "Revising Immersion." (n.d.). <http://lmc.gatech. edu/~cpearce3/DiGRA07/Proceedings/011.pdf>.

Carr, Nicholas, "Avatars Consume as Much Electricity as Brazilians," *Rough Type* (December 5, 2006). <www.roughtype.com/?p=611>.

——. *The Shallows: What the Internet is Doing to Our Brains.* NY: Norton, 2010.

Castells, Manuel. *The Rise of the Network Society. Volume 1.* Malden, MA: Blackwell Press, 2000 (2nd edition).

Castronova, Edward. *Exodus to the Virtual World: How Online Fun is Changing Reality.* NY: Palgrave McMillan, 2008.

Catfish Pictures and MTV, prods. "Catfish: The TV Show." 2012+.

Center for History and New Media. Website. (n.d.). <http://chnm.gmu.edu>.

Chambers, Tod. "Virtual Disability: On the Internet No One Knows You Are a Sick Puppy," in Lester D. Friedman, ed., *Cultural Sutures: Medicine and Media.* Durham, NC: Duke University Press, 2004 (pp. 386–398).

Chan, Dean. "Playing with Race: The Ethics of Racialized Representation in E-Games." *International Review of Information Ethics* 4 (December 2005). <www.i-r-i-e.net/inhalt/004/chan.pdf>.

China Watch. "Apple's Supplier Pegatron Group Violates Workers' Rights." (2013). <www.chinalaborwatch.org/news/new-459.html>.

Chow-White, Peter A. "Genetic Databases and an Emerging Digital Divide in Biotechnology," in Lisa Nakamura and Peter Chow-White, eds., *Race after the Internet.* NY: Routledge, 2012 (pp. 29–309).

Christen, Kimberly, and the Warumungu people. *Mukurtu Project.* Website. (n.d.). <www.mukurtu.org>.

Christensen, Neil. *Inuit in Cyberspace: Embedding Offline Identities Online.* Copenhagen, DK: Museum Tusculanum Press, 2003.

Coleman, Stephen, and Jay G. Blumler. *The Internet and Democratic Citizenship: Theory, Practice and Policy.* London and Cambridge: Cambridge University Press, 2009.

Coming Home. Website. (n.d.). <http://projects.ict.usc.edu/force/coming home/>.

Connolly, Thomas M., Elizabeth A. Boyle, Ewan MacArthur, Thomas Hainey and James M. Boyle. "A Systematic Literature Review of Empirical Evidence on Computer Games and Serious Games." *Computers and Education* 59.3 (2012): 661–686 <www.sciencedirect.com/science/article/pii/S0360131512000619>.

Corneliussen, Hilde, and Jill Walker Rettberg, eds. *Digital Culture, Play, and Identity: A World of Warcraft® Reader.* Cambridge, MA: MIT Press, 2008.

Couldry, Nick, and Angela McRobbie. "The Death of the University, English Style." *Interzone* (November 2010): 1–3. <www.culturemachine.net>.

Coupland, Douglas. *Microserfs.* NY: Harper Collins, 1995.

Crawford, Susan. *Captive Audience: The Telecom Industry and Monopoly in the New Gilded Age.* New Haven: Yale University Press, 2013.

"Cyber/Bullying Statistics." *Statistic Brain* (May 7, 2013). <www.statisticbrain.com/cyber-bullying-statistics/>.

Cyberbullying Resource Center. Website. (n.d.). <www.cyberbullying.us/cyberbullying_identification_prevention_response.php>.

"Cyber Sexual Harassment Statistics." *American Psychological Association* (August 2012). <www.apa.org/news/press/releases/2011/08/cyberworld.aspx American Psychological Association citing US Dept of Justice>.

Cybracero. Website. (n.d.). <Cybracero.org>.

Damasio, Antonio. *Self Comes to Mind: Constructing the Conscious Brain.* NY: Pantheon, 2010.

Danet, Brenda. "Text as Mask: Gender, Play and Performance on the Internet," in Steven G. Jones, ed., *Cybersociety 2.0.* Thousand Oaks, CA: Sage, 1998 (pp. 129–158).

Daniels, Jessie. *Cyber Racism: White Supremacy Online and the New Attack on Civil Rights.* Lanham, MD: Rowman & Littlefield, 2009.

Davis, Sheila, and Ted Smith. "Corporate Strategies for Electronics Recycling: A Story of Two Systems." *Silicon Valley Toxics Coalition* (June 25, 2003). <http://svtc.org/wp-content/uploads/prison_final.pdf>.

Deleuze, Gilles, and Felix Guattari. *A Thousand Plateaus: Capitalism and Schizophrenia.* Trans. Brian Massumi. Minneapolis: University of Minnesota Press, 2007.

Digital Humanities Now. Website. (n.d.).<http://digitalhumanitiesnow.org>.

Digital Meets Culture: The Art of Video Games. Exhibit. Smithsonian Institution (n.d.). <www.digitalmeetsculture.net/article/the-art-of-video-games-smithsonian/>.

Digital Sabbath. Website. (n.d.). <www.sabbathmanifesto.org/unplug>.

Dill, Karen E., Brian P. Brown and Michael A. Collins. "Effects of Exposure to Sex-stereotyped Video Game Characters on Tolerance of Sexual Harassment." *Journal of Experimental Social Psychology* 44.5 (2008): 1402–1408.

"DOCCs." *FemTechNet.* (n.d.) <http://femtechnet.newschool.edu/docc2013/>.

Doctorow, Cory. *Context.* San Francisco: Tachyon, 2011.

Drahos, Peter, and John Braithwaite. *Information Feudalism: Who Owns the Knowledge Economy.* NY: Earthscan/Routledge, 2002.

"Droid." TV commercial. (n.d.). <www.youtube.com/watch?v=U8K83gR7 Qmc&feature=related>.

Drummond, Katie. "Pentagon's Brain-Powered Videogame Might Treat PTSD." *Wired* (July 2012). <www.wired.com/dangerroom/2012/07/neurofeedback/>.

Duster, Troy. "Lessons from History: Why Race and Ethnicity Have Played a Major Role in Biomedical Research." *Journal of Law, Medicine & Ethics* 34.3 (Fall 2006): 2–11.

Dyer-Witheford, Nick, and Greig de Peuter. *Games of Empire: Global Capitalism and Video Games.* Minneapolis: University of Minnesota Press, 2009.

Earl, Jennifer, and Katrina Kimport. *Digitally Enabled Social Change: Activism in the Internet Age.* Cambridge, MA: MIT Press, 2011.

Edwards, Paul N. *The Closed World: Computers and the Politics of Discourse in Cold War America.* Cambridge, MA: MIT Press, 1996.

End Violence Against Women Project (United Nations). Website. (n.d.). <www. un.org/en/women/endviolence/>.

Escobar, Arturo. "Welcome to Cyberia: Notes on the Anthropology of Cyberculture," in Ziauddin Sardar and Jerome R. Ravetz, eds., *Cyberfutures: Culture and Politics on the Information Superhighway.* NY: New York University Press, 1996 (pp. 111–137).

"Essential Facts about the Computer and Video Game Industry" *Entertainment Software Association.* (2013). <www.theesa.com/facts/pdfs/ESA_EF_2013.pdf>.

Everett, Anna. "The Revolution Will Be Digitized: Afrocentricity and the Digital Public Sphere." *Social Text* 20.2 (2002): 125–146.

——, ed. *Learning Race and Ethnicity: Youth and Digital Media.* Cambridge, MA:. MIT, 2007. <http://mitpress.mit.edu/sites/default/files/titles/free_download/9780262550673_Learning_Race_and_Ethnicity.pdf>.

——. *Digital Diaspora: A Race for Cyberspace.* Albany, NY: SUNY Press, 2009.

——. "Have We Become Postracial Yet? Race and Media Technology in the Age of Obama," in Lisa Nakamura and Peter Chow-White, eds., *Race after the Internet.* NY: Routledge, 2012 (pp. 146–167).

——, and John Caldwell. *New Media: Theories and Practices of Digitextuality.* NY and London: Routledge, 2003.

Everyday Sexism Project. Website. (n.d.). <www.everydaysexism.com>.

"Fat, Ugly, or Slutty." *Fat, Ugly or Slutty* blog post. (n.d.). <http://fatuglyorslutty.com/>.

Farman, Jason. *Mobile Interface Theory: Embodied Space and Locative Media.* NY: Routledge, 2011.

Fascendini, Flavia, and Katerina Fialova. "Voices from Digital Spaces: Technology-related Violence against Women" (December 2011). *Association for Progressive Communications.* <www.apc.org/en/system/files/APCWNSP_MDG3advocacypaper_full_2011_EN_0.pdf>.

"February 15, 2003 Anti-War Protest." *Wikipedia.* (n.d.) <http://en.wikipedia.org/wiki/February_15,_2003_anti-war_protest>.

Ferguson, Christopher J. "Blazing Angels or Resident Evil? Can Violent Video Games Be a Force for Good?" *Review of General Psychology* 14.2 (2010): 68–81. <www.apa.org/pubs/journals/releases/gpr-14–2-68.pdf>.

Fischer, Claude. *America Calling: A Social History of the Telephone to 1940.* Berkeley: University of California Press, 1992.

Fuchs, Christian. *Internet and Society: Social Theory in the Information Age.* NY: Routledge, 2008.

Gabry, Jennifer. *Digital Rubbish: A Natural History of Electronics.* Ann Arbor: University of Michigan Press, 2011.

GAMBIT: Hate Speech Project. Website. (n.d.). <http://gambit.mit.edu/projects/hatespeech.php>.

Gamers Against Bigotry. Website. (n.d.). <http://gamersagainstbigotry.org>.

Games for Change. Website. (n.d.). <www.gamesforchange.org>.

Gardening Superfund Sites. Website. (n.d.). <www.futurefarmers.com/superfund>.

Gardiner, Beth. "Charting the Impact of Everyday Sexism across the World." *New York Times* (May 31, 2013). <http://global.nytimes.com/2013/06/01/world/europe/charting-the-impact-of-everyday-sexism-across-the-world.html?pagewanted=all>.

Geere, Duncan. "Sukey Apps Help Protesters Avoid Police Kettles." *Wired* (January 31, 2011). <www.wired.co.uk/news/archive/2011–01/31/sukey-protest-app>.

Gellman, Barton. "NSA Broke Privacy Rules Thousands of Times Per Year, Audit Finds." *Washington Post* (August 15, 2013). <www.washingtonpost.com/world/national-security/nsa-broke-privacy-rules-thousands-of-times-per-year-audit-finds/2013/08/15/3310e554–05ca-11e3-a07f-49ddc7417125_story.html>.

Gender Equality Evaluation Portal (United Nations). Website. (n.d.). <http://genderevaluation.unwomen.org/Reports/Default.aspx>.

Gentrification: The Game. Website. (n.d.). <www.atmosphereindustries.com/gentrification/>.

Gentzkow, Matthew, and Jesse M. Shapiro. "Ideological Segregation Online and Offline." *Quarterly Journal of Economics* 126.4 (2011): 1799–1839.

Gerbaudo, Paolo. *Tweets and the Streets: Social Media and Contemporary Activism.* London: Pluto Press, 2012.

Gibson, William. *Neuromancer.* NY: Ace Books, 1994.

Gitelman, Lisa. *Always Already New: Media, History, and the Data of Culture.* Cambridge, MA: MIT Press, 2006.

Gladwell, Malcolm. "Small Change: Why the Revolution Will Not Be Tweeted." *New Yorker*, (October 14, 2010). <www.newyorker.com/reporting/2010/10/04/101004fa_fact_gladwell>.

Goggin, Gerard, and Christopher Newell. *Digital Disability: The Social Construction of Disability in New Media.* Lanham, MD: Rowman and Littlefield Publishers, Inc., 2003.

Goldman, Eric. "Lara Croft's Animated Origins." *IGN*, (July 11, 2007). <http://ca.ign.com/articles/2007/07/11/ign-exclusive-lara-crofts-animated-origins>.

Google. Data Centers Gallery. Website. (n.d.). <www.google.com/about/datacenters/gallery/#/>.

Gordon-Levitt, Joseph, dir. "Don Jon." Film, 2012.

Gould, Stephen Jay. *The Mismeasure of Man.* NY: Norton, 1981.

Gray, Chris Hables. *Cyborg Citizen.* NY: Routledge, 2002.

——. *Peace, War and Computers.* NY: Routledge, 2004.

——, with Heidi Figueroa-Sarriera, and Steven Mentor, eds. *The Cyborg Handbook.* NY: Routledge, 1995.

Green Grid, The. Website. (n.d.). <www.thegreengrid.org/Home/about-the-green-grid/TGGCSCI.aspx>.

Gross, Doug. "Lessons from the Sorority Girl E-mail Rant." *CNN Tech Online* (April 25, 2013).

Grossman, Elizabeth. *High Tech Trash: Digital Devices, Hidden Toxins, and Human Health.* Oncan, UK: Shearwater, 2007.

Gustin, Sam. "Is Broadband Internet Access a Public Utility?" *Time Magazine online* (January 1, 2013). <http://business.time.com/2013/01/09/is-broadband-internet-access-a-public-utility/#ixzz2K9Smb0u0>.

Gutierrez, David. "Cyberstalking more Traumatic than Physical Stalking, Study Finds." *Natural News* (February 19, 2013). <www.naturalnews.com/039148_cyberstalking_fear_trauma.html>.

Hald, Gert Martin, N. N. Malamuth and T. Lange. "Pornography and Sexist Attitudes among Heterosexuals." *Journal of Communication* 63.4 (2013). <http://onlinelibrary.wiley.com/doi/10.1111/jcom.12037/abstract;jsessionid=1350509F6DA33449730EB1BC04DA97C1.f04t01?deniedAccessCustomisedMessage=&userIsAuthenticated=false>.

Hall-Stigerts, Lauren. "Body Image in Tomb Raider: Lara Croft's Changing Look." *Big Fish* (April 22, 2013). <www.bigfishgames.com/blog/tomb-raider-body-image-lara-crofts-changing-look/>.

Halter, Ed. *From Sun Tzu to X-Box: War and Video Games.* NY: Public Affairs, 2006.

Hands, Joss. *@ Is for Activism: Dissent, Resistance and Rebellion in a Digital Culture.* London: Pluto Press, 2011.

Haraway, Donna. "Situated Knowledges: The Science Question in Feminism and the Privilege of Partial Perspective." *Feminist Studies* 14.3 (1988): 575–599.

——. "The Actors are Cyborg, Nature is Coyote, and the Geography is Elsewhere." Postscript to "Cyborgs at Large," in Constance Penley and Andrew Ross, eds., *Technoculture.* Minneapolis: University of Minnesota Press, 1991 (pp. 21–26).

——. *Modest_Witness@Second_Millenium.Female_Man©_Meets Oncomouse™: Feminism and Technoscience.* NY: Routledge, 1997.

——. "A Manifesto for Cyborgs," [1984] in *The Haraway Reader.* NY: Routledge, 2003 (pp. 7–46).

HarassMap. Website. (n.d.). <Harassmap.org/en>.

Hargittai, Eszter. "Open Doors, Closed Spaces? Differential Adoption of Social Network Sites by User Background," in Lisa Nakamura and Peter A. Chow-White, eds., *Race after the Internet*. NY: Routledge, 2012 (pp. 223–245).

Harnad, Stevan. "Post-Gutenberg Galaxy: The Fourth Revolution in the Means of Production and Knowledge." *Public-Access Computer Systems Review*, 2 (1991): 39–53.

Harry Potter Alliance. Website. (n.d.). <http://thehpalliance.org/what-we-do/>.

HASTAC (Humanities, Arts, Science and Technology Alliance and Collaborative). Website. (n.d.). <www.hastac.org>.

Hayles, N. Katherine. *How We Became Posthuman: Virtual Bodies in Cybernetics, Literature, and Informatics*. Chicago: University of Chicago Press, 1999.

Hesse-Biber, Charlene Nagy. *The Handbook of Emergent Technologies in Social Research*. London and Oxford: Oxford University Press, 2011.

Hillis, Ken, Michael Petit and Kylie Jarrett. *Google and the Culture of Search*. London and NY: Taylor and Francis, 2013.

Hilty, Lorenz. *Information Technology and Sustainabilty*. Norderstedt: Books on Demand, 2008.

Hollaback! Website. (n.d.). <www.ihollaback.org>.

Holt, Robert Lee. "When Gaming is Good for You: Hours of Intense Play Change the Adult Brain; Better Multitasking, Decision-Making and Even Creativity." *Wall Street Journal* (March 13, 2012). <http://online.wsj.com/article/SB10001424052970203458604577263273943183932.html?mod=wsj_share_tweet>.

Horst, Heather A., and Daniel Miller. *The Cell Phone: An Anthropology of Communication*. Oxford, UK: Berg, 2006.

Huizinga, Johan. *Homo Ludens*. Boston: Beacon Press, 1971.

I Am Bradley Manning. Website. (n.d.). <Iambradleymanning.org>.

Indy Media. Website. (n.d.). <https://publish.indymedia.org/or/index.shtml>.

Internet World Stats. Website. (n.d.). <www.internetworldstats.com/stats.htm>.

Ito, Mizuko, Heather A. Horst, Matteo Bittanti, Danah Boyd, Becky Herr Stephenson, Patricia G. Lange, C. J. Pascoe and Laura Robinson. *Living and Learning with New Media*. Pew/MacArthur Foundation Report (November 2008). <http://mitpress.mit.edu/books/living-and-learning-new-media>.

Jarrett, Kylie. "Interactivity is Evil! A Critical Investigation of Web 2.0." *First Monday* 13.3 (March 3, 2008). <http://firstmonday.org/ojs/index.php/fm/article/view/2140/1947>.

Jenkins, David. "Interview with Toby Gard." *Gamasutra* (October 23, 1998). <www.gamasutra.com/view/feature/3292/interview_with_toby_gard.php>.

Jenkins, Henry. *Convergence Culture: Where Old and New Media Collide*. NY: New York University Press, 2008 (revised edition).

Joost, Harry and Ariel Schulman, dirs. "Catfish: The Movie." Film, Rogue Pictures, 2010.

Jordan, Chris. Intolerable Beauty. Photographic art. <www.chrisjordan. com/gallery/intolerable/#cellphones2>.

Joyce, Mary, ed. *Digital Activism Decoded: The New Mechanics of Change.* NY: International Debate Education Association, 2010. <www.cl.cam. ac.uk/~sjm217/papers/digiact10all.pdf>.

Jurgenson, Nathan. "The IRL Fetish." *The New Inquiry* (June 28, 2012). <http://thenewinquiry.com/essays/the-irl-fetish/>.

Juris, Jeff. *Networking Futures.* Durham, NC: Duke University Press, 2008.

Khaled, Rilla. "Overview of PTSD-Related Digital Games and Research." *Games for Health* (June 2011). <http://gamesforhealth.dk/sites/ gamesforhealth.dk/files/PTSD%20overview%20(2).pdf>.

Karaganis, Joe, ed. *Structures of Participation in Digital Culture.* NY: Social Science Research Council, 2007.

Kee, Jac S. M. "Cultivating Violence through Technology? Exploring the Connections between Internet Communication Technologies (ICT) and Violence Against Women (VAW)." *GenderIT* (April 16, 2005). <www. genderit.org/content/cultivating-violence-through-technology-exploring-connections-between-internet-communication>.

Kember, Sarah, and Joanna Zylinska. *Life after New Media: Mediation as a Vital Process.* Cambridge, MA: MIT Press, 2012.

Kennedy, Helen W. "Lara Croft: Feminist Icon or Cyberbimbo?" *Game Studies* 2.2 (2002). <gamestudies.org/0202/kennedy/>.

Kerr, Jennifer. "Teens Migrating to Twitter." *Pew Internet* (May 21, 2013). <www.pewinternet.org/Media-Mentions/2013/Poll-Teens-migrating-to-Twitter.aspx>.

King, Katie. *Networked Reenactments: Stories Transdisciplinary Knowledges Tell.* Durham, NC: Duke University Press, 2012.

King, M. L., Jr. "Letter from Birmingham Jail" (1963). <www.stanford. edu/group/King/frequentdocs/birmingham.pdf>.

Klein, Adam. *A Space for Hate: The White Power Movement's Adaptation into Cyberspace.* Duluth, MN: Liktwin Books, 2010.

Klein, Marty. "You are Addicted to What? Challenging the Myth of Sex Addiction." *The Humanist* (July–August 2012). <http://thehumanist. org/july-august-2012/you're-addicted-to-what/>.

Kleinman, Zoe. "Facebook Sexism Campaign Attracts Thousands Online." *BBC Online* (May 28, 2013). <www.bbc.co.uk/news/technology-22689522>.

Klose, Simon, dir. "TPB AFK—The Pirate Bay Away from Keyboard." Documentary film, Nonami Films, 2013.

Klosterman, Chuck. *Sex, Drugs, and Cocoa Puffs: A Low Culture Manifesto.* NY: Scribners, 2004.

Kolko, Beth, Lisa Nakamura and Gilbert Rodman, eds., *Race in Cyberspace.* NY: Routledge, 2000.

Kreutz, Christian. "Maptivism: Maps for Activism, Transparency and Engagement." *Crisscrossed* blog post (September 14, 2009). <www. crisscrossed.net/2009/09/14/maptivism-maps-for-activism-transparency-and-engagement/>.

Kuhl, Stefan. *The Nazi Connection: Eugenics, American Racism and German National Socialism.* NY: Oxford University Press, 1994.

Lambert, Nathaniel M., Sesen Negash, Tyler F. Stillman, Spenser B. Olmstead and Frank D. Fincham. "A Love That Doesn't Last: Pornography Consumption and Weakened Commitment to One's Romantic Partner." *Journal of Social and Clinical Psychology* 31.4 (2012): 410–438.

Landzelius, Kyra, ed. *Native on the Net: Indigenous and Diasporic Peoples in the Virtual Age.* NY: Routledge, 2006.

Lanier, Jared. *You Are Not a Gadget.* NY: Knopf, 2010.

Latour, Bruno. *Science in Action: How to Follow Scientists and Engineers through Society.* London: Open University Press, 1987.

Lee, R. C., and S.-L. C. Wong, eds. *AsianAmerica.Net: Ethnicity, Nationalism and Cyberspace.* NY: Routledge, 2003.

Leonard, David. "High Tech Blackface: Race, Sports Video Games and Becoming the Other." *Intelligent Agent* 4 (2004): 1–5.

——. "Virtual Gangstas, Coming to a Suburban House Near You: Demonization, Commodification, and Policing Blackness," in N. Garrelts, ed., *The Meaning and Culture of Grand Theft Auto.* Jefferson, NC: MacFarland, 2006.

Li, Joyce H.-S. "Cyberporn: The Controversy." *First Monday* 5.8 (August 7, 2000). <http://journals.uic.edu/ojs/index.php/fm/article/view/777/686>.

Lievrouw, Leah. *Alternative and Activist New Media.* Boston: Polity, 2011.

MacKinnon, Catherine, and Andrea Dworkin. *Pornography and Civil Rights: A New Day for Women's Equality.* Minneapolis: Organizing Against Pornography, 1988.

Madden, Mary Amanda Lenhart, Sandra Cortesi, Urs Gasser, Maeve Duggan, Aaron Smith, Meredith Beaton. "Teens, Social Media, and Privacy." *Pew Internet* (May 21, 2013). <www.pewinternet.org/Reports/2013/Teens-Social-Media-And-Privacy.aspx>.

Madigan, Jamie. "The Psychology of Immersion in Video Games." *The Psychology of Video Games* (July 27, 2010). <www.psychologyofgames.com/2010/07/the-psychology-of-immersion-in-video-games/.

Mallan, Kerry, and Natasha Giardina, "Wikidentities." *First Monday* 14.6 (June 1, 2009) <http://firstmonday.org/ojs/index.php/fm/article/view/2445/2213>.

Maravita, Angelo, and Atusushi Ikiri. "Tools for the Body (Schema)." *Trends in Cognitive Science* 8.2 (2008): 79–86.

Margolis, Jane, and Allan Fisher. *Unlocking the Clubhouse: Women in Computing.* Cambridge, MA: MIT Press, 2006.

Marie, Meagan. "Lara Croft: The Evolution." *Game Informer* (December 7, 2010). <www.gameinformer.com/b/features/archive/2010/12/06/lara-croft_3a00_-the-evolution.aspx?PostPageIndex=5>.

Martens, Todd. "'Grand Theft Auto V' Review: Stubborn Sexism, Violence Ruin Game Play." *Los Angeles Times* (September 20, 2013). <http://herocomplex.latimes.com/games/theft-is-the-least-of-the-sins-of-grand-theft-auto-v/>.

Martinez, Marion. "The Art of Marion Martinez." *Pink Tie Promotions* (n.d.). <www.pinktieproart.com/Pages/ArtofMarionMartinez.aspx>.

Matthew, Emily. "Study: Sexism in Video Games," *Price Charting* (October 6, 2012). <http://blog.pricecharting.com/2012/09/emilyami-sexism-in-video-games-study.html>.

McChesney, Robert. *Digital Disconnect: How Capitalism is Turning the Internet against Democracy.* NY: New Press, 2013.

McCullagh, Declan, and Anne Broache "FBI Taps Cellphone Mic as Eavesdropping Tool." *CNet News* (December 1, 2006). <http://news.cnet.com/FBI-taps-cell-phone-mic-as-eavesdropping-tool/2100–1029_3–6140191.html>.

McGlaughlin, Rus. "The History of Tomb Raider." *IGN* (February 29, 2008). <http://ca.ign.com/articles/2008/03/01/ign-presents-the-history-of-tomb-raider>.

McGonigal, Jane. *Reality is Broken: Why Games Make us Better and How They Can Change the World.* NY: Penguin, 2011.

——. *You Found Me.* Website. (n.d.). <http://janemcgonical.com>.

McPherson, Tara. "I'll Take My Stand in Dixie-Net: White Guys, the South and Cyberspace," in Beth Kolko, Lisa Nakamura and Gilbert Rodman, eds., *Race in Cyberspace.* NY: Routledge, 2000 (pp. 117–131).

McLuhan, Marshall. *Understanding Media.* Cambridge, MA: MIT Press, 1994 [1964].

MediaNOLA. Website. (n.d.). <http://medianola.org>.

Melendez, Elisa. "What's It Like to Be a Girl Gamer?" *Slate.com* (August 13, 2012). <www.slate.com/articles/double_x/doublex/2012/08 sexual_harassment_in_the_gaming_world_a_real_life_problem_for_female_gamers_.html>.

Mendelsohn, Ben, dir. "Bundled, Buried and Behind Closed Doors." Documentary film, 2011. Available on many sites online.

Minecraft Educational. Website. (n.d.). <http://minecraftedu.com/page/>.

Molinari, Aleph. "Bridging the Digital Divide with Learning and Innovation Networks." *LI4E* (February 4, 2012). <www.li4e.org/2012/02/aleph-molinari-bridging-the-digital-divide-with-learning-and-innovation-networks/>.

Monroe, Barbara. *Crossing the Digital Divide: Race, Writing, and Technology in the Classroom.* NY: Teachers College Press, 2004.

Moore, Bret. "Video Game or Treatment for PTSD?" *Psychology Today* (May 24, 2010). <www.psychologytoday.com/blog/the-camouflage-couch/201005/video-game-or-treatment-ptsd>.

Mossberger, Karen. *Virtual Inequality: Beyond the Digital Divide.* Washington, D.C.: Georgetown UP, 2003.

Mozorov, Evengy. *Net Delusion: The Dark Side of Internet Freedom.* NY: Public Affairs, 2011.

Mullins, Aimee. "The Opportunity of Adversity." *TED Talk* (February 17, 2010) <www.ted.com/talks/aimee_mullins_the_opportunity_of_adversity.html Mullins,>.

Nakamura, Lisa. *Cybertypes: Race, Ethnicity, and Identity on the Internet.* NY: Routledge, 2002.

——. *Digitizing Race: Visual Cultures of the Internet.* Minneapolis: University of Minnesota Press, 2007.

——. "Don't Hate the Player, Hate the Game: Racialization of Labor in *World of Warcraft.*" *Critical Studies in Media Communication* 26.2 (2009): 128–144.

——. "Five Types of Online Racism." *TEDx Talks* (October 11, 2011). <www.youtube.com/watch?v=DT-G0FlOo7g>.

—— and Peter Chow-White, eds., *Race after the Internet.* NY: Routledge, 2012.

Nanotechnology in Medicine. Website. (n.d.). <www.understandingnano.com/medicine.html>.

Nayar, Pramod. "The Sexual Internet." *EconPapers* (2008) <www.academia.edu/738319/The_Sexual_Internethttp://econpapers.repec.org/paper/esswpaper/id_3a1391.htm>.

Negroponte, Nicholas. *Being Digital.* NY: Vintage, 1995.

Nelkin, Dorothy, and M. Susan Lindee. *The DNA Mystique: The Gene as Cultural Icon.* Ann Arbor: University of Michigan Press, 2004.

Nelson, Alondra, and Jeong Wong Hwang. "Roots and Revelation: Genetic Ancestry Testing and the YouTube Generation," in Lisa Nakamura and Peter Chow-White, eds., *Race after the Internet.* NY: Routledge, 2012 (pp. 271–290).

Nelson, Alondra, and Thuy Lihn N. Tu, with Alicia Headlam Hines, eds., *Technicolor: Race Technology, and Everyday Life.* NY: New York University Press, 2001.

Norris, Kamala O. "Gender Stereotypes, Aggression, and Computer Games: An Online Survey of Women." *CyberPsychology Behavior* 7.6 (2004): 714–727.

Norris, Pippa. *Digital Divide: Civic Engagement, Information Poverty, and the Internet Worldwide.* Cambridge University Press, 2008.

Ogas, Ogi, and Sai Gaddam, *A Billion Wicked Thoughts: What the Internet Tells us About Sexual Relationships.* NY: Dutton, 2011.

O'Leary, Amy. "In Virtual Play, Sex Harassment Is All Too Real." *New York Times* (August 2, 2012). <www.nytimes.com/2012/08/02/us/sexual-harassment-in-online-gaming-stirs-anger.html?_r=0>.

Owens, Eric W., R. J. Behun, J. C. Manning and R. C. Reid. "The Impact of Internet Pornography on Adolescents: A Review of the Reseach." *Sexual Addiction & Compulsivity* 19.1/2 (2012): 99–122. <www.psych.utoronto.ca/users/tafarodi/psy427/articles/Owens%20et%20al.%20(2012).pdf>.

"Panel on Homophobia in Virtual Communities." *GLAAD.* (n.d.). <www.glaad.org/2009/07/28/video-glaads-panel-on-homophobia-virtual-communities/>.

Papadoupoulus, Linda. "The Sexualization of Young People." (n.d.). <http://dera.ioe.ac.uk/10738/1/sexualisation-young-people.pdf>.

Parry, David. "Knowledge Cartels versus Knowledge Rights." *Enculturation* 10.10 (2012). <www.enculturation.net/knowledge-cartels>.

Participatory Chinatown. Website. (n.d.). <www.participatorychinatown.org>.

"Participatory Design." *CPSR (Computer Professionals for Social Responsibility).* (n.d.). <cpsr.org/issues/pd>.

Payne, Charles. *"I've Got the Light of Freedom": The Organizing Tradition and the Mississippi Freedom Struggle.* Berkeley: University of California Press, 2001 [1995].

Pellow, David Naguib, and Lisa Sun-Hee Park. *Silicon Valley of Dreams: Environmental Injustice, Immigrant Workers, and the High-Tech Global Economy.* NY: New York University Press, 2002.

Phillips, David J., and Kate O'Riordan, eds. *Queer Online.* London: Peter Lang, 2007.

Phone Story. Video game. Molleindustria, 2011. <www.phonestory.org>.

Pinchefsky, Carol. "Sexual Harassment in Online Videogames: How to Fix the Problem." *Forbes Magazine* (August 3, 2012). <www.forbes.com/sites/carolpinchefsky/2012/08/03/sexual-harassment-in-videogames-how-to-fix-the-problem/>.

Podlas, Kimberlianne. "Mistresses of Their Domain: How Female Entrepreneurs in Cyberporn are Initiating a Gender Power Shift." *CyberPsychology and Behavior* 3.5 (2000): 847–854.

"Porn Sex vs. Real Sex." Video. <www.huffingtonpost.com/2013/07/30/porn-vs-real-sex-video_n_3677746.html>.

"Pornstar Nina Hartley: Pornography is 'Not Meant to Be a Rulebook'." *Huffington Post* (August 8, 2013). <www.huffingtonpost.com/2013/08/05/porn-star-nina-hartley-real-sex_n_3708132.html>.

Postman, Neil. *Technopoly: The Surrender of Culture to Technology.* NY: Vintage, 1993.

Potter, Amelia Bryne. "Zones of Silence: A Framework beyond the Digital Divide." *First Monday* 11.5 (May 1, 2006). <www.firstmonday.org/ojs/index.php/fm/article/view/1327/1247>.

Powers, Richard. *Galatea 2.2.* NY: Picador, 2004.

"Public Knowledge of Current Affairs Little Changed by News and Information Revolution." *Pew Internet* (April, 15, 2007). <www.people-press.org/2007/04/15/public-knowledge-of-current-affairs-little-changed-by-news-and-information-revolutions/>.

Pullen, Christopher, and Margaret Cooper, eds. *LGBT Identity and Online New Media.* NY: Routledge, 2010 (2nd edition).

Putnam, Robert. *Bowling Alone: The Collapse and Revival of American Community.* NY: Simon and Schuster, 2000.

"Racism in WoW." YouTube videos. <www.youtube.com/watch?v=AFPpXUI5Kl4>.

Rajagopal, Indhu and Nis Bojin. "The Globalization of Prurience." *First Monday* 9.1 (January 5, 2004). <http://journals.uic.edu/ojs/index.php/fm/article/view/1114/1034>.

Raley, Rita. *Tactical Media.* Minneapolis: University of Minnesota Press, 2009.

Rampell, Catherine. "Freebees for the Rich." *New York Times Magazine* (September 29, 2013): 14–15.

Ray, Thomas S. "Kurzweil's Turing Fallacy." (n.d.). <http://life.ou.edu/pubs/kurzweil/>.

"Re: Activism." *Petlab.* (n.d.). <http://petlab.parsons.edu/newWeb/index.php?content=none&project=reactivism>.

Reed, T. V. *The Art of Protest: Culture and Social Activism from the Civil Rights Movement to the Streets of Seattle.* Minneapolis: University of Minnesota Press, 2005.

Rheingold, Howard. *Virtual Community: Homesteading on the Electronic Frontier.* Cambridge, MA: MIT Press, 2000 [1994].

Road Less Taken, The. Website. (n.d.) <http://lindsaysminzy.wordpress.com/page/3/>.

Ruvolo, Julie. "How Much of the Internet is Actually for Porn?" *Forbes* (August 7, 2011). <www.forbes.com/sites/julieruvolo/2011/09/07/how-much-of-the-internet-is-actually-for-porn/>.

Sarkeesian, Anita. *Feminist Frequency.* Blog. (n.d.). <www.feministfrequency.com>.

Sassen, Saskia. "Digital Networks and Power," in M. Featherstone and S. Lash, eds., *Spaces of Culture: City, Nation, World.* NY: Sage, 1999 (pp. 49–64).

Scarleteen: Sex Ed for the Real World. Website. (n.d.). <www.scarleteen.com>.

Schäfer, Mirko Tobias. *Bastard Culture! How User Participation Transforms Cultural Production.* Chicago: University of Chicago Press, 2011. Also online at <http://mtschaefer.net/media/uploads/docs/Schaefer_Bastard-Culture_2011.pdf>.

Selfe, Cynthia L., and Richard J. Selfe, Jr. "The Politics of the Interface." *College Composition and Communication* 45.4 (1994): 480–504.

Shaw, Adrienne. "Putting the Gay in Games." *Games and Culture* 4.3 (2009): 228–253.

Silicon Valley Toxics Coalition. Website. (n.d.). <http://svtc.org>.

Silver, David "Introduction: Where is Internet Studies?" in David Silver, ed., *Critical Cyberculture Studies.* NY: New York University Press, 2006.

Singer, P. W. *Wired for War: The Robotics Revolution and Conflict in the 21st Century.* NY: Penguin, 2009.

Sisler, Vit. *Digital Islam.* Website. (n.d.). <www.digitalislam.eu/article.do?articleId=1704>.

Slade, Giles. *Made to Break: Technology and Obsolescence in America.* Cambridge, MA: Harvard University Press, 2007.

"Slow Technology Movement." *Technopedia.* (n.d.). <www.techopedia.com/definition/28641/slow-technology-movement>.

Smith, Ted, David Pellow, and David Sonnenfeld, eds. *Challenging the Chip: Labor Rights and Environmental Justice in the Electronic Industry.* Philadelphia: Temple University Press, 2006.

Snow, Keith Harmon. "High Tech Genocide in the Congo." *El Corresponsal.* (n.d.). <www.elcorresponsal.com/modules.php?name=News&file=article&sid=4862>.

Social Science Research Council (U.S.). *Structures of Participation in Digital Culture*. NY: Social Science Research Council, 2007.

Sofia, Zoe. "Exterminating Fetuses: Abortion, Disarmament and the Sexo-Semiotics of Extraterrestrialism." *Diacritics* 14.2 (1984): 47–59.

SOPA Strike. Website. (n.d.). <http://sopastrike.com>.

Southworth, Cindy, Toby Cremer, Sarah Tucker and Cynthia Frasier "A High-Tech Twist on Abuse: Technology, Intimate Partner Stalking, and Advocacy." (June 2005). Minnesota Center Against Violence and Abuse. <www.mincava.umn.edu/documents/commissioned/stalking andtech/stalkingandtech.html>.

Statistic Brain. Website. (n.d.). <www.statisticbrain.com>.

Steiner, Peter. "On the Internet, Nobody Knows You're a Dog." Cartoon. *The New Yorker* (July 5, 1993): 61.

Sturgeon, Noel. *Environmentalism in Popular Culture*. Tucson: University of Arizona Press, 2009.

Stuster, J. Dana. "Mapped: Every Protest on the Planet since 1979." *Foreign Policy* (August 22, 2013). <www.foreignpolicy.com/articles/2013/ 08/22/mapped_what_every_protest_in_the_last_34_years_looks_ like>.

Sukey Apps. Website. (n.d.). <sukey.org>.

Sunstein, Cass. *RepublicDotCom*. Princeton: Princeton University Press, 2000.

"Systemic Bias." *Wikipedia*. <http://en.wikipedia.org/wiki/Wikipedia: Systemic_bias>.

The Wall-The World. Website. Paula Levine and Christopher Zimmerman, designers. (n.d.). <http://thewalltheworld.net>.

Think B4 You Speak. Website. (n.d.). <www.thinkb4youspeak.com>.

Thoreau, Henry David. *The Portable Thoreau*, ed. by Carl Bode. NY: Penguin, 1982.

Tomlinson, Bill. *Greening Through IT: Information Technology for Sustainability*. Cambridge, MA: MIT Press, 2010.

Tsatsou, Panayiota. "Digital Divides Revisited: What is New About Divides and Their Research?" *Media, Culture and Society* 33 (2011): 317–331.

Turkle, Sherry. *Life on the Screen*. NY: Simon and Schuster, 1995.

——. *Alone Together: Why We Expect More from Technology and Less from Each Other*. NY: Basic Books, 2012.

Turner, Fred. *From Counterculture to Cyberculture: Stewart Brand, the Whole Earth Network, and the Rise of Digital Utopianism*. Chicago and London: University of Chicago Press, 2006.

UNESCO Institute for Statistics. Website. (n.d.). <www.uis.unesco.org/ Pages/default.aspx>.

Urbina, Ian. "A Growing Hazard," *New York Times* (March 19, 2013): 1, 16.

Usable Web. Website. (n.d.). <UsableWeb.com>.

Utne, Eric. "Signs of the Zeitgeist." *Utne Reader* (May–June 2013): 92.

Vaidhyanathan, Siva. *The Googlization of Everything: (And Why We Should Worry)*. University of California Press, 2011.

Vegh, Sandor. "Hacktivists or Cyberterrorists? The Changing Media Discourse on Hacking." *First Monday* 7.10 (October 7, 2002). <http://firstmonday.org/ojs/index.php/fm/article/view/998/919>.

Videogamerability. Website. (n.d.). <https://sites.google.com/site/videogamerability/home>.

Wardrip-Fruin, Noah, and Pat Harrigan. *First Person: New Media as Story, Performance, and Game*. Cambridge, MA: MIT Press, 2004.

——. Second *Person: Role-Playing and Story in Games and Playable Media*. Cambridge, MA: MIT Press, 2007.

——. *Third Person: Authoring and Exploring Vast Narratives*. Cambridge, MA: MIT Press, 2009.

Warschauer, Mark. "Reconceptualizing the Digital Divide." *First Monday* 7.7 (July 1, 2002). <http://journals.uic.edu/ojs/index.php/fm/article/view/967/888>.

——. *Technology and Social Inclusion: Rethinking the Digital Divide*. MIT Press, 2003.

Webster, Frank, ed. *Theories of the Information Society*. NY: Routledge, 2006 (3rd edition).

Weiser, Mark. "The World is not a Desktop." (1993). <www.ubiq.com/hypertext/weiser/ACMInteractions2.html>.

Whitson, Jennifer R., and Claire Dormann. "Social Gaming for Change: Facebook Unleashed." *First Monday* 16.10 (October 3, 2011).

WikiLeaks. Website. (n.d.). <http://wikileaks.org>.

Wills, Amanda. "Another Snowden Leak: NSA Program Taps Everything You Do Online." *Mashable.com* (July 31, 2013). <http://mashable.com/2013/07/31/nsa-xkeyscore/>.

Wilson, Gary. *Your Brain on Porn*. (n.d.). Website. <http://yourbrainonporn.com>.

Winfrey, Oprah. Interview. "Craigslist Rape Victim." *Oprah* (September 23, 2010). <www.oprah.com/oprahshow/Craigslist-Rape-Victim/print/1>.

WISAT (Women in Global Science and Technology). Website. (n.d.). <http://wisat.org/home/>.

Wolf, Mark, J. P., and Bernard Perron. eds. *The Video Game Theory Reader*. NY: Routledge, 2003.

Women Watch. Website. (n.d.). <www.un.org/womenwatch/>.

Woolgar, Steve. *Virtual Society? Get Real! Technology, Cyberbole, Reality*. Oxford University Press, 2003.

World Internet Stats. Website. (n.d.). <www.internetworldstats.com/stats.htm>.

World Wide Web Accessibility Initiative. Website. (n.d.). <www.w3.org/WAI/>.

Wu, Tim. *The Master Switch: The Rise and Fall of Information Empires*. NY: Vintage, 2011.

Yao, Mike Z., Chad Mahood, and Daniel Linz. "Sexual Priming, Gender Stereotyping, and Likelihood to Sexually Harass: Examining the Cognitive Effects of Playing a Sexually-Explicit Video Game." *Sex Roles* 62.1/2 (2009): 77–88.

Young, Jeffrey. "As Technology Evolves, New Forms of Online Racism Emerge." *Chronicle of Higher Education* (March 13, 2011). <http://chronicle.com/blogs/wiredcampus/as-technology-evolves-new-forms-of-online-racism-emerge/30351>.

Zaremba, Alan. *The Deepening Divide: Inequality in the Information Society.* Thousand Oaks, CA: Sage, 2006.

Glossary

Concepts for Digital Cultural Analysis

This brief glossary is not a comprehensive list of information technology and cultural analysis terms, but provides a basic tool kit of key terms used in this book and elsewhere to better characterize and understand the variety of technocultural issues, devices and processes.

ACA-FAN An academic student of popular culture, including digital culture products like video games, who is also a user or fan of the culture they study. Aca-fans try to avoid criticizing from some supposedly pure or higher intellectual plane above mere players of popular culture.

ACTOR–NETWORK THEORY Actor–network theory is an approach to the social and cultural study of society. Associated with figures like Bruno Latour, ANT views technological devices as actors (agents), with something resembling human agency (power to impact events), with the caveat that like humans, technological actors are always caught up in larger networks of power and causality. Technologies and humans are equally entangled in economic relations, political relations, social relations, and cultural relations that shape what they can and cannot do.

ADBUSTING Coined by the editors of *Adbusters* magazine, the term refers to the creation of counter-advertising, mock advertisements that satirize commercial ads or provide anti-consuming messages in a form normally used for promoting consumerism. This practice precedes but has been greatly expanded through the use of digital technologies for creating and especially disseminating subversive ads, or subvertisements.

ADVERGAMING Following in the footsteps of product placement in Hollywood films—the prominent display of brand-name consumer items in movie scenes—advergaming refers to the increasingly common parallel practice of brand-name placement in scenes within digital games. Like product placement in movies, corporations pay to have a character in a game drink their soda or wear their clothes or drive their cars, with labels, logos or hood ornaments clearly visible.

AFFINITY PORTALS Portals, points of access to the Web that collect and organize sites, built for particular demographic groups, based upon any of a limitless number of kinds of collective interest (ethnic cultures, business, hobbies, education, sports, etc.). These portals can be defined as broadly as for women to as narrowly as supporters of a particular football club. They seek to be more focused than general portals like Yahoo or AOL.

AGENCY; SOCIAL AGENCY In cultural studies, agency refers to a given subject's ability to have social impact. One's agency is one's social power, the capacity of an individual to act independently and to make (relatively) free choices. Agency is always performed in relation to social structures that limit and shape the potential power of any individual subject. Debates about the relative power of social structure versus personal choice are at least as old as theological debates about the relation between "free will" (agency) and "determinism" (control from outside the person). Contemporary social theory has sought to get beyond simple either/or dualisms or dichotomies, and to speak of mutually constitutive or dialectical interactions between agency and structure.

ANALOG Often used vaguely to mean the opposite of digital, technically speaking, analog is actually a representation of an object that mimics (is analogous to) an original. Put crudely, an analog image attempts a one-to-one correspondence between the representation and the thing represented. In contrast, a digital image is a kind of sampling approximation of the thing represented. On the down side, this means some nuances are lost in digital imaging standardization. On the plus side, this allows for far greater compression of data so that digital images are far more easily and quickly reproduced and disseminated. Since humans actually perceive the world in analog form, that is, everything we see, feel, taste, smell and hear is a continuous transmission of information to our senses, analog is in one sense a more accurate or fuller reflection of the everyday reality we experience. By contrast, digital information translates or estimates analog data using only ones and zeros as samplers. A vinyl record is an analog representation, while a CD is digital, because the bumps and grooves from a record are a continuous signal, while a CD is a sampled set of excerpts. Vinyl is said to have a more naturally variable sound, while digital is crisper and more regular. Analog is also slangily used as a put-down by the tech savvy, as in "Oh, that's *so* analog" (i.e., hopelessly out of date).

APPARATGEIST A term developed by Katz and Aakhus combining the words "apparatus" (device, material product) and "geist" (spirit, mind), to characterize the ever present elements of material and mental construct that together make up any digital experience.

ASYNCHRONOUS literally means not at the same time, and it is used in digital culture to indicate things like online courses where instead of all students being in the same classroom at the same time, their participation is scattered over time through things like posts that represent discussion spread over hours or days rather than talking face to face in the same time frame. Online live chat rooms, by contrast, replicate synchronous conversation in the same time frame, while being dispersed across space. Dislocations of time and space represent two of the key features of life online.

BLOG; BLOGGER; VLOG Short for web log, an online journal maintained by an individual (blogger). A vlog is a blog done in video form rather than written text. Blogs, along with personal space on social networking sites, have to a large degree supplanted the "personal homepage," a genre particularly popular in the 1990s and still used by some on the Web.

BLOGEBRITY: BLOGOSPHERE A blogger who has achieved the status of a celebrity in (and sometimes beyond) cyberspace (cf. Perez Hilton or Arianna Huffington) or the blogosphere—the combined space of blogs.

BRAIN–COMPUTER INTERFACE (BCI) is a direct connection between the human brain and an external, digitally controlled device. Such devices have been used to restore elements of human sight, hearing and movement (known technically as neuroprosthetics).

CATFISH Someone who systematically misrepresents themselves in online profiles, dating sites or other digital spaces. The term was popularized by the documentary film "Catfish" (2010) on this topic, and given further cache by the reality docu-drama series "Catfish: The TV Show" (2012+) on MTV dealing with deceptive relationships online.

CONVERGENCE (of media) is a term used in media studies to note the ways in which previously separate media are converging into one digital mode. This refers to both the convergence among new media in the Web 2.0 era (like accessing the Web on a smartphone), but also the convergence of old media (TV, film, radio) and new (like watching a TV show on your smartphone or listening to radio over the Net or reading a book on a Kindle). The assumption is that this convergence will continue and expand such that increasingly all media, old and new, will be accessed through a small set of digital devices and platforms. *Remediation* is one key aspect of convergence.

CONSUMERISM/TECHNO-CONSUMERISM As cyberspaces have become increasing commercialized by e-business, advertising, and other prods to greater consumption, new media have added to the excessive consumerism long a part of US culture. More particularly, techno-consumerism refers to the intensely pushed consumer desire for every smaller, faster, cooler high-tech/digital toy. No business has more effectively built quick obsolescence into their marketing processes than the new media device business.

CROWDSOURCING Sending a task or problem out to be worked on by a largely undefined general population, as opposed to a specific group of people. On the Web, wikis are in effect "crowdsourced," as have been many other problems and projects. This form of mass collaboration is intended to tap hidden human resources.

CULTURAL COMPETENCY acknowledges that, while people develop a more or less automatic depth of understanding of the subject positions and cultures into which we are born and socialized, achieving something like that depth of understanding of other subject positions and other cultures is far more difficult, but not impossible. The process of gaining depth of understanding of subject positions and cultures other than your own is the process of gaining various degrees of cultural competency.

CULTURAL IMPERIALISM is hegemonic influence over cultural production (movies, TV, music, etc.) by one culture over others. The culture subject to cultural imperialism (CI) is overwhelmed and overridden by the dominant culture from outside such that local traditions are lost or transformed beyond recognition The US and to a lesser degree Europe have been accused of cultural imperialism vis-à-vis most of the rest of the world. Japan has been accused of CI with regard to the rest of Asia (and sometimes with regard to the US). Smaller-scale cultural imperialism can occur within countries, between ethnically dominant and minority cultures, and between the dominant culture and subcultures.

CYBER-BALKANIZATION A notion, most associated with Cass Sunstein, that the Web leads to political Balkanization, or *silo effect,* in which users seek out only news and opinion sources that echo and often intensify their already existing political views and biases.

CYBER-ETHNOGRAPHY is the close study of online communities, using techniques derived from sociology and anthropology. Cyber-ethnography employs techniques like interviews, focus groups, and participant observation in online communities to get a more detailed sense of how users interact in cyberspaces.

CYBERPUNK Genre of science fiction typically set in a dystopian near future in which digital culture is more deeply embedded in every area of a world divided between a wealthy corporate class and a poor majority. Influential on a variety of cultural phenomena, from fashion to political dissent.

CYBERSPACE(S) Term coined by sci fi author William Gibson in his novel *Neuromancer* that has come to be widely used to name the virtual "spaces" of interaction created by the Internet and associated techno-devices. Since the term can falsely imply a single, homogenous territory, for the purpose of analysis it is best used in the plural, cyberspaces. Like all metaphors, this one both illuminates and misleads, since it is precisely the illusion of spacelessness, or no place-ness, that characterizes much wired experience.

CYBER-TERRORISM The use of computer hacking to inflict serious direct or indirect psychological or physical damage to human targets.

CYBERTYPING The appearance of social stereotypes in cyberspaces, and/or the generation of new stereotypes by and in cybercultures (coined by Lisa Nakamura).

CYBORG The term cyborg names a being that is part human, part machine. The best known cyborgs in popular culture are the title character in the "Terminator" and "Robocop" movie series. In digital culture studies, the figure of the cyborg has been invoked to characterize the increasing entanglement of many humans with digital devices. The metaphor of the cyborg was given great prominence in a highly influential 1984 essay, "A Manifesto for Cyborgs," by feminist techno-science scholar Donna Haraway. While recognizing that the cyborg was the "illegitimate offspring of militarism and corporate capitalism," Haraway also saw positive potential in thinking about the metaphor of the cyborg as a figure that could break down one of the rigid boundaries that has defined putative human nature. Because throughout much of human history describing certain traits as *naturally* male or female, or placing races in a natural hierarchy, have provided the justification for social inequalities, Haraway puts forth the *un*natural image of the cyborg as one possible counter to this discriminatory naturalizing of human variety.

CYBRARIAN A term noting that much of the work of librarians has come to include digital resource management, in addition to, or, alas, at times instead of, printed books and other non-virtual materials.

DATA MINING The practice of companies who scour social media and other websites to gather personal information about people's website visiting habits and expressed preferences that they can sell to corporations as marketing research. Much of the revenue for social media sites comes from this practice of selling private information to marketers.

DATA PROFILING is the use of information gained by tracking users' site visits and other web habits in order to create a marketing profile. This is the process by which ads that seem tailored to your interests appear on your social media page or as part of your Google searches. While some people enjoy this profiling when it correctly identifies preferences, it can also be used to exclude users from certain privileges (see *weblining*) and can narrow the options presented to users. More importantly, these surreptitiously garnered data have the potential to be used in a variety of undesirable ways, including government surveillance and criminal activity.

DATAVEILLANCE A compound word made from data and surveillance, it refers to the surveillance of a person's activities by studying the data trail created by actions such as credit card purchases, mobile phone calls, and Internet use. The term is used by critics concerned that various web spaces like Google and Facebook gather far too much information on users, and fail to protect the misuse of that material for commercial and criminal activity.

DEFAULT IDENTITY All technical devices and processes are designed and built consciously or unconsciously, with particular users in mind. Thus, technologies tend to be biased by the cultural assumptions and identities of designers. Default identity refers to this presumed user. Historically, it refers to the process by which straight, white, middle-class, Euro-American cultural assumptions, values and ideas were (mostly unintentionally) built into early hardware, software and cybercultures. Just as it is possible to change the default settings on most programs, it has been possible to move beyond this default identity to welcome more subject positions online. But just as default settings often remain invisible to most users and don't get changed, default identities have to be intentionally changed, and there are still a number of ways and a number of places where the default identity dominates cyberspaces. *Participatory design* has been one approach to lessening biases, as has, more fundamentally, improving the diversity of design teams in terms of class, race/ethnicity, gender and other social markers.

DIGERATI Modeled on the term literati, this new coinage refers to those deeply knowledgeable about new media culture; often used ironically or in a critical way to suggest the digerati are arrogant in their flaunting of digital hipness and/or excessive in their trendy obsession with the latest digital devices.

DIGITAL A method of coding data about the world through abstraction as binary numbers (0s and 1s), as opposed to *analog* form. While analog coding is closer to the way humans perceive data in the world, digital coding is far more versatile and far more easily and cheaply replicated, two factors that account for the massive explosion of digital devices (computers, smartphones, dvd players, etc.), platforms (the Internet, video game consoles, etc.) and digitized genres (music, movies, photography, videos, etc.) since the late twentieth century. Digital means numerical, and is derived from the word digit, referring to fingers and toes (still widely used counting devices among humans).

DIGITAL DIVIDES The digital divide is a concept gaining popularity during the 1990s to describe the gap between those who had access to computers and high-tech devices, versus those who did not. The term was made prominent through a series of US government reports, beginning during the Clinton Administration, laying out the statistics regarding the technological "haves" and "have nots," a discrepancy attributable largely to race/ethnicity, income bracket and/or rural vs. urban location. Analysis of the digital divide began as a discussion of simple access to hardware, but evolved to look at a number of social and cultural factors that additionally impacted one's ability to fully utilize new technologies. More complex understanding of the full nature of various digital divides has led to a multifaceted approach often labeled *technology for social inclusion.*

DIGITAL NATIVE; DIGITAL IMMIGRANT A digital native is an individual who grew from infancy in a technology-rich environment. For digital natives, high-tech devices and practices seem natural and are taken for granted. In contrast, a digital immigrant is a person who began interacting with high-tech devices later in life; for these generationally older individuals, or individuals introduced to ICTs later in life, comfort with and immersion in digital culture is generally less fulsome. While digital natives generally have the advantage of deeper integration of technologies into their lives, digital immigrants often have the advantage of understanding more fully the contrast between life in digital and non-digital environments.

DIGITEXTUALITY Coined by Anna Everett, this concept plays off the literary term "intertextuality" (Kristeva), and refers to the complex relationships among digital texts and among various digitized media. Everett uses the term in conjunction with the concept of media convergence, arguing that on the one hand digital media reduce all media to certain "zeros and ones," to sameness, but on the other hand older media like TV and radio are given new life and intensity as they move through the Net onto laptops, tablets and smartphones.

DISINHIBITION means the lessening of social inhibitions and taboos. In online environments disinhibition stems largely from the anonymity or invisibility provided by written content without identifiable visual or aural clues to identity. In some cases, this can be a good thing, allowing people to talk frankly about issues they are not comfortable addressing face to face. In other cases, it provides cover for those who choose to launch hate speech or other forms of denigration without identifying themselves.

DOMESTICATION (OF TECHNOLOGY) The processes by which computers and new media devices moved increasingly from work environments (businesses, schools) into the home and other personal spaces, beginning perhaps with the first "personal computers" and proceeding apace, due to both technical innovations (decreasing size, increasing speed) and cultural value changes.

DOTCOM BOOM refers to the frenzy of activity in the 1990s when the potential of the Internet and digital culture suddenly led to a massive growth of start-up tech firms, the vast majority of which crashed and burned in a dotcom bust a few years later. Analysts now see this period as an earlier example of the kind of overreach that led to the economic crash of 2008, and also as premature in getting ahead of the curve of audience interest in new technologies.

EARLY ADOPTERS is a term used to characterize the first groups of users of any new digital device, app, program, etc. It is also sometimes used more particularly to name people who habitually seek to have the newest hi-tech stuff, or who love the challenge of experimenting with the latest products.

EDUTAINMENT is a derogatory term used by opponents of multi-media and digital teaching techniques presumed because of their similarity to popular forms of entertainment to be less effective or serious pedagogically. While certainly capable of being overused and abused, empirical studies clearly show multi-media and online approaches that get beyond the traditional lecture/textbook model of teaching can expand the range of effective learning for many students.

ENVIRONMENTAL JUSTICE Environmental justice is the branch of environmentalism that documents and fights against the fact that environmental hazards are far more prevalent in working-class neighborhoods and neighborhoods with high concentrations of people of color in the Global North, and in the poorest communities of the Global South. Its relevance to digital culture lies in the fact that electronic waste is highly toxic, and increasing at alarming rates. The vast majority of workers endangered by e-waste around the global are the poor, women, and people of color, because they do most of the toxic assembly and because most of the e-waste is exported from the developed world and dumped on the Global South where protections for disassemblers are largely non-existent. Most of the toxic waste from electronic devices ends up leaching into the land, air and water in the poorest parts of Africa, India, China, and other parts of the less industrialized world, as well as poorer neighborhoods in the Global North.

ESSENTIALISM is the generally false belief that there are certain "essential," innate human traits that are unchanged by history, as opposed to a "social constructionist" view that traits that seem essential were in fact created over time through social interactions that can therefore be changed. Racial essentialists argue that all members of a racial group share certain basic characteristics or qualities that mark them as inherently different from members of other racial groups. Biologists, however, have abandoned the category of race as genetically meaningless. Gender essentialists believe certain inherent features of masculinity and femininity exist across all cultures and all time, a point of view challenged by the sheer diversity of women across the time and geography around the globe.

ETHNIC PORTALS Particular kinds of *affinity portals* built around historically defined ethnic groups (Serb, Laotians, Puerto Ricans, etc.).

E-WASTE; ELECTRONIC WASTE Toxic waste from computers, TVs, cellphones and other electronic devices is one of the fastest growing environmental hazards around the globe (though largely dumped on the Global South).

FAN CULTURES Various cultural products, from pop music celebrities to soap operas, have long had avid groups of fans who communicate with each other (fan clubs) and as much as possible with the people behind the object of their fan affection. But fandom has been taken to a whole new level by the Web and other digital technologies. Fan fiction, mashups of favorite shows, communication between fans and with celebrities (via web pages, tweets, etc.) have grown exponentially. While fans are a somewhat atypically intense type of user, the existence of fan sites and other products of fan culture have proven to be an especially accessible way for scholars to study what people make out of popular culture in the digital era.

FEMINIST TECHNOSCIENCE STUDIES Associated with figures like Donna Haraway, Sandra Harding, Evelyn Fox Keller and Sharon Traweek, this transdisciplinary field views science as deeply embedded in cultural forces of gender, race and class, and seeks a deeper form of scientific objectivity in which sociocultural factors are included alongside technical elements.

FRAMING NARRATIVE In game studies, the storyline surrounding the action in any given game, in contrast to the "in-game" narrative.

GAME GAZE Modeled on the concept of the "cinematic gaze" widely used in film studies, game gaze refers to the positioning of a game player in different types of game play. The term is useful in studying how, for example, a "first-person shooter" game shapes the experience of a user differently from a game set up in the third person. Analysis of the game gaze also seeks to understand the qualitative difference between "gazing" at a digital game screen as compared to gazing at a film, painting or TV program.

GAME WORLD; GAME PLAY The partly explicit and partly implicit environment in which a given game is enacted. Each game world has a structure and a logic of its own, with varying degrees of similarity to or difference from our everyday world. Often contrasted with game play, the activity going on within a game.

GAMIFICATION Use of game-like processes and game-world motivations (the incentives and mechanics of games, like points or rewards) and applying them to something that's not a game (credit card or store reward programs are familiar examples). This includes use of games in the marketing of products and services, a practice criticized by game designer/ theorist Ian Bogost as "exploitationware." In her work on using game-like elements to deal with real-world problems, Jane McGonigal prefers the term "gameful design."

GOLD FARMING The practice of playing multiplayer online games to earn in-game currency that can then be sold to other players for real-world currency. Gold farming is most widespread in China and other developing nations where wealthier individuals within or more often outside the country in richer nations, effectively buy the labor of gold farmers to enhance their power in *MMORPGS* and other games.

GREEN COMPUTING; SUSTAINABLE IT Efforts to eliminate the many toxic substances found in computers, recycle computers, and otherwise deal with the substantial problem of *electronic waste* and energy consumption by digital devices.

HACKTIVISM Online activism that includes civil disobedience in the form of breaking into and altering websites or other digital spaces for the purpose of parody or critical commentary on political opponents, or in support of dissenting political positions. While "black-hat hacking" or "cracking" computers is used maliciously or for personal gain, hactivism refers only to breaking into and manipulating digital systems for specific political reasons, for challenging existing economic, social or political power structures.

HARDWARE–SOFTWARE–WETWARE The trio of terms denoting the main elements of any baseline digital culture device/process—"hardware" (computers, cable networks, game consoles, cellphones, etc), "software" (the digitally coded programs that run or are run on a device) and "wetware" (the humans who design, distribute and/or use the hardware and software). In digital culture studies, each of these elements is subject to historical, *technocultural* analysis of the economic, social and political choices that determine its technical nature and sociocultural use.

HEGEMONY is cultural domination without overt force or coercion. Hegemony is a process by which groups with greater power lead those with lesser power to adopt their dominant ideas as common sense, even when those ideas work against fairness, justice or the self-interest of the dominated group. In ICT terms, hegemony has meant greater power to shape cyberculture in the hands of certain cultural groups and the default subject position. The concept was originally developed by the Italian Marxist cultural theorist, Antonio Gramsci.

ICT is shorthand for Information Communication Technology and refers to all the digital devices (computers, cellphones, tablets, digital music handhelds, etc.) that play a role in the creation of new media modes of interaction between people. The move from the term IT to ICT exemplifies the increasing degree to which communication between people, rather than mere information storage and retrieval, has come to define the world of new media technology.

IDENTITY TOURISM Pretending to be someone you are not online, often by crossing gender or ethnic boundaries. Coined by Lisa Nakamura, the term indicates a superficial effort to elude ascribed characteristics of identity.

INTERACTIVE One of the most common claims about new media is that they are more interactive than older media like film and TV. The claim is that new media like video games and Web 2.0 features allow more room for the user/player to shape the activity. There is no doubt that this is true in certain cases, but media scholars have shown both that older media audiences are far more active than has been assumed, and that much of the interactivity in new media is more scripted than we might suppose. Thus, degrees of interactivity should be seen as existing along a spectrum, and differing kinds of interactivity should be specified, rather than simply accepting the claim (or commercial hype) that new media are a major breakthrough in interaction.

LEET (or ELEET or LEETSPEAK) is an alternative English alphabet that uses ASCII characters, numbers and symbols to create an insider language in certain communities of cyber-techies. The leet designation for the Web, for example, is 1n73rw3b. Originally used to disguise discussions of illegal hacking practices or to elude web search engines, 1337 (leet for leet) slowly crept into gamer circles and then out into popular usage.

LOCATIVE MEDIA Digital media targeting or attached to particular real-world places. An example would be a city tour in which tourists are guided to particular places around town where their smartphones provide information about the nature or history of each site.

LUDOLOGY; NARRATOLOGY Ludology is the study of all kinds of games. Analysis of video and computer games has been enriched by drawing upon this wider field that looks historically at games of every type; especially relevant is the history of board games, one of the main bases of many new media variations. Much ludology looks for underlying patterns or structures found across different games and different genres and types of games. Sometimes contrasted with narratology, an approach to game studies that emphasizes story telling over other aspects of game world activity, and places game narratives in the context of other kinds of story-telling forms like novels and fiction films. While sometimes portrayed as competing approaches, ludology and narratology both have important things to offer game studies, and can be synthesized in interesting ways.

MAINSTREAMING OF PORNOGRAPHY One impact of the free and easy access to pornography provided by the Net has been what some call the mainstreaming of porn, the movement of porn from the dark corners of society closer to the center, as evidenced by things like casual jokes about watching porn that pervade television and film, and porn actors becoming celebrities mingling with rock icons and movie stars.

MAPTIVISM Combining the words map and activism, this is a form of online activism that uses digital tools to map sites of political contestation. HarassMap.org, for example, in Egypt maps places of sexual harassment across the country to better organize against these practices, and ToxicRisk.com traces sites of pollution via Google maps.

MATERIALITY In analysis of digital cultures, materiality refers to the physical dimension often lost in discussions of virtual realities. All digital interactions take place over devices with a material basis, one linked to a long material production process, and all interactions involve the material body of the user, no matter how much the illusion of disembodiment or placelessness may take mental precedence. There are no virtual spaces not also grounded in material ones.

MEDIA MONOPOLY refers to the increasingly narrow ownership of various old and new media by a small number of very powerful media mega-corporations (Time Warner, Viacom, Bertelsmann, Disney, NewsCorp, GE, CBS and a few others). Critics worry that monopolies lead to higher prices, more censorship of controversial issues, and less variety of media content.

MEDIATION In a communication studies context, mediation names the process entailed by the use of any particular medium of communication, whether it be the human voice, language, drawings, old media (TV, film, radio) or new media (the Internet, smartphones). Mediation is a central fact of human existence. We are never in truly *imm*ediate contact with one another because all modes of communication, even the most basic, seemingly natural ones like gesturing, or speaking, are culture bound in ways that enable and also constrain the range of information that can be exchanged between interlocutors. This point about mediation is crucial in new media studies because digital means of communication have frequently been denigrated as less natural, less human, or otherwise less real and desirable than face-to-face or forms of non-digital written communication. Most digital culture scholars would reply to this claim by saying that digital media are simply different from, not lesser than, other older forms of (always also mediated) communication.

MICROBLOGGING A broadcast form of blogging (i.e., Twitter) limited to a small number of characters.

MMORPG Massively Multiplayer Online Role-Playing Game. Short-hand for online digital games like World of Warcraft where massive numbers (millions in some cases) of players interact in an ongoing way via the Net.

MOBILE; MOBILITY Mobility, while first popularly associated in a digital context with mobile phones, has come to be a characteristic of much new media culture. Theorizing the impact of mobility on people's sense of place, time and identity has been a major component of cyberculture analysis.

NEOLIBERAL GLOBALIZATION The form of global marketing and cultural networks driven since the latter decades of the twentieth century by transnational corporations in league with a few key international financial institutions like the World Bank and the International Monetary Fund (IMF). Neoliberal in this context is a synonym for "free-market" ideology (rather than referring to liberals in the US sense of left of center). This latest phase of globalization has been characterized by the privitization of many public institutions, dismantling many social safety nets, severe austerity programs and cuts in services to the lower classes, and growing economic inequality within and between nations. The growing poverty caused by neoliberal policies has been challenged by a broad alliance of organizations networked as a worldwide Global Justice or Alter-Globalization Movement (sometimes misleadingly referred to as the anti-globalization movement).

NET NEUTRALITY (aka network neutrality or Internet neutrality) is a movement seeking to minimize commercial and government control of the Net, treating it instead as a public resource or commons. Prominent supporters of this position have included one of the key creators of the Internet, Vint Cerf, and World Wide Web inventor, Tim Berners-Lee.

NETROOTS ACTIVISM Online political or social movement organizing, meant to parallel the term, grassroots, but applying to activism emerging or developing significantly on the Internet and through digital devices.

OPEN-SOURCE MOVEMENT The open-source movement seeks to replace expensive corporate-produced software and related digital technology with freely available, collectively created free products. The effort to expand the use of open-source programs is part of a movement that critiques the commercialization of computing, and unnecessary expense created by the monopoly on such products by corporations like Microsoft, Apple and IBM. Proponents often demonstrate that these free programs and processes are as good as if not superior to the costly corporate ones. Most of these products are associated by the Linux programming language. While initially user-friendliness was a barrier to wider adoption of these products, the prime barrier currently is simply that they are not as well known as the highly hyped and advertised commercial versions. Many of these folks also favor *net neutrality*.

PARTICIPATORY DESIGN Recognizing the limits of hardware and software design from the *default identity* position, participatory design involves diverse actual users in the creation of new technologies, and aims to make sure that a culturally diverse group is part of the design process. Ideally, this process moves beyond consulting diverse users to working to increase the diversity of engineers and other technology creators. This has proven particularly important in working with users who have disabilities, and with varied ethnic groups around the world who don't share default norms of Western designers.

PERSONALIZATION The ability of users to transform digital culture processes, devices and spaces to fit individual personality choices. This can range from choosing the color of a cellphone cover to the layout of a person's Facebook page. Increased personalization is said to be a key feature of *Web 2.0*.

PLANNED OBSOLESCENCE The creation of commercial products that are intended to go out of date relatively quickly so that new purchases are required. While the term predates the digital era, electronics corporations have become the true masters of planned obsolescence, often by the incremental release of slight improvements in software or hardware that are touted as major breakthroughs driving consumers toward new purchases. *Early adopters* are the ideal consumers for planned obsolescence.

PRIVILEGE; SOCIAL PRIVILEGE Social privileges are built-in advantages based on the *subject position* (combined impact of class, gender, ethnicity, dis/ability, etc.) you are born into or placed into by circumstances not of your own making. Privilege is typically invisible to people who have it because one key privilege is not having to think about people who do not have your privileges. Usually, privileged people believe their privilege was earned rather than conveyed upon them automatically by luck of birth, the "genetic lottery."

PROSUMER; PROSUMING Prosumer (David Marshall) is a term used to express the idea that some consumers of technocultural devices and processes have become producers too via Web 2.0 features like online product reviews, iReport news items, YouTube video uploads, Facebook "likes" etc.

PROTOCOLS Protocols are the systematic sets of rules that act as control mechanisms in information technologies. Largely invisible to most users, protocols shape every aspect of ICTs, including such things as domain names and addresses, bandwidth and type of access, and surveillance capabilities. "Protocology" (Galloway) studies the social choices that go into the creation and implementation of IT protocols. The creation of the domain suffix "xxx," for example, reflects the social choice to attempt to isolate pornography from other web spaces, but also a certain acceptance of porn as a valid domain.

RACIAL CROSS-DRESSING Cross-dressing usually refers to the practice of wearing clothing typically worn by a gender other than the one you have been socialized to see as your natural one. But in digital culture studies, the concept was extended to describe a number of online masquerades, including pretending to be from an ethnic/racial group to which you do not belong in life offline (hence *racial* cross-dressing). See also *identity tourism.*

REMEDIATION In digital culture studies remediation refers most often to processing one type of media through another, like watching a movie on television or television on a smartphone or a website on a television. New media have increasingly moved forms from one platform (mode of display) to another, and remediation theory seeks to understand how this changes the experience for users. Remediation notes the connection between newer media and older media that preceded and influenced the subsequent form. The process can also be reversed, as when television news frames come to look more and more like web pages.

RL vs. VL (Real Life/Virtual Life) These terms meant to contrast life off- and online can be useful, but are often misleading by suggesting too much of a break between our lives online and offline. We are never not offline when we are online (our bodies remain solidly present somewhere in RL, for example) and our online and offline lives interweave in a myriad of ways that can never be fully disentangled.

RSS Shorthand for Real Simple Syndication, or Rich Site Summary. A process by which news or other time-sensitive information is conveyed automatically to online subscribers.

SCOPOPHILIA refers to the pleasure of looking at objects of desire. It has primarily been used as a term in critiques of the fact that historically and in the present much art and media is built around the active male gaze looking upon passive women. This includes not only soft and hardcore pornography, but less overt forms of sexualizing images in TV, films and other visual media, and in the female nudes of high art painting. But old and new media also develop other forms of pleasure in looking that may be as intense as sexual desire but are more like a kind of generalized voyeurism.

SEMIOTICS; SEMIOTIC ANALYSIS A method of cultural study that treats cultural expressions as sets of "signs" (written, verbal, visual, aural) subject to laws of interaction similar to the way words, grammar and syntax function to make sense in a language. Signs are broken down into "signifiers" and "signifieds." "Signifiers" (words, images, sounds) have only conventional or arbitrary relation to what they "signify" (meanings). A furry, four-legged domesticated feline, for example, is a cat, chat, gato or billi, depending on the signifying system (in this case a written language) in which it is located. Each variation on the word "cat" would carry with it certain particular cultural connotations that vary its signification (and a culture that does not domesticate felines might have no word for this creature at all). A more complex image, a black cat, say, would have very different connotations in an American horror movie (where it might signify bad luck or witchcraft) from those on a French banner (where it might signify sabotage). Semiotic analysis applied to a digital device would, for example, look at how each of its aspects (color, shape, size, sound [e.g., ringtones], name, etc.) carries particular significance that will vary across cultural and subcultural domains and contexts. A pink cellphone, for example, signifies femininity in Anglo-American culture, but signifies trust in an non-gendered way in Korea. A cellphone would also have a very different social connotation amidst the Arab Spring uprising (where phones were often "signs" of dissent in the semiotics of revolt) from those in non-revolutionary contexts in other times and places where it might signify something about class, degree of connectedness, or subcultural consumer taste.

SEXTING Sending sexually explicit photographs or messages via text or e-mail.

SILO EFFECT in digital culture analysis has been used especially in looking at the political impact of the Web. Political advisor Cass Sunstein and other proponents of this view argue that many Web users, rather than broadening their social views or political knowledge by visiting many sites with differing ideologies, stick to a narrow range of sites that not only echo but amplify their existing views, leading to greater rigidity and political polarization. Also known as *cyber-balkanization*.

SITUATED KNOWLEDGE Associated especially with cultural theorist Donna Haraway, the concept of situated knowledges aims to deepen the idea of objectivity by factoring in the inevitably culture-bound nature of all viewpoints on the world. Haraway rejects relativism (the idea that all points of view are equal), arguing instead that knowledge claims must be evaluated in relation to the host of social forces (especially class, gender, ethnicity and related bases of social inequalities) that confer historically varying degrees of power to shape and represent what counts as reality.

SLACKTIVISM Sometimes also called "clicktivism," slacktivism is a derogatory term for online activists who allegedly delude themselves into thinking "clicking" to dislike or like a social issue contributes to real change. While a term useful for pointing to some superficial elements of some social change activism online or activism that relies too heavily or exclusively on technology, it has also been used misleadingly to characterize all of the (often quite effective) movement organizing that uses digital technologies as one tool among many.

SLOW TECHNOLOGY MOVEMENT A social movement seeking to avoid the downside of digital technologies, and to celebrate the positive dimensions of being offline. Not an anti-tech phenomenon, many of its advocates have been and still are deeply involved in high-tech industries or as users, but they wish to counter the excessive hype that seems to suggest online life is better in every way, or that there are no downsides to being constantly online.

SNAIL MAIL Slightly sneering name for traditional post service-delivered mail that, compared with e-mail, moves at the pace of a snail (and leaves a gooey trail of stamp glue?).

SOCIAL NETWORKING SITES (SNSs) Sites like MySpace and Facebook, designed to facilitate communication between and among subscribing individual members, and cohorts defined by a variety of possible commonalities (professional, institutional, geographic, recreational, political, etc.).

SUBJECT POSITION refers to the social positioning—race/ethnicity, gender, age, class, sexuality, nationality, etc.—that plays a major role in structuring a person's view of the world. By definition, subject positions are given by society, not chosen by individuals. Whenever you view a film or website, or read a book or article, you are doing so from a particular subject position. While it is possible to get outside your subject position, it is more difficult to do so than most of us think, and it requires the development of serious new *cultural competencies* to truly view the world through the eyes of someone whose subject position is far different from your own.

SUBVERTISEMENT is a portmanteau word (subvert + advertisement) to name anti-commercials offered in typical commercial ad format designed to subvert traditional comsumerist advertisements. See also *adbusting*.

TACTICAL MEDIA Techniques used to disrupt mainstream cultural processes, especially cybercultural processes. These may include cyber sit-ins, electronic civil disobedience, *adbusting* or *subvertising*, meme infowar, *hacktivism* and a host of other dissident cultural practices. Tactical also suggests that these practices are often meant to be temporary, rather than part of a broader set of objectives, though they can also be used as part of wider campaigns for change.

TECHNOLOGICAL DETERMINISM argues that technology has an independent, causal power in changing society; some argue that technologies are even the main force in social life, beyond economics, culture or politics. Technological determinists often see technology as a force larger than human control. Technological determinists come in both utopian versions (technology will solve all social problems) and dystopian versions (technology will doom us all). Digital culture scholars reject strong versions of technological determinism (preferring "technocultural" analysis), while recognizing that technologies do have impacts not fully under social control.

TECHNOCULTURAL analysis approaches, in contrast to *technological determinism,* argue that technologies like the Internet always have cultural assumptions built into them by culturally shaped producers. Technologies are always created by individuals and groups deeply shaped by cultural assumptions and biases. Choices about which technologies to develop are always partly economic and partly social. Choices about which technologies become popular are deeply social and cultural. The uses to which technologies are put are deeply social and cultural. The adoption and use of technologies is always a social process. Technologies are subsequently adapted, changed or replaced by ongoing social processes. Technologies are always therefore technocultural, always shaped by culture even as they shape culture in turn.

TECHNOLOGICAL IMAGINARY refers to our imagined relations to technologies, as interwoven with (and sometimes in contradiction to) what we actually do with them and through them. Whenever we use or think about a technical device, we invest a certain amount of imaginary energy in it; we form a mental image of what the device is or is doing to us. These fantastical imaginings are a real part of technoculture, are a real element in how technology shapes and is shaped by culture. If we imagine robots mostly as polite helpful creatures like C-3PO from "Star Wars" we will have a very different relationship to robotics than if we mostly think of the Terminator or Robocop.

TECHNOLOGY FOR SOCIAL INCLUSION refers to a multi-factor approach to overcoming gaps between those with full access to new digital technologies and those who lack such access. This proactive approach stresses multiple cultural factors as well as simple access to hardware and software, and often uses *participatory design* and other interactive practices to engage underserved communities desiring greater degrees of access to the economic, political, social and cultural opportunities available through digital technologies.

TEXT/TEXTUAL ANALYSIS in the context of cultural studies argues that the social text is any unit of meaning isolated for the purpose of analysis. In cyberculture analysis the "text" may be as small as one word or image on a web page, or as large as a whole community of users. Web "texts" include words, images, sounds, page layout, links and their interrelationships. When talking about "text-based" cyberspaces, however, the reference is to writing, as opposed to visual or aural representation. Textual analysis is a major technique used in digital culture studies to get at the meanings projected by websites, online conversations and other manifestations of cyberculture.

TEXTING is the use of Instant Messaging or similar programs for communication among cellphones or other messaging-capable devices. The world record for thumbed texting is less than 22 seconds to type "The razor-toothed piranhas of the genera Serrasalmus and Pygocentrus are the most ferocious freshwater fish in the world. In reality they seldom attack a human." A quadriplegic man named Hank Torres has the current Guinness World Record for "Fastest Hands-Free Typing." In about 83.09 seconds, Torres typed the same phrase.

THUMBERS Another term for the digital generation (derived from usage in Asia) based upon the use of the named digits in speedy texting. One sign of the digital generation gap is that those raised before the digital revolution often text with fingers like typing, while the younger, digital native set often uses only thumbs.

VIRAL; GOING VIRAL Analogous to the spread of a computer virus (itself analogous to the spread of a biological virus), a cultural product goes viral on the Net when it has a sudden explosion in popularity, receiving a huge number of hits, sometimes in the millions. While a relatively rare phenomenon, the occasional viral success gives inflated hope to independent cultural producers that they may gain sudden fame without help from major media channels (record companies, news outlets, etc.).

VIRTUAL COMMUNITY First lauded by digital culture early adopter Howard Rheingold, a virtual community is any group of individuals, from a handful to thousands, who share a particular interest or passion that they share primarily if not exclusively through interactions online or through other elements of digital culture. Skeptics unfavorably compare such digital groupings with offline communities they claim are superior.

WEARABLE COMPUTERS While people have been wearing computers in a sense at least since the advent of digital watches, the concept of wearable computers generally refers to more fulsome integration of digital connection via clothing. There have been many kinds of wearable computers for a couple of decades that had limited adoption (virtual reality suits constitute an extreme early example, but one whose costs prohibited wide adoption). Google Glasses arguably represent the first widely known example of a wearable product that directly connects users to the Net.

WEB 2.0 refers to the more interactive dimensions developing on the World Wide Web in the twenty-first century, and the increasing *convergence* of digital forms on single devices (e.g. phoning, e-mailing, texting, Web surfing, photography and videography all on a smartphone), and the *remediation* of old media into digital spaces such that movies, television shows, recorded music, radio stations and other older media are being digitized and made available via the Web. Other elements frequently tied to this concept include *personalization, domestication,* participatory production, *crowdsourcing, prosuming* and other modes of interaction by which new media productions differ from the one-way flow—from creators to a more passive audience—typical of older, broadcast media like radio and TV.

WEBLINING is the use of information gathered legally or illegally from an individual's social media page or other online identity cache that is used to exclude that user from certain marketing offers based on economic and racial profiling done through tracking one's online traffic patterns and expressed preferences. The term is meant to echo "redlining," a practice outlawed in 1977 whereby individuals, typically from ethnic minority groups, were excluded from certain mortgage offers to protect the racial "purity" of neighborhoods.

WIKI A website, typically informational or educational (e.g. Wikipedia), that allows open, collaborative editing directly online.

WIKIDENTITIES A concept arguing that people, especially young people, deeply immersed in *social networking sites* like MySpace and Facebook, create their identities collectively with help from online friends, and with a sense that identity construction is always partly a fictional process. Part of a larger argument that Web 2.0 features like "wikis" are changing the way that people, especially young people, think about how knowledge is produced (see Mallan and Giardina 2009).

ZOMBIE COOKIE A zombie cookie is a cookie illegally planted that remains even after it has been deleted by the removal option on a browser. It continues to gather information about a user's activities usually for the purposes of surreptitious marketing research. Zombie cookies can work across several browsers on the same computer, and can gather information about user login IDs.

Index

CPSIA information can be obtained at www.ICGtesting.com
Printed in the USA
LVOW07s0457010815

448359LV00017B/152/P

9 780415 819312